**SHIPS
BENEATH
THE SEA**

Also by the Author

The Mystery of Mound Key
A Time for Tigers
Where Condors Fly
The Sharks
Sinkings, Salvages and Shipwrecks
Exploring a Coral Reef

SHIPS BENEATH THE SEA

A History of Subs and Submersibles

ROBERT F. BURGESS

McGraw-Hill Book Company
New York St. Louis San Francisco
Düsseldorf London Mexico Sydney Toronto

Book design by Elaine Gongora.

123456789KPKP798765

Library of Congress Cataloging in Publication Data

Burgess, Robert Forrest.
    Ships beneath the sea: A history of subs and submersibles
    Bibliography: p.
    1. Submarine boats—History.   I. Title.
V857.B87   387.2'57   75-8659

ISBN 0-07-008958-2

This book is dedicated to all men
Who have gone down to the sea in submarines
And especially
To those who never returned

Contents

Illustrations facing page 1; also following pages 50, 112, and 169

Foreword

". . . No defects to be afraid of, for the double shell is as firm as iron; no rigging to attend to; no sails for the wind to carry away; no boilers to burst; no fire to fear, for the vessel is made of iron, not of wood; no coal to run short, for electricity is the only mechanical agent; no collision to fear, for it alone swims in deep water; no tempest to brave, for when it dives below the water, it reaches absolute tranquillity. There, sir! that is the perfection of vessels! . . ." Captain Nemo, speaking of the *Nautilus*

Jules Verne, *Twenty Thousand Leagues under the Sea,* 1869

Jules Verne has often been thought of as the man who prophesied the submarine. Indeed, the septuagenarian French novelist wrote the American submarine inventor Simon Lake in 1898, "My book is entirely a work of the imagination." But what the famous author had forgotten was that at least twenty-five practical versions of the submarine had navigated underwater successfully before he wrote his eternally delightful *Twenty Thousand Leagues under the Sea.* This, then, is the story of those machines, of the men who built them, of the men who lived or died because of them, and all that has happened since.

An early engraving of Dr. Cornelius Van Drebbel who in 1620 became the first of a
long line of farsighted men responsible for the invention of the submarine.
(Courtesy: Submarine Museum, New London, Connecticut)

CHAPTER 1

The First Submariners

 Over four hundred years ago a British naval officer named William Bourne penned an idea so bizarre that had he not been so well regarded by Queen Elizabeth she might have sent him to the Tower to see if her headsman could separate him from some of his outlandish ideas. Instead of an executioner's block, however, Bourne's mental meanderings earned him immortality for dreaming up what was generally considered a workable idea for a submarine boat. Bourne's book *Inventions and Devices,* published in 1578, describes an enclosed vessel of leather and wood designed to be submerged and rowed underwater. The sub-title of his "18th Devise" suggests that, after he was smitten by this bright idea, Bourne wondered who in the world would want to go rowing underwater anyway. He therefore made it perfectly clear by stating that this particular invention was "Very Necessary for All Generals and Captains, or Leaders of Men as Well by Sea as by Land."

After this catchall caption the author proceeded to outline his theory in the laborious jargon of the times:

> It is possible to make a shippe or boate that may goe under the water unto the bottome, and so to come up againe at your pleasure. Any magnitude of body that is in the water, if that quality in biggnesse, having alwaies but one weight, may be made bigger or lesser, then it shall swimme when you would, and sinke when you list: and for to make anything doo so, then the jointes or places that doo make the thing bigger or lesser must bee of leather; and in the inside to have skrewes to winde it in and also out againe: and for to have it sinke, they must winde the thing in to make it lesse, and then it sinketh unto the

1

bottom: and to have it swimme, then to winde the sides out
againe, to make the thing bigger, and it will swimme according
unto the body of the thing in the water.

With that he launched into the mechanics of his idea,
describing in great detail a ballasted wood-frame boat enclosed
in greased leather. The flexible sides of the vessel could be
expanded or contracted at will by crewmen inside the hull
manipulating large winding screws attached to the leather
bulkheads. Screwing in the boat's sides decreased its volume,
allowing it to sink. A reverse action made it rise. Air was
supplied by a hollow mast. Interestingly, Bourne equipped
his theoretical diving boat with double decks, or as he said, it
was "fitted with two close orloppes," considering perhaps
both the need for structural strength and the desirability of an
enclosed air pocket for safety.

As detailed as his verbal description was, Bourne failed to
include any layout or sketch of what he was talking about.
Nor is there any record that he ever built the device.
Consequently, we are left simply with whatever mental
picture we can imagine to fit his words.

Still, Bourne's name heads the list of ancestral submarine
pioneers because his was the first attempt to design a
navigable underwater vessel. There may have been others
before him who actually ventured underwater in various
contraptions, but they had no control over their mobility.
Legend says that Alexander the Great (356–323 B.C.) was
lowered into the sea in a device that kept its occupants dry
and admitted light. This vessel has variously been described
as a diving bell, a skin-covered box with glass windows and a
glass barrel. Numerous early French, English and Persian
paintings depict the event from which Alexander not surprisingly is supposed to have returned telling stirring tales about
seeing sea monsters.

Centuries later even the renowned Leonardo da Vinci
(1452–1519) claimed to know how to remain for a prolonged
period underwater. But the genius who fathered the flying
machine, tank tactics, the machine gun and a scheme where-
by armored divers in swim fins and snorkels sank empty

ships by ripping open their bottoms refused to tell his secret because he felt it was too destructive. He said, "I do not publish or divulge [my method] on account of the evil nature of men who practice assassination at the bottom of the sea." One wonders what the creator of *Mona Lisa* would have done if he had suspected how future generations were to use the airplane, tank and machine gun.

While Leonardo kept at least this one secret for humanitarian reasons, the submarine had to wait another hundred years before it appeared.

Then in 1620, the same year that the Mayflower set off on her famous voyage, a Dutch guest at the court of King James I, Dr. Cornelius Van Drebbel,* was strolling along the Thames River one evening when he saw something that started him thinking. Fishermen were dragging heavy baskets of fish behind their boats. Each time the ropes grew taut, the boats sank low in the water. But each time the ropes slackened, the boats rose to the surface. "Would it be possible," Dr. Van Drebbel wondered, "for a boat to be held underwater in this fashion and then propelled by oars?"

The idea intrigued him. The more he thought about it, the more it excited him. Certainly he knew little about nautical matters but he saw no reason why the problems could not be resolved with the proper application of scientific principles. And those matters he did know about.

Later that evening when there was an appropriate moment, Dr. Van Drebbel confided his thoughts to his royal host. The King listened attentively while the physician described what he had seen and what he theorized might be done. Others present stifled sniggers, for who but a madman would want to go rowing underwater? The King, however, did not laugh. Indeed, the idea appealed to him. But he was thinking along different lines. Who could say what a long-boat of British seamen might accomplish against an enemy warship if by some scientific miracle the boat could be made to travel underwater? The King therefore offered to help the inventor in any way he could.

---

*Also spelled Drebel, Dreble, Drebell and Trebel.

Thus, financed by funds from the royal treasury, Dr. Van Drebbel started experimenting with fishing boats and heavy drags. The results were unimpressive. While the doctor found that he could sink or raise a boat with sufficient ballast, drag and river current, he quickly realized that the method was impractical because it limited him to these factors.

There had to be another way. He puzzled over the principles involved. A boat sank from a heavy load of ballast or when it holed its hull and took on, rather than displaced, the water supporting it. If there was a way to take the water in and then get rid of it at will, would that not make a boat alternately sink and float? He toyed with this thought for several days before the solution finally came to him. And then it was so incredibly simple he wondered why he had not thought of it before.

"Pigskins!" he shouted to his co-workers the next day, his eyes dancing brightly behind his spectacles. "That's the answer, my good fellows!" and forthwith he sent off to the local tannery for as many large whole pigskins as his men could carry. No doubt the men considered the request quite strange, but nevertheless they obliged his whims and carted back a fine load of big empty pigskins, the kind still used in some countries as large flexible wine containers.

However, it was not wine that Dr. Van Drebbel had in mind for the hides. They were to be the secret of his diving boat. The bags, thoroughly greased to assure their being waterproof, were installed under the thwarts along both sides of an ordinary wooden longboat. The necks of the bags were coupled to brass flanges passing through the boat's hull. Their opposite ends were lashed to short cylindrical sections of oak which when turned would twist the bags tightly. This then was the method Dr. Van Drebbel had figured out for making his boat sink or float at will. When the restraining cinches were removed from the necks of the flexible skin bags, they would fill with water taken in through the holes in the hull. The added weight of this water ballast would make the boat sink. Reversing the process by twisting the bags expelled the water back into the river so that the boat would rise again and float.

Although the Dutchman would not admit it to himself, it was really quite an ingenious idea, one that would have made the naval officer, William Bourne, proud, particularly since it was essentially his idea updated by only forty-two years. But if Dr. Van Drebbel had been told this, he probably would have stared over the top of his spectacles and asked in all seriousness, "Dr. Bourne who?" Then laughing, he would most likely make some joke about his "beautiful boatful of balloons." Whether or not the pigskins would do what they were supposed to do remained to be seen. But anyone who listened long to the affable Dutch doctor would surely believe that it was already an accomplished fact.

With all his bags finally installed, he completed the rest of the boat. The vessel's sides were built higher and a wooden framework was added over the cockpit. The entire boat was then enclosed in layers of greased leather with one central opening high in the middle of the strange superstructure. Two pairs of port and starboard oars protruded through collars in the leather covering which were then fitted snugly around each oar with brass straps. The leather's flexibility allowed the oars to move forward and backward as in rowing.

The day the diving machine was tested has to have been one of the more exciting moments in old English history. Dr. Van Drebbel, accompanied by four sturdy seamen, rowed the leather-covered boat a short distance from shore, guided by the doctor standing amidships with his head protruding through the open hatchway.

At what was judged an appropriate point, he closed and sealed the hatch and gave orders for the men to untie the ropes encircling the necks of the ballast bags, allowing water to enter the leather containers.

The boat immediately began to sink lower in the water until she reached a point about the level of her gunwales where she remained, still floating like a half-submerged bubble.

"All the hides are full," reported one of the seamen.

"Then we need more ballast," said Van Drebbel. "Empty and secure the hides, then return to port," he ordered.

Back on shore half a cartload of cobblestones were rounded

up and laid evenly along the bottom of the longboat under the ballast bags.

The heavily ballasted boat rode so low now as the seamen rowed back into the Thames that the water rose well up her sides. Van Drebbel battened down the boat's hatch and again ordered the bags opened to take on water.

Now, there was no doubt about it, the longboat submerged slowly but surely with a creaking framework and a gradual dimming of light as water crept up and over the vessel's leather-bound superstructure.

"We're under!" cried Van Drebbel. "Cinch off the necks of the bags and row!"

And row they did, blindly and awkwardly, the boat moving forward sluggishly while the air inside their pigskin cabin grew stale and steamy with their efforts. But most importantly, the basic principle of the underwater boat worked. Using water for part of the ballast, Van Drebbel's diving machine was submerged and being propelled underwater. With this event, the first page of submarine history was written.

In the next four years the inventive Dutch physician went on to build two more diving boats, both similar but larger than his first successful effort. It was said that one of these boats was large enough to carry twelve rowers plus passengers and that King James himself risked a ride in the underwater craft. On this pleasure trip down the Thames River, the royal party reputedly spent several hours underwater at a depth of from twelve to fifteen feet.

What miracle had the wily Dutchman worked that enabled his passengers to breathe comfortably during this remarkable underwater joyride? The answer has long been forgotten. Some writers believe that Van Drebbel supplemented the boat's air with bellows that pumped surface air down through a snorkel-like pipe at one end of the boat while expelling stale air through another pipe at the opposite end. But Dr. Van Drebbel's associates spoke of his using a bottle of some kind of "magic" liquid which immediately rejuvenated the cabin air when it became stale. Whichever method he used, the secret was well kept. Since Van Drebbel left no record of how he performed the feat, all we have are the facts as attested to by his eminent friend Robert Boyle, the English chemist, physicist and theologian, who wrote in 1662, "Van Drebbel conceived that it is not the whole body of the air but a certain quintessence, or spiritous part of it that makes it fit for respiration, which being spent, the grosser body, or carcase of the Air, is unable to cherish the vital flame residing in the heart."

What an amazing statement to make at a time when neither Van Drebbel nor Boyle knew that oxygen* comprised one fifth of the atmosphere—a fact not revealed for at least another century when scientists learned how to analyze air.

But even more astounding is Boyle's subsequent implication that the Dutchman may have hit upon a method for making that life-giving "quintaessentia" of air long before anyone else. For he wrote, "Besides the mechanical contrivance of his [Van Drebbel's] vessel, he had a chemical liquor, which he accounted the chief secret of his submarine navigation. For when from time to time he perceived that the finer and purer part of the air was consumed or over-clogged by the respiration and steames of those that went in his ship, he would, by unstopping a vessel full of the liquor, speedily restore to the troubled air such a proportion of vital parts as would make it again for a good while fit for respiration."

Some scientists have speculated that Van Drebbel knew the secret of making oxygen from saltpeter and this was what he used to rejuvenate the air in his diving machine. A British diving historian, Sir Robert Davis, thought he may have used soda ash to absorb the carbon dioxide. Whatever it was and however he used it, the doctor kept the secret to himself. While it is recorded that Van Drebbel's underwater boat traveled back and forth on the Thames between Greenwich and Westminster for the next few years, it was considered little more than a tourist attraction.

Although the Dutch inventor's benefactor, King James I, died in 1625, the English government was sufficiently impressed with Van Drebbel's achievements that Sir William

---

*Discovered as a gas first by Joseph Priestley in 1774, then independently by K. W. Scheele in 1775, and later named oxygen by A. L. Lavoisier.

Heydon was ordered to procure water mines and "boates to go under the water." Whether or not he ever did, history fails to tell us. We do know, however, that Cornelius Van Drebbel went to work for the British Admiralty at a substantial salary and was engaged in some kind of secret work for that department. Unfortunately, however, it was so secret that history never found out what it was. In fact, when Van Drebbel died in 1634, at the age of sixty-two, his project became so hush-hush that according to a royal directive "none but kings successively and their heirs must know it."

Oddly enough almost a century would go by before anyone seemed able to pick up where Van Drebbel left off. But this did not bother the would-be inventors. When they were not editorializing about their theoretical diving machines, they were drawing pictures of them. Needless to say, few ever got built and those that did were failures. Such was the case of French inventor De Son's so-called submarine boat built in Rotterdam in 1653, nineteen years after Van Drebbel's death. What distinguishes De Son's effort is that we know exactly how the boat looked because his were the first drawings to survive the centuries. At the risk of ruining De Son's reputation for modesty, it might have been better if the Old English caption accompanying the drawings had been lost along the way. But since it wasn't, we are told that the inventor "doeth undertake in one day to destroy a honderd Ships," Furthermore, the vessel "can goe from Rotterdam to London and back again in one day, and in 6 weeks to goe to the East Indiens, and to run as Swift as a bird can flye. No fire, nor Storme, or Bullets, can hinder her, unless it please God. Although the Ships meane to bee safe in their hauens [havens], it is vaine, for shee shall come to them in any place, it is impossible for her to bee taken, unless by treacherie, and then can not bee governed by any but himself . . ."

The illustration of this wondrous vessel shows a crude slope-sided Rube Goldberg contraption of wood, seventy-two feet long with an eight-foot beam, reinforced by iron girders. Bow and stern are pointed to rams running fore and aft through the vessel's midsection. Permanent ballast would supposedly submerge the boat no deeper than its small, railing-enclosed upper deck surmounted by a huge flag. The boat was to be powered by a paddle wheel located amidships and rotated by clockwork. But so far as anyone knows, De Son never got around to installing this mechanism and persuading it to run for the eight-hour voyages which he claimed. When all else failed, including all his water trials, De Son finally recouped some of his production costs by putting his "Strange Ship" on exhibit and charging the public to look at it.

Typical of De Son's difficulties, progress in the development of the submarine was agonizingly slow. However, this was not the case for another kind of diving machine in use almost a century before Van Drebbel's first underwater boat. This was the diving bell. The earliest reliable record of this simple device appears in Francesco de Marchi's book *Architettura Militare,* first published in 1599 and later reprinted in 1810. In discussing the 1531 attempts to raise Caligula's sunken pleasure galleys in Lake Nemi, Marchi says that a diving machine invented by Guglielmo de Lorenca enabled him to examine one of the sunken wrecks for an hour. Marchi described the apparatus as a small diving bell that fitted down over the diver's upper body. Its weight was supported by chains from the surface and from a yoke resting on the diver's shoulders. A glass-covered opening served as a viewing port. Although Marchi failed to mention how air was renewed in the bell, this was apparently accomplished without too much difficulty.

Seven years after Lorenca's Lake Nemi dives, two Greeks are reported to have put on a diving exhibit in Toledo, Spain, before Emperor Charles V and several thousand spectators. The performers used a machine resembling a large inverted kettle, the mouth of which was loaded with lead. After their dive the men emerged dry and carrying a lighted candle. In 1552, Adriatic fisherman performed a similar exhibition in Venice before the doge and senators. Their diving machine measured ten feet high and ten feet wide. In 1597, Buonaiuto Lorini described a wooden diving contrivance resembling a packing case reinforced by iron bands. The case was attached to a wooden platform where divers could stand with their heads inside the enclosed air pocket while the whole thing was raised or lowered from the surface by a double-rope pulley system.

Periodically throughout the seventeenth century a variety of diving bells were built and used. In 1616, Franz Kessler designed a lightweight bell attached to a wooden frame that covered the diver down to his ankles. Small round portholes encircled the top of the tumbler-shaped apparatus. The harnessed diver apparently carried his own ballast ball because the bell had no visible means of suspension from above. In 1640, Frenchman Jean Barrié patented a diving bell said to have been used to salvage cargo from a shipwreck near Dieppe. Another bell was used with some success in 1665 to salvage cannon from a Spanish galleon sunk in Tobermory Bay, Mull, an island of the Inner Hebrides.

In 1677, a Dr. Panthot of Lyons employed Spanish methods to salvage treasure with a diving bell from two wrecked ships in the port of Cadaques, Spain. The French physician was obviously an astute observer and an accurate reporter because his description of the event in his book *Journal des Scavans* published in 1678 is one of the finest detailed accounts on record. Dr. Panthot wrote:

> The whole machine and everything connected with it was quite simple. Two boats supported a transverse beam between them and from this beam hung the diving-bell, thirteen or fourteen feet high by about nine feet across. It was constructed of wood supported by hoops of iron. The bottom hoop had numerous rings and from each hung metal balls weighing between 60 and 80 pounds apiece.
>
> The diver was seated on a crossbar in the middle. In his hand he held a rope by means of which he could signal when the bell was far enough down. He had a sack suspended from his neck and this he filled with money, emptying it when it was full into other sacks which were kept inside the bell under which he breathed. When the bell became uncomfortably hot he would ring a little bell and the big bell would be hoisted out of the water by means of a cable. A diver's reward consisted of as many piastres as he could carry in both hands and in his mouth.

Panthot goes on to say that one of the Moorish divers could distinctly hear voices from those on the surface but that they were unable to hear any noise made by the diver from inside the bell. Pursuing this further, the hardy Moor took a hunting horn down into the bell and rendered a mighty blast. Whether or not it was heard on the surface was not reported, but the sound almost burst the Moor's eardrums and turned him so giddy he nearly fell out of the bell.

Until the last decade of the seventeenth century, all diving bells were dependent upon the amount of air trapped under the apparatus as it was lowered into the water. When this was exhausted by the occupants, the bell had to be raised and the air replenished. But in 1689, a celebrated French physicist, Dr. Denis Papin, suggested that force pumps or bellows be used to keep up a constant, pressurized, fresh air supply that would enable bell divers to go deeper and stay longer. Before the end of the century this idea was used to great advantage by Dr. Edmund Halley, the man who built what is generally accepted as the forerunner of the modern diving bell. More than that, he was an exceptional man. Contrary to most real-life situations, Halley had everything going for him right from the beginning. Born of a well-to-do English family in London in 1656, young Edmund received the best schooling money could provide. He was an outstanding student with a wide range of interests and talents. Despite the ease with which he could have squandered everything, he matured into a personable young man with fewer than the usual vices who went through life making as many friends and as few enemies as possible. His one burning desire was to gain knowledge about the scientific world and to share this with his fellow men.

A small sampling of Halley's accomplishments should give some idea of his interests and abilities. At fifteen, young Halley charted all the magnetic variations of the compass, something that had never been done accurately until then. At twenty, he published an outstanding paper on the planetary orbits, then headed for St. Helena in the Southern Hemisphere where he catalogued 341 stars and made other important astronomical observations. Returning to England he observed a comet in 1682, calculated its orbit and correctly predicted its return in 1757, the first time such a feat had ever been accomplished. Forever after, that heavenly body would bear his name—Halley's Comet. Astronomy was his forte, but in addition to plumbing the depths of outer space, he methodically turned his questing mind to the problems of plumbing the depths of inner space—the ocean. He devised a diving bell so superior to anything that had ever preceded it that it marked a turning point in man's exploration of the sea. Here is how Halley described it:

> The Bell I made was of Wood, containing about 60 Cubick Foot in its concavity, and was of the form of a Truncate-Cone, whose Diameter at Top was three Foot, and at Bottom five. This I coated with Lead so heavy that It would sink empty, and I distributed its weight so about its bottom, that it would go down in a perpendicular situation and no other.
>
> In the Top I fixed a strong but clear Glass, as a Window to let in the Light from above, and likewise a Cock to let out the hot Air that had been Breathed; and below, about a Yard under the Bell, I placed a Stage which hung by three Ropes, each of which was charged with about one Hundred Weight, to keep it steddy. This Machine I suspended from the Mast of a Ship, by a Spritt which was sufficiently secured by Stays to the Mast-head, and was directed by Braces to carry it over-board clear of the Ship side, and to bring it again within-board as occasion required.

Although Halley's bell was superior it was by no means original. The originality was in his method of replenishing the bell's air while it was still submerged. The obvious way would have been to use pressure pumps or bellows as Papin had suggested earlier. But Halley purposely avoided the Frenchman's suggestion for one of his own. So it was this and not the bell that he said was the "principal invention I can boast of."

Halley used two lead-lined barrels of air which were lowered beside the bell. Each barrel had a bung hole in its top and bottom. From the top hole there extended a long leather hose weighted at its end so that it normally hung lower than the barrel, the water pressure thereby imprisoning the air in the barrel. But when the bell's atmosphere needed freshening, the occupant had only to fish up the loose end of the weighted leather tube until it was inside the bell and the water pressure acting through the bung hole on the bottom of the barrel pushed its contents into the bell.

The barrels were raised or lowered alternately to provide a constant supply of fresh air. The method worked so well that Halley and two others remained submerged in a bell at sixty feet for an hour and a half without feeling any ill effect.

The royal astronomer next designed a diving suit of leather employing a glass helmet so that a diver could extend his range from the bell. He breathed through "a leathern hose, well-lacquered with bees-wax and oyl," whose extremity was held inside the bell by the diver's assistant.

Old illustrations show Halley-type bells being used in various salvage operations. But cannon, not gold, were the objects most often recovered. The large armament was easily located with a bell and raised by block and tackle from a surface support vessel. Finer treasure—coinage and jewelry—had to wait until a later day when more sophisticated diving equipment was invented.

While most underwater exploration of the seventeenth century used diving bells as a kind of underwater elevator, men still dreamed of more mobile submersibles. In 1680, Giovanni Alfonso Borelli, a wealthy Italian with a penchant for theorizing about subnautical matters, published a book on the subject of fish and submarine construction. Borelli pictured his vessel as an inverted rowboat with its cockpit planked over. In an arrangement similar to Van Drebbel's, submersion occurred when water filled rows of leather bags installed over holes in the bottom of the boat. Surfacing occurred in the same manner as the Dutchman's boat when water was squeezed out of the bags. But Borelli's boat had a slightly new twist. It was propelled by rowers whose oar blades collapsed like fish fins. There is no record that the Italian ever built this boat. But over a half-century later, in 1747, an illustration in reverse of Borelli's boat appeared in London's *The Gentleman's Magazine* with the claim that it had been invented and built by one Nathaniel Symons (also spelled Symonds and Simons). According to the article the vessel was used extensively on the Thames River. This information touched off a flurry of counterclaims by other would-be originators of the boat. Among the letters to the editor was one from an Englishman, John Lethbridge, who claimed to have made hundreds of deep ocean dives in an apparatus of his own design. And apparently he had. About 1715, Lethbridge decided to build some kind of machine that would enable him to recover wrecks lost at sea. Looking about his farm for suitable building materials, he found a hogshead at the lower end of his orchard which was big enough to hold him. But how long could he breathe inside of it? Since there was only one way to find out, he crawled inside, bunged it up tight, and sat there for half an hour as he later said, "without communication of air."

So much for living inside a hogshead on land, but what about one surrounded by water? Since there was no lake nearby, Lethbridge cleverly dug a trench from his well to below his orchard and flooded it with enough water to cover his hogshead. Again he got inside, bunged it tight and was pleased to note that "without air pipes or communication of air . . . I could stay longer underwater than upon land."

Lethbridge then hired a cooper to build him a diving machine which not surprisingly resembled a modified hogshead. Made of six-foot-long wainscot (oak panels) reinforced with iron hoops, it was the shape of a truncated cone slightly tapering from three and a half feet wide at the upper end to two and a half feet at the bottom. The diver entered through a cover on top which could be bolted in place. Once inside he slipped his arms out through two holes waterproofed by well-greased leather sleeves tied tightly at the diver's biceps. A four-inch-wide, one-and-a-quarter-inch-thick glass window in front of his face allowed him to see out. With Lethbridge inside and the machine heavily ballasted with iron castings outside, the device was suspended horizontally on a cable from a surface vessel.

Lethbridge reported that he could stay down in his diving engine for thirty-four minutes before having to be hauled up for air. Then, instead of opening the container, air was pumped in to him through valves in its top and bottom. In case of an emergency the diver could release his ballast from inside and the rig would surface under its own buoyancy. Documents of the period indicate that Lethbridge and his diving machine were often hired to recover lost treasure from shipwrecks. A depth of sixty feet was about his normal operating range, however he did dive to seventy-two feet "with great difficulty." Although Lethbridge patented his diving engine and used it successfully for three years, it enjoyed only a brief period of popularity.

Periodically there were rumors of submersible craft being built and operated successfully, but in most cases few records remained behind to verify the stories. In 1772, a Frenchman named Le Sieur Dionis was said to have perfected an underwater craft capable of carrying people on a four-and-a-half-hour underwater journey. If that was true, then he must have stumbled on to the secret of making Van Drebbel's fabulous "chemical liquor" for restoring air. And if he did, someone forgot to tell history about it.

Facts of an equally nebulous nature document the submarine-building adventures of the Englishman John Day. Usually it is a toss-up among historians trying to decide whether Day was a carpenter, a wagon builder, a dockyard laborer or a combination of all three. But one who knew him well felt his personality eclipsed his profession. He said he was "a man very illiterate and indigent in circumstances. His temper was gloomy, reserved and peevish, his disposition penurious; he was remarkably obstinate in his opinion and jealous of his fame." Lest it seem that he did not like the fellow, the chronicler tempered his remarks by adding that Day was also "penetrating in his observations, acute in his remarks, faithful to his patron and unshaken in his resolutions."

So now we have a picture of this poor, faithful, not too sharp fellow gloomily hammering and sawing away on what he stubbornly believes to be an underwater boat but which his historians tell us was in fact a "tub."

In any event, John Day trundled his tub to Norwich, climbed inside and sank to the bottom of a 30-foot-deep pool. And from then on Day's historians sharpened their focus on the young do-it-yourself submariner. While they were later not too sure of the mechanics of how he did it, there was certainly no doubt *what* he did.

Since he was "indigent," but "resolute," Day searched for a way to get funds to continue his project on a grander scale. Failing to obtain any local backing he finally wrote to Christopher Blake, a wealthy gambler notorious for betting on anything that took his fancy. If Blake would finance the venture, said Day, he would build an underwater boat that would make them both rich.

Blake considered the possibilities and wrote back that he appreciated the offer to become associated with such a worthy scientific endeavor. Not only would he be glad to finance the project but he would pay Day £100 for every £1,000 he won betting that Day could stay submerged in his boat for a long time without harm.

The deal was made. Blake advanced Day £350 with which he bought a fifty-ton sloop, *Maria,* and got busy converting her into an underwater boat. First he collected seventy-five empty hogsheads for buoyancy tanks and enclosed them in a watertight cabin that he built amidships. Then he loaded ten tons of ballast in the ship's hold and attached twenty tons more to the bottom of the hull so that they could be released from inside the cabin. After painting the *Maria* red, Day announced that he would submerge in his "submarine" to 130 feet, remain there for twelve hours, then drop his twenty tons of ballast and float to the surface with the buoyancy of his built-in hogsheads.

The great day arrived. Large crowds gathered on the wharfs and along the beach at Plymouth. Passing among them were Blake's men making bets with those who doubted that Day could stay the agreed length of time on the bottom without difficulty.

When everything was ready, the *Maria* was towed out into Plymouth Harbor to the melodic accompaniment of a brass band on shore. At a point in the harbor where soundings revealed a depth of 130 feet, the gloomy, obstinate Day climbed aboard his "submarine" carrying a candle, biscuits and a bottle of water. They sealed him in his cabin, added the necessary outside ballast and Day was on his way.

As one eyewitness described it: "She sank at two o'clock in the afternoon of the 20th of June 1774, and Mr. Day descended with her into perpetual night."

And that was the last anyone ever saw of Day or his boat.

Of course when the twelve hours were up and he did not appear, Blake and others tried to grapple up the boat but without success. Theories were rampant as to what had befallen him. "Considering the depth," said a doctor at the scene, "I can assure you that Mr. Day froze to death."

And so it was dutifully noted that after 150 years of submarine navigation, John Day was history's first recorded fatality to take place on a submarine.

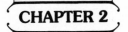

CHAPTER 2

The Eagle and the Turtle

 Two years and an ocean away from the unfortunate John Day, the first blows for freedom in the American Revolution had already been struck. Lexington and Concord, Breed's Hill and Bunker Hill, were history. With the taking of Ticonderoga and Dorchester Heights by the colonists, the great seige of Boston was on. Surrounded by a ragtag army of 16,000 American patriots, the pleasure-loving British general Sir William Howe wisely decided that retreat was the better part of valor. On March 17, 1776, he evacuated the city, loaded his troops and some one thousand weeping Tories aboard his ships and departed.

Although no one knew his destination, George Washington suspected that Howe might be heading for New York to capture the Hudson River and split the thirteen colonies. Hastily he sent half his army to fortify Brooklyn Heights, Long Island. Meanwhile, the British landed at Halifax, Nova Scotia, where they licked their wounds and awaited reinforcements from England.

In late June, Washington's suspicions were confirmed. Four heavily armed men-of-war sailed into New York Bay and dropped anchor. The next day, forty more followed. Within the week there were over a hundred. Ten thousand British soldiers occupied Staten Island. And still the ships came. General Howe was awaiting arrival of his brother, admiral of the navy, Lord Richard Howe, whom his sailors affectionately nicknamed "Black Dick" because of his dark complexion. Parliament had authorized the Howe brothers to put down the rebellion as quickly as possible. But what neither man knew was that it was already too late to negotiate. On July 4, the Continental Congress in Philadelphia signed the Declaration of Independence. The Howes could pardon and make recommendations, but they could not negotiate with an independent congress or independent states.

On July 9, two British men-of-war, the *Phoenix* and the *Rose,* sailed disdainfully past ineffectual fire from the American shore battery and proceeded up the Hudson to anchor near Tarrytown. That evening, to the thunderous cannon salutes of every British man-of-war, the great flagship of the fleet, the sixty-four gun *Eagle,* stood in from the sea and loomed large against the Staten. Island shoreline. Word swept through New York town that the admiral, Black Dick, had arrived.

The massed British fleet now comprised the largest fighting force the Americans had ever seen—350 ships, 10,000 sailors, and 32,000 professional soldiers including some 9,000 German mercenaries. And against this imposing force Washington had less than 20,000 ill-prepared, poorly equipped patriots, one quarter of them down with dysentery or fever.

Futilely the Americans prepared for the onslaught. Ex-farmer and Indian fighter Gen. Israel Putnam—"Old Put" to his men—concentrated on stopping the attack by water. He scuttled four large vessels linked together with iron-spiked logs to block the channel. Fourteen others loaded with combustibles and soaked with turpentine were readied as fireships to be launched flaming into any enemy warships crossing their bows. And finally, an urgent request was sent through channels for a little-known inventor of a strange "water machine" which some officials felt might be the secret weapon to stem the threatening tide. His name was David Bushnell.

Not too many years earlier this Connecticut Yankee was a reluctant farmer. After his father died, his mother remarried, and David sold his farm inheritance to his brother Ezra. He spent this pitifully small amount of money on something he had always wanted—an education that would enable him to enter Yale. And this he did at the relatively advanced age of thirty-one.

Whether it was the nature of the time or the fact that all his life David Bushnell nurtured a profound interest in ships and gadgets, he became obsessed with experimenting with ways to explode gunpowder underwater. His efforts resulted in his inventing an ingenious submarine mine, the first of its kind, that was triggered by a clockwork mechanism. David called his infernal contraption a "powder magazine." Both his professors and fellow students were enormously impressed when the quiet, publicity-shy Bushnell showed them his miniature models that blasted geysers in the river with monotonous regularity. When he learned what two ounces of gunpowder could do, he calculated that it would take a 150-pound gunpowder mine to blow one of his Majesty's men-of-war to kingdom come. And that was his goal.

Such were Bushnell's extracurricular activities at Yale in January 1775 as the country braced itself for a rebellion. Indeed, the ardent young inventor had high hopes that his mines might someday be used to sink the entire British fleet. All he needed was a vehicle to deliver his 150-pound surprise packages under the hulls of the enemy ships. And this, he decided, had to be a "sub-marine."

Slowly and carefully he designed an underwater boat the likes of which had never been seen before. It was egg-shaped, as if two gigantic tortoise shells were joined together and stood on end. Noting this resemblance, Bushnell laughingly called his creation a "turtle." The name stuck. There would be no model; it had to be built full size the first time.

When Yale let out for spring vacation, many of Bushnell's friends dashed off to Cambridge to tag along behind the troops of hotheaded patriot-hero Capt. Benedict Arnold. But just as eagerly Bushnell hurried home to Saybrook, Connecticut, to get his brother, Ezra, to help him build the *Turtle.*

They located a suitably secret building site on the long since eroded away Poverty Island near Sill's Point in the Connecticut River. There they built a small shed and let it be known locally that they were to become fisherman. The locals must have thought the brothers were constructing some fantastic fishing gear when they noticed all the heavy oak lumber, tar, cork, rope, brass and iron fittings that were ferried out to the island. But then if anyone saw their secret project, it is doubtful that they would have guessed what manner of thing it was anyway. Even Ezra Bushnell may have had moments of indecision when he found out what kind of gadget his older brother was building. To say the least, it was a far cry from farming; and in some people's minds it could be considered pure treason.

But somehow, despite the lack of funds and technical know-how, the thing took shape. It took over a month of almost around-the-clock labor to do it, but Bushnell's "barrel-stave" submarine was almost finished by the first of June when classes began again at Yale. The underwater vehicle was as cleverly constructed as the clockwork bomb it was intended to carry. Measuring seven and a half feet long, eight feet deep and four feet wide, the *Turtle* was just large enough to hold its single operator and enough air to sustain him underwater for thirty minutes. Its inverted egg shape was formed by tightly fitted vertical lengths of oak planking bound by iron hoops. All joints were corked and tarred for waterproofing. The operator entered through a brass hatch in a wide iron hoop mounted atop the domed hull. From his seat astride one of the oaken beams that strengthened the hull, he looked out through portholes in the six-inch high conning tower—about all of the vessel that was visible above water when she was afloat. Enough controls surrounded the operator that he had more than his hands full. To make the boat go forward or backward his right hand twisted a crank in front of him that windmilled a pair of oar blades joined together on the outside of the hull. Cranking another oar-bladed propeller mounted vertically through the upper hull drove the boat up or down. His left hand grasped a rudder bar behind his back to steer the boat right or left while his foot opened or closed a valve that flooded the boat's ballast tank. Two hand-operated force pumps, one in front and one behind him, emptied the ballast tank so that the boat could surface. In addition, turning a hand-operated auger in front of the conning tower screwed a line to the underside of an enemy hull so that, when the *Turtle* moved away, its 150-pound clockwork bomb, carried piggyback outside the submarine, remained behind, set to explode at another time.

One thing was certain, there would never be a dull moment aboard Bushnell's submarine. So eager was he to put the finishing touches on the boat and start testing it that he almost failed to return to his classes in June. But return he did and somehow he managed to control his enthusiasm until late July when he finally accomplished his long-desired goal—graduation from Yale.

Then back to his *Turtle* and Ezra for the tests. When final adjustments were made, the awkward-looking craft was loaded aboard a small sloop late one afternoon and taken out into Long Island Sound. David climbed aboard, secured the hatch and put the *Turtle* through her paces. He took on just enough water to allow the vessel's 900 pounds of lead ballast carried beneath the boat to take her down. As an added safety factor he had attached a chain to 200 pounds of this ballast which could be dropped quickly in an emergency, allowing the boat to rise.

He had no trouble other than some difficulty cranking the propellers, job enough for a strong man. He stayed submerged for forty-five minutes until he nearly fainted from the stale air, then he worked the force pumps and slowly rose to the surface.

As he climbed out of the conning tower he was both happy and sad. Happy that the *Turtle* had performed so well, but sad to admit that he was not physically capable of propelling the submarine for the prolonged period he knew would be necessary to accomplish his mission.

Then Ezra wanted to try the *Turtle.* David agreed only after securing a safety line to the submarine before his brother climbed aboard and took her down. Contrary to David's dive, Ezra had a minor problem with one of the two air intake and exhaust ventilation pipes behind the operator. But other than that, he easily propelled the boat in whatever direction he wished. David quickly realized that his brother was far better qualified than he to handle the submarine. So from then on

Ezra, not David, was trained for the dangerous mission ahead.

The next few months were spent making minor alterations to the *Turtle* and running practice dives in the Sound. David added a compass to take some mystery out of the underwater navigation and a water gauge or barometer to enable the operator to keep track of the submarine's depth.

Then one seemingly simple but very important problem plagued him. The operator had to be able to read his instruments at night or submerged when the interior of the *Turtle* would be dark. David tried a candle, but it consumed too much valuable oxygen. His best result was with fox fire, a phosphorescent fungi in rotting wood. Small amounts of this material on his compass needle and water-gauge float worked well until winter came; then frost killed the fungi and put out the light. For want of a nail a battle was lost. For want of a light, the *Turtle* could not possibly go to battle before spring when the fox fire glowed again. A major obstacle was understandable, but to be hamstrung by something as small as this was bitterly disappointing to the Bushnells.

But then not even the scientific genius of Benjamin Franklin was able to solve the dilemma. Earlier in October, the sixty-nine-year-old Franklin had left the Continental Congress in Philadelphia on his way to Cambridge to confer with Gen. George Washington. En route he stopped in Connecticut to see an old colleague, Dr. Benjamin Gale. The doctor, a close friend of the Bushnells, brought Franklin to see the *Turtle.* Obviously quite impressed by both the submarine and its inventor, Franklin urged David to bring his boat to New York to see if it could be used against the British fleet there. But not long after that historic encounter, the fox fire failed and David prevailed upon Dr. Gale to write Franklin to see if he had a solution. Apparently he did not, because it was the following spring before David was again able to illuminate his instruments with fox fire. Now Ezra made practice dives that simulated an attack on a ship. David moored a borrowed sloop offshore, and Ezra "attacked" it. Since neither sloops nor gunpowder were expendable items, his attack consisted of diving beneath the boat, attaching the screw that would be roped to the mine, then returning to shore again. David made his brother go through this maneuver each day until he performed it quickly and perfectly. Then they practiced at night until Ezra became equally proficient.

By now the British fleet was gathering in New York Bay. Franklin had told General Washington and others about the submarine. Washington doubted that it would be of any great benefit. But others thought that it might be one of the most persuasive weapons that the Americans would have. "Where is Bushnell?" they asked. "Where is that Water Machine we've been hearing about?"

Finally, convinced that the *Turtle* was in as good a shape as it would ever be, and that his brother was fully capable of handling her, David rented a sloop, somehow managed to get the ponderous *Turtle* aboard and set sail for New York.

He arrived without fanfare, hoping that his odd cargo would not attract undue attention, especially from any Tory spies in the area. Fortunately, it didn't. But when General Putnam learned that the *Turtle* had arrived, he excitedly sent a young aide named Aaron Burr to inspect it and bring him the news. Burr's report must have been complimentary, because Old Put was soon expounding the virtues of the *Turtle* and telling everyone that Billy Howe and his Redcoats didn't have a lick of a chance against this newfangled Yankee invention. According to Put it was going to sink the whole British fleet.

And maybe it might have to because General Putnam's other far-out schemes for defending the Hudson were not working too well. Two of his fireships took off up river to attack the British men-of-war, the *Phoenix* and the *Rose,* which were disturbing the peace around Tarrytown. The first fireship missed the *Phoenix* in the dark but got a tender, a smaller boat, which she took down in flames with her. The second fireship reached her target, the *Rose,* but the alert British crew cut her loose before any damage was done. The next morning, as if to add insult to injury, the two British ships sailed contemptuously down the Hudson, found a narrow passage near shore to skirt the General's scuttled ship blockade and slipped past the American batteries so close that their guns could not be lowered enough to land a shot.

Somehow it seemed that every grand strategy Old Put was sold on had a way of backfiring. And then it was the *Turtle's* turn.

Ezra Bushnell, who had trained for almost a year with the *Turtle,* the only man capable of operating the submarine, came down with a virulent case of fever, the same malady that had struck down so many of Washington's troops. It meant that he would be hospitalized for weeks. And by then the plan might be useless.

David already had spent almost every shilling he owned building the boat, then almost a year training Ezra. What could he do? He had invested too much to give up now, the very moment that they had been waiting for. There had to be another way. He had to find and train someone else. But even as he realized this, David doubted that it could be done soon enough. Still, he had to try.

He searched for a replacement. Days, then weeks, passed. Finally with the help of a brigadier general under Putnam's command he located three men who had volunteered for fireship duty but were willing to try Bushnell's new machine.

David took them aboard a sloop with the submarine and headed back to Saybrook, stopping briefly along the way to let the volunteers try the *Turtle* in various isolated coves on Long Island Sound. One of the men, twenty-seven-year-old Sgt. Ezra Lee, caught on quickly. He seemed more proficient than the others in handling the *Turtle,* but this time David was taking no chances. He would train all three soldiers equally. The best man would get the job, leaving him two reserves just in case General Putnam's jinx was still running true to form.

Meanwhile, the war would not wait. On August 22, 1776, General Howe landed on Long Island with 15,000 British troops. In the fierce fighting that followed, the British forced the Americans back to their fortifications at Brooklyn Heights. But then, instead of pursuing his advantage and capturing the outflanked American army, General Howe waited two days too long, and Washington slipped through his grasp. On the foggy night of August 29, Washington evacuated Long Island with the help of his skilled fisherman-soldiers from Marblehead and Salem who ferried 9,500 soldiers with all their baggage, artillery, ammunition, cattle and supplies across the East River to Manhattan before dawn the next morning. This successful maneuver relieved some of the depression which the defeat had brought to the army. The battle of Long Island had taken some 1,500 American lives, but Washington had salvaged the bulk of his army to fight another day.

When Bushnell heard the news, he knew he could delay no longer. If the *Turtle* was to be of any help to the patriots, now was the time. A sloop was found, the *Turtle* was loaded aboard, and David and the volunteers sailed back along the Sound, landing at New Rochelle. From there they carted the submarine overland to the East River where once again it was put on a small boat that carried it downriver to the tip of Manhattan. There it was tied to the wharf under the protective guns of Whitehall Battery to await the most opportune moment to strike.

As luck would have it, the very night the *Turtle* arrived conditions seemed perfect. There was the merest sliver of a moon, the waters of the bay hardly rippled, and the tide appeared to be barely moving out. So David decided that this was the night to try. His choice of operator, the man who had shown the most proficiency from the beginning of the tests was Sgt. Ezra Lee.

Spread across the bay before them in the faint glow of moonlight lay the enemy fleet. Although at that distance it was impossible to tell one ship from another, the *Turtle's* target was to be the mighty sixty-four gun flagship of the fleet, Black Dick's *Eagle,* with the Admiral himself aboard.

Shortly after midnight on September 6, the *Turtle* was readied for attack. Only General Putnam, Aaron Burr and a handful of others watched the preparations for the historical event. The boat was carefully checked and tested for a couple hours, then the 150-pound gunpowder mine was carefully attached to her hull just above the rudder. Finally, when everything was ready, Sergeant Lee climbed aboard and squeezed down through the narrow hatchway. Two whaleboats drew alongside and attached tow ropes to the one-ton vessel. Then with a few whispered words of good luck, the whaleboat crews leaned on their muffled oars, the dripping ropes tautened, and the strange vessel moved off slowly into the darkness.

Sergeant Lee later wrote, "The whaleboats towed me as nigh the ships as they dared to go and then cast me off." By then he had zeroed in on the unmistakable outlines of Admiral Howe's flagship, the *Eagle*. All Sergeant Lee had to do was dive under the ship, attach his bomb, set its clockwork mechanism working and get out of there before it blew.

Unfortunately, however, it was not that easy. About the time Lee's whaleboat escort disappeared in the darkness, Sergeant Lee discovered that someone had miscalculated the tide. It was not ebbing, but picking up speed, pushing him and the *Turtle* well below his target ship.

Lee cranked frantically on his forward propeller, but the ponderous *Turtle* barely moved against the outsurging waters of the bay. Still, for the unfortunate Sergeant there was no alternative but to crank endlessly on the propeller shaft. To pause even for a moment meant losing ground; to stop altogether meant being swept away by the outgoing tide.

Lee fought a near-losing battle for over an hour before the tide finally slackened and he gradually gained against it. With every fiber of his body aching from the ordeal, the stubborn Sergeant once again drew abreast of the *Eagle,* but even as he did he realized that the delay had cost him his cover of darkness. It was beginning to grow light.

Cautiously he propelled the *Turtle* closer to his massive target. So far no one had detected him. It was still dark enough that it would take a sharp-eyed sentry to spot the little more than six inches of turret that showed above the water. And even if he saw it, Lee knew it was unlikely the man would suspect it was anything but floating debris.

He eased the *Turtle* under the *Eagle's* broad counter. Above him he heard sailors moving about the deck and talking in soft voices. Quietly he closed and battened down the hatch. His foot nudged the valve, and water gurgled into the ballast tank. As soon as the *Turtle* submerged, Lee cranked the overhead propeller to help her go down. He had half an hour to do the job. Beads of sweat stood out on his brow, but his hands were clammy cold.

He watched the faint green glow of the fox-fire cork as it inched down the water gauge, tracing his descent. At three fathoms he judged he was deep enough to move under the curve of the hull. Gingerly he cranked the forward propeller until he figured he had gone far enough. Looking through the portholes revealed nothing but Stygian darkness. Finally he reached down and pushed the two pump handles that forced water out of the ballast tank. The *Turtle* rose a short way, then thudded to a halt against the bottom of the *Eagle.* Praying that no one noticed the bump, Lee grasped the handle of the vertical auger and began cranking.

Moments later he realized nothing was happening; the auger's screw tip was not penetrating the ship's bottom. The oak hull was copper sheathed to protect it against teredo worms. But Bushnell had foreseen this; the auger would penetrate the soft metal. Lee pondered what was wrong. Instead of copper maybe he had hit the iron bar connecting the rudder hinge to the stern.

He decided to move the *Turtle* and try another spot. When he twisted the forward propeller crank the boat suddenly lurched upward as she cleared the keel. Before the inexperienced Lee could correct his trim the *Turtle's* positive buoyancy sent her bumping and scraping up the ship's curved hull until she popped to the surface not three feet from the British man-of-war. Daylight streamed through the *Turtle's* portholes. Aware that he was now in immediate danger of being seen and discovered, Lee quickly flooded his ballast tank and submerged.

The Sergeant was going to try for the *Eagle* again until he realized how exhausted he was and decided against it. Besides, he knew that British longboats would soon be moving back and forth on the bay.

With four miles to go before he reached safety, Lee started cranking for home. A short while later, something went wrong with his compass. With no way to tell where he was going underwater, he was forced to surface and keep a lookout. Even then he had difficulties. The tide kept pushing him closer to British-held Governor's Island. To avoid washing ashore he steered a zigzag course. But just as he came opposite the island's fort, the enemy spotted him.

"Three or four hundred men got upon the parapet to observe me;" Lee wrote later, "at length a number came down to the shore, shoved off a 12 oar'd barge with 5 or 6 sitters and pulled for me. I eyed them, and when they got within 50 or 60 yards of me I let loose the magazine in hopes that if they should take me they would likewise pick up the magazine, and then we should all be blown up together."

But the soldiers were not too sure that they wanted to catch what they were chasing. When the 150-pound oddly shaped oak cask of gunpowder popped to the surface with its clockwork mechanism merrily ticking away, the British broke all records sculling back to shore, much to Sergeant Lee's relief.

Without further difficulty he propelled the *Turtle* safely to Manhattan and rejoined the anxious group awaiting him at Whitehall Battery.

Twenty minutes later, as Sergeant Lee was describing his adventures to David Bushnell and the others, the *Turtle*'s floating mine went off with a resounding explosion that rattled every window in the neighborhood.

"Glory be to God!" shouted General Putnam. "That'll do for 'em!"

People rushed from their houses expecting to see a fallen meteor, or at the very least, an earthquake. The towering column of water that erupted from New York Bay with such a fearful sound threw the British fleet into instant confusion. Bo's'ns immediately slashed their anchor cables so that the ships could drift out of harm's way. Officers shouted orders, bugles blew, sailors raced fore and aft, and men made ready to fend off attackers. But from which quarter? In the general pandemonium some ships drifted into each other, while others, fearing a Yankee trick, hoisted sails and scurried away.

Before any semblance of order came about, the routed British fleet, including Lord Richard Howe's mighty *Eagle,* was scattered far and wide to the safer extremities of New York Bay. It was the first time a submarine had ever been used in naval warfare. No one was hurt, but for once British reserve was shaken. Never again would the British ever feel quite so certain of their position in dealing with the damnably unpredictable Americans.

Shortly after its historic debut, the *Turtle* vanished. No one knows whether it was destroyed accidentally by the British, scuttled purposely by the Americans to prevent capture or dismantled secretly by its inventor. After the war, for some unaccountable reason, David Bushnell left his home, changed his name and chose to live out the remainder of his life in complete anonymity.

CHAPTER 3

Fulton: Submarine
Round the Bend

 On the afternoon of July 29, 1800, a party of picnickers along the banks of the River Seine near Rouen, France, hardly noticed the small sailboat moving sluggishly downriver on a light breeze. A few commented on the vessel's unusual appearance, particularly its sail—a large fan-shaped affair standing well above the deck. But even as they spoke, the boat swung about, two men lowered and folded the sail, then disappeared into the small cabin—nothing in the least unusual. But what suddenly shook the picnickers out of their lethargy was to see the vessel continue upriver with no visible sign of locomotion, then slowly sink from sight.

Some rubbed their eyes in disbelief; others raced off to spread the alarm that a boat with two passengers had foundered in the river. Those left standing on the riverbank five minutes later were further confounded to see the boat suddenly reappear on the surface, proceed some distance upriver, then again sink from sight.

Seventeen minutes later, if there had been anyone left behind, they would have seen an even more incredible sight, for the boat surfaced once more, the men hoisted her peculiar sail and calmly sailed away.

What the picnickers had unknowingly witnessed was the first trial run of a remarkable submarine designed by the even more remarkable man at her helm, a young American artist-turned-engineer named Robert Fulton. It was twenty-eight years before French novelist and fictional submarine forecaster, Jules Verne, would be born, but Fulton had successfully dived to a depth of twenty-five feet for seventeen minutes and surfaced in his submarine *Nautilus,* first of a long line of underwater boats to be given this name.

The success of the venture had not surprised him. After all, Fulton had scrupulously planned and carried out everything to the last detail. Still, he was highly elated. It meant that at thirty-five, an age when most of his contemporaries had already made their marks, he was at last on the threshold of the fame and fortune he had always sought. Not too bad for a farmer's son from Conowingo Creek, Little Britain Township, Pennsylvania.

How much of a Pennsylvania farmer he was is another story, but he was born to Mary Smith and Robert Fulton, Sr., on November 14, 1765. Three years later his father died. Since the elder Fulton had not been a successful farmer, his mother was hard-pressed taking care of her five children. Yet it was from her that Robert got his education and inherited two of her finest qualities—a keen mind and a strong will to succeed, assets which served him well throughout his life. Still he was a less than average student, preferring to sketch or work mechanical experiments rather than study. At seventeen he left home and went to Philadelphia to seek his fortune. Little is recorded of those early years, but we do know that he soon became enough of an artist that he was registered as a painter of miniatures under the patronage of Benjamin Franklin. And in 1786, Franklin sent him to England to sharpen his talents under the tutelage of the renowned painter and eventual president of the Royal Academy, Benjamin West. When he reached London, he had no more than 40 guineas (about $118) and a letter of introduction to West. In the next few years the young apprentice's lot did not much improve. Like most who have followed the artist's profession, he was frequently broke and in debt. On several occasions he was forced to borrow money from more affluent friends to pay off his more demanding creditors.

Seven years later, however, Robert Fulton had become an accomplished and moderately successful artist whose work was accepted by the Royal Academy. Then, inexplicably, in 1793, Fulton turned his back on his chosen profession and took up the science of engineering.

From then on he threw himself into his new endeavor with all the vigor and enthusiasm he had previously reserved for his art. He wrote a treatise pointing out the value of a proposed canal system for England. He spent three years studying the construction of canals, then designed inclined planes to replace locks. And through it all the same financial troubles still plagued him.

Finally Fulton borrowed enough money to return to America, hoping possibly that his own country would be interested in his canal schemes. But before he left, he visited Paris. The city, the people, the country and in particular the political flavor of the time caught his fancy, and he did not get around to leaving for the next seven years.

Fulton's first ambitious undertaking was to sell France on his canalization ideas. He translated and published his English treatise on the subject, adding some new material of interest to the French. In 1798, he patented some of his ideas and upon learning that Napoleon Bonaparte had expressed some interest in his work, Fulton promptly sent him a copy of his treatise. Included was a flattering letter to the French general in which the enterprising engineer expressed his hope that France would soon succeed in her efforts to defeat England in the war that was being waged between the two countries. So much for Fulton's English sympathies.

The year Fulton changed his profession, he was already considering the problems of powering vessels by steam. The idea was not new. James Rumsey did it on the Potomac in 1785 and took out British patents; John Fitch was running a steamboat on the Delaware River in 1790 and patented it in France the next year. Rumsey operated a steamboat on the Thames River in 1793, so it is likely that Fulton was fully aware of these efforts. The difficulty with some steamboats then invented was that they were impractical. Fulton felt that he could do a better job than his competitors by designing a more practical steamboat, which is, of course, what he eventually did and is most famous for.

Possibly it was a natural progression from the idea of powering a surface vessel to designing one to operate underwater. Again the idea was not new, but sometime between 1793 and 1797, Fulton designed a submarine he named the *Nautilus*. While some biographers have suggested that he and David Bushnell of *Turtle* fame knew each other in Paris and that Fulton borrowed some of his countryman's ideas, it is unlikely that the two ever met. Despite the contention that in 1797, fourteen years after the American Revolution, "someone tried to sell France an invisible means" to break the British blockade, there is not valid evidence that this was Bushnell or that he ever went abroad. Not until the reading of his will in 1884 was it learned that after the American Revolution Bushnell moved to Georgia, changed his name to Bush, practiced medicine and lived in comparative obscurity until his death at eighty-four when his real identity became known.

It is probable that Fulton knew about the *Turtle* and may have even borrowed some of Bushnell's ideas. In any case the results were a marked improvement. Fulton's early ideas about a submarine seem to have had less appeal to him than his canalization or steamboat schemes. But once he considered the unlimited potentials of his *Nautilus,* he soon focused all his energies on the new project.

For the purpose of "lessening the power of the English fleet," he proposed to the French Directory that the government build his *Nautilus*. They turned him down. He submitted his proposals again, asking no financial remuneration for himself until after the submarine had proved itself by sinking English ships. And then he asked for a modest sum equivalent to a fraction of the value of the ships destroyed. Still his proposal was rejected.

The more he thought about it the more Fulton saw his submarine as an "ultimate weapon" capable of bringing the naval powers of the world to one gigantic stalemate. After that, he reasoned, there was nothing for them to do but get along peaceably with each other. Such was Fulton's altruistic dream, and it appears that he was genuinely sincere about it. With the unrelenting passion of a man who believes he is right, Fulton sat down and wrote a masterpiece of argumentation to the Minister of Marine, picking out every possible objection to his proposals and obliterating them with keen logic. Unable to stand up under such withering fire, official resistance gave way, and Fulton was granted permission to build his submarine.

So off to Rouen he went, and at the Perrier boatyard the first *Nautilus* submarine took shape. She was twenty-one feet three inches long with a six-foot-four-inch beam. Her streamlined shape could only be described as an imperfect ellipsoid. With her forward-mounted observation dome and collapsible fan-shaped sail, the *Nautilus* bore a remarkable resemblance to a modern-day research submersible. She was operated by a three-man crew. Power was by a hand crank geared to a screw propeller at the stern. The boat would submerge upon flooding her hollow iron keel. Angle of dive was controlled by horizontal fins on the rudder, both of which could be manipulated from inside. Pumping the water ballast from the keel brought her to the surface where she could be sailed.

Interestingly the submarine was designed to carry a torpedo or "carcass" as Fulton called it. Deployment was much like that on Bushnell's *Turtle*, but with Fulton's refinements. A thin rope threaded through a detachable spike in the top of the *Nautilus'* observation dome. One end was attached to a winding spool in the bow of the boat; the other to the explosive charge. In use, the submarine was to dive beneath an enemy warship and come up against its bottom. A blow on the end of the spike from within the dome drove the iron thorn into the ship's oak planking. As the submarine moved away, the spike detached from the dome. The submarine continued to a safe distance, trailing the gunpowder torpedo behind it on its rope until it drew up to the eye of the spike. On contact with the ship's hull the charge exploded.

After a successful test of the submarine in the Seine, Fulton found that the river's swift current interfered with the boat's operation underwater, so he decided to take it to Le Havre for a trial run in the ocean.

This time he took a candle down with him and found that it did not deplete the oxygen from the boat's air as quickly as he thought it would on his first dive. Fulton reported that, on one of the test dives, he and his two crewmates remained submerged for six hours without difficulty. During this time they renewed their air through a tube attached to a surface float. In another test he checked the *Nautilus'* speed with two men cranking the submarine submerged against two men rowing a boat on the surface. The hand-cranked submarine covered the 360-foot distance two minutes faster than the rowboat. Still, Fulton was disappointed with certain features. The short horizontal rudder and the Archimedes' screw were inefficient. He replaced the screw with a four-bladed propeller similar to the sails on a windmill and named it "Flier."

Finally pleased with the results, Fulton returned to Paris and got back to the serious business of promoting his invention in the upper echelons of the French government. Some of the better things Fulton had going for him were his youthful good looks, personable charm and his brilliant mind. Whether by chance or intention his closest friends were some of the most influential people of the times. And not surprisingly each one played an important role in Fulton's climb toward fame and fortune. One of the young inventor's first and closest friends in Paris was the American poet Joel Barlow, a personal friend of Napoleon Bonaparte. During Fulton's more destitute days trying to sell France canals, he was obliged to borrow funds from his friend the Earl of Stanhope. Being an inventor and a student of the sciences himself, Stanhope and Fulton had a common interest in moving boats by steam. Two other of his close friends were also highly reputable men of science—the mathematician Gaspard Monge and Pierre Simon de Laplace, the famous astronomer whose masterful explanation of heavenly movements earned him the highly acclaimed position of president of the French Academy. Both men possessed two identical characteristics—they were each enthusiastically loyal to Robert Fulton, and each also enjoyed the personal friendship of Napoleon Bonaparte. So when the young American inventor returned to Paris excited over his successful trial runs with the *Nautilus,* they urged him to lay his proposals before the First Consul himself.

Fulton confidently complied, presenting his offer of the *Nautilus* to the French government in return for whatever they felt he deserved. Monge personally presented Fulton's letter to Napoleon, who in turn sent it on to the Minister of Marine with this marginal note: "Je prie le Ministre de la Marine de me faire connaitre ce qu'il sait sur les projets du capitaine Fulton.—BONAPARTE."

A few days later, Monge and Laplace arranged a meeting between Fulton and the First Consul, Napoleon Bonaparte. Both were aspiring young men, one a brash, headstrong inventor, the other an arrogant, ambitious dictator who believed himself destined to conquer the world. And what did the two have in common? Interestingly, without either realizing it, each could have solved the other's problem. Fulton, as Napoleon well knew, was an unsuccessful American artist-turned-inventor anxious to sell France an admittedly crude and highly unorthodox war machine which he claimed would make all navies defenseless. Napoleon on the other hand wanted to conquer a world empire, but one obstacle stood in his way—the all-powerful English navy. Fulton offered Bonaparte the means of eliminating this obstacle. Napoleon said he would think it over.

Fulton went home convinced that the little dictator could not afford to pass up his magnanimous offer. Six days later, however, he was not so sure. "Who in his right mind would take this long to decide such an obviously simple decision?" raged Fulton. "Here I am offering the man world dominion with my *Nautilus* and he ponders whether or not he wants it!"

Finally reaching the end of his patience, Fulton dashed off a tactless letter to the Minister of Marine, saying, "Although I retain the most ardent desire to see the English Government beaten . . . the cold and discouraging manner with which all my exertions have been treated . . . will compel me to abandon the enterprise in France if I am not received in a more friendly and liberal manner."

With the usual bureaucratic dispatch of his office, Minister of Marine Admiral Decrés was considering Fulton's proposal when the inventor's letter arrived and settled the question. Prompted by Fulton's veiled threat Admiral Decrés reacted as any sailor might to a contrivance designed to put his branch of service out of business. He vetoed the idea and sent his adverse report to Bonaparte.

Monge and Laplace rallied round their temperamental friend, warned him about writing letters to officials and patched up the whole affair with remarkable finesse. Indeed, when they finished, not only had they persuaded Napoleon to overlook his Minister's opinion of the Fulton project but they got the First Consul's permission to go ahead with the development of the *Nautilus* under the watchful eye of a new investigative committee. That committee: Monsieurs Monge, Laplace and Volney, the latter an eminent scholar. Fulton could not have gotten a better deal if he had masterminded the arrangement himself, which he probably did.

Off to Le Havre he went to collect his *Nautilus* and take it to Brest where the boat was altered and improved. Then on July 3, 1801, he and three others made their first dive in the remodeled submarine. Excitedly he wrote of the results in a Paris letter addressed to the "Commissioners appointed by the First Consul to promote the invention of Submarine Navigation"—citizens Monge, Laplace and Volney.

"On the 3d of thermidor* I commenced my experiment by plunging to the depth of 5 then 10 then 15 and so on to 25 feet but not to a greater depth than 25 feet as I did not conceive the Machine Sufficiently Strong to bear the Pressure of a Greater column of water. At this depth I remained one hour with my companions and two candles burning without experiancing the least inconvenience. . . ." He went on to tell how before he left Paris a mathematician had calculated that in the 212-cubic-foot *Nautilus* there would be enough

---

*July in the calendar of the First French Republic.

oxygen to supply four men and two small candles for three hours. But he decided to do away with the candles in favor of adding "a Small window in the upper part of the Boat near the bow which window Is only one inch and a half diameter and of Glass 9 lines thick." After diving the boat to a depth between twenty-four and twenty-five feet he found he had "Sufficient light to count the minutes in the Watch. . . ." He therefore concluded that such windows located in various parts of the boat would give him sufficient daylight illumination.

On the surface he found that the *Nautilus* sailed along at about two knots an hour.

> I tacked and retacked tryed her before and by the wind And in all these operations found her to Answer the helm And Act like a common dul Sailing boat, After exersising thus About An hour I lowered the mast and Sails and commenced the operation of Plunging this required about two Minutes. I then placed two men at the engine which gives the Rectileniar Motion, And one At the helm, while I governed the machine which keeps her balanced between two waters. With the bathomater before me And with one hand I found I could keep her at any depth I thought Proper the men then commenced movement and continued about 7 Minutes when mounting to the Serface I found we had traveled 400 Matres . . .

He was pleased to note in turning his submarine around underwater that his compass worked the same above as below the surface. To extend the submarine's air supply Fulton constructed a copper globe he called a "bomb" into which he compressed 200 cubic feet of air. Then he and two companions dove the *Nautilus* five feet underwater and tested it. At the end of an hour and forty minutes Fulton began to let off measured amounts of air from his reservoir for the next four hours and twenty minutes that the crew remained submerged without experiencing any discomfort.

Next Fulton turned his attention to his vessel's attack capabilities. "I Quit the experiments in the Boat to try those of the Bomb Submarine," he wrote. "It is this bomb which is the Engine of Destruction the Plunging boat is only for the purpose of carrying the bomb to where it may be used to Advantage."

Fulton's bombs were different-sized copper cylinders containing from 10 to 200 pounds of powder. Each device was armed with a gunlock mechanism that triggered the charge upon contact with a ship's hull. Fulton tested his "Bomb Submarine" before a small crowd of spectators including French Admiral Vellaret. The target was a forty-foot sloop provided by the Admiral and the Brest Maritime Prefect. With the *Nautilus* trailing a bomb containing twenty pounds of gunpowder, Fulton submerged 650 feet from the vessel and continued underwater, "So as to pass near the Sloop I Struck her with the bomb in my Passage the explosion took Place and the Sloop was torn into Atoms, in fact nothing was left but the buye and cable, And the concussion was so Great that a Column of Water Smoak and fibres of the Sloop was cast from 80 to 100 feet in Air, the Simple Experiment at once Proved the effect of the Bomb Submarine to the Satisfaction of all the Spectators. . . ."

Along with the details of his Brest experiments to his faithful Paris friends, Monge, Laplace and Volney, Fulton included the proposal that two such submarines at least thirty-six feet long and twelve feet wide be built, each capable of carrying a crew of eight and an air supply for eight hours. The brass-hulled underwater boats were to be made strongly enough to permit submerging to sixty- or eighty-foot depths and also be capable of carrying provisions and twenty-five to thirty bombs at a time. Fulton suggested that these charges not only be used to destroy enemy shipping but that hundreds of floating bombs be dispersed by the submarines at the mouths of various bays, rivers and harbors so that tidal currents would carry them in to do their deadly business. "And this is Perhaps the most Simple and certain means of convincing England that Science can put her in the Power of France and of compelling her to become a humble Pleader for the liberty of the Seas She now denies to her Neighbors . . . it is Probable in a few years England will See it her best policy never to give france reason to exersise this invention against her—if England cannot prevent the Blockade of the Thames by the means of plunging boats and

Bombs submarine, of what use will be her boasted navy. . . ."

Two months later Monge, Laplace and Volney requested additional information regarding the cost of Fulton's proposed scheme. They also mentioned that Bonaparte would like to see the *Nautilus.*

Fulton supplied the cost information, then tossed them a bomb: He had destroyed the *Nautilus!*

"I am Sorry that I had not earlyer information of the Consuls desire to See the Plunging boat, when I finished my experiments," he wrote them on September 20, 1801.

> She leaked Very much and being but an imperfect engine I did not think her further useful hence I took her to Pieces, Sold her Iron work lead and Cylinders and was necessitated to break the greater part of her movements In taking them to Pieces So that nothing now remains which can give an Idea of her Combination. . . . You will be so good as to excuse me to the Premier Consul, when I refuse to exhibit my drawings to a committee of Engineers for this I have two reasons, the first is not to put it in the Power of any one to explain the Principles or movements lest she Should Pass from one to another til the enemy obtained information, the Second is that I consider this invention my Private Property the Perfectionment of which will give to france incalculable advantages over her most Powerful and Active enemy. . . .

Fulton said that since he had labored on this project for three years at a considerable expense to himself he now felt that it was time for his invention to "Secure to me an ample Independence" (financial, that is) and "that consequently the Government Should Stipulate certain terms with me before I proceed to further explination. . . ."

Fulton apparently felt that his Brest demonstration was proof enough for acceptance, that the government could take his word on how well his submarine performed and what a great service it could render France. Indeed, the Prefect Maritime at Brest had passed on a favorable report of the *Nautilus'* performance and attack demonstration. But he also added that he considered the whole idea somewhat suicidal. "This manner of making war against an enemy carries the adverse criticism that the person using the device and sinking with it would be lost. Certainly that is not a death for military men."

The impetuous Fulton had done it again. He came home from Brest elated over the results of his experiments, positive that he would hear shortly from Bonaparte himself, praising him for his success and complying with his wishes to give France the "ultimate weapon." But Napoleon had more pressing matters on his mind. As the days passed without word from the First Consul, Fulton finally wrote a personal letter to Bonaparte urging him to take positive action on his appeal.

Napoleon did not even give him the courtesy of a reply. As time passed Fulton heard that the French dictator was calling him a charlatan and a swindler bent only on obtaining money from the government under false pretenses.

Fulton was outraged. During the silence he had at least hoped. But now he knew that the matter was closed; this was the end of any further negotiations with France. Historians have wondered why Napoleon passed up the golden opportunity of Fulton's offer, but in retrospect it is not surprising. New innovations are often opposed by those who stand to benefit most from them. Considering the manner of warfare in Fulton's day this was particularly true about the submarine. Many saw it as a sneaky way to attack an opponent's undefended underbelly from the invisible anonymity of the water's depths. "And what kind of war is that?" Napoleon might well have asked. "When my armies do battle they fight openly and with honor. Fulton's proposals are for cowards; his methods are a threat to proper warfare."

Not even Monge and Laplace could patch up this situation. Still they remained faithful to their American friend while he temporarily shelved his submarine ideas and turned his attention to the problems of powering a boat by steam. This time another of Fulton's influential friends encouraged and financially supported his efforts—the American minister to the French government, Robert R. Livingston. The statesman was fond of mechanical contrivances and was more than ordinarily interested in helping one of his gifted countrymen try to perfect a practical steam-powered boat. Fulton corresponded with various pioneers in the field including the famous inventor of the condensing steam engine, James C. Watt; and in 1803 he built a steamboat which he tried out on the Seine.

Although Napoleon and the French government were no longer interested in Fulton's activities, others were. While he was trying to sell France a submarine to sink the English navy, the British secret service was noting his every move. Moreover, Fulton, himself, made sure that England was well appraised of his projects by detailing them in letters to his old friend the Earl of Stanhope who in turn became so "alarmed" that he made a public speech on the subject in the House of Lords. In any event, on June 19, 1803, a month after England and France went to war, the British Admiralty issued a secret circular to their naval commanders at Sheerness, Portsmouth, Downs, Plymouth and at sea, warning them that "a plan has been concerted by Mr. Fulton, an American resident at Paris, under the influence of the First Consul of the French Republic, for destroying the Maritime Force of this Country; I am commanded by their Lordships to send you herewith the substance of the information they have received thereto. . . ." The enclosed detailed specific though slightly exaggerated facts about the *Nautilus* and its attack demonstration off Brest.

Along with this information England knew that Napoleon had turned down Fulton's submarine proposals and that the American inventor was now marking time with steamboats. Rather than have him loose in the enemy camp England thought it wiser to woo Fulton over to their side so they could keep an eye on him. Consequently, a gentleman named Smith approached Fulton in Paris, explained that the English wanted to use his subs against the French and offered him £800 to go to England to explain his invention to the ministers. He would, said Smith, be rewarded accordingly.

Fulton, no longer the idealist offering his efforts for whatever a government cared to give him, sent Smith back to England to say that he required the following: First, £10,000 for leaving France and his present pursuits and, second, a committee to be formed within three weeks of his arrival in London to appraise his principles of submarine navigations. If these were accepted he would then sell England all his plans for the construction and development of the submarine and its bombs for £100,000.

Fulton thought he had the British lion by the tail. It was a nice feeling being sought after. While awaiting England's decision he retired to a neutral corner: Amsterdam.

There England let him languish for three months. Thinking that negotiations had foundered, Fulton finally returned to Paris where he was again confronted by Smith with a coded letter from Lord Hawkesbury, the foreign secretary. It stated that England could not afford to pay Fulton such sums of money as he requested without proof of his invention by actual experiment before a government-approved board. But if Fulton cared to trust His Majesty's government by offering England his invention, then, "you may rely on being treated with the utmost liberality and Generosity. . . ."

Since it was his best and only offer, Fulton left France and arrived in London on April 28, 1804, only to find that his correspondent Lord Hawkesbury was no longer in office and William Pitt was about to become prime minister. Pitt was not interested in their original proposals; rather he wanted Fulton to build a submarine that would prove itself in action against the French. When Fulton agreed, they drew up a contract granting £7,000 for the vessel's construction, full use of His Majesty's dockyard for the purpose, a salary of £200 a month for Fulton with the added stipulation that he would receive half the value of all enemy vessels destroyed by his "engines" in fourteen years. Fulton was satisfied with the arrangement, and the wily William Pitt must have been equally pleased. After all he had in effect eliminated the submarine threat against England by coaxing Fulton over to their side to build that same weapon for use against France— all for the amazingly small down payment of £800.

Britain's new prime minister was far more receptive to Fulton's submarine ideas than Napoleon Bonaparte. At a country-house breakfast with Pitt and his aide, Sir Home Popham, near Putney Common, Fulton reported this conversation: When Sir Home Popham went into an adjoining room Pitt said, "This remarkable invention of yours seems to go to the destruction of all fleets."

"It was invented with that in view," said Fulton. "Indeed, I think that this invention will lead to the total annihilation of the existing system of marine war."

"But in its present state of perfection," said Pitt, "those who command the seas will be benefited by it while the minor maritime powers can draw no advantage from what is now known."

"True," agreed Fulton, "unless submarines were introduced into practice, but it will probably be some years before any nation can bring such a vessel to perfection. So for the moment if French warships could be destroyed by submarine attack, it would convince Bonaparte and the whole world that any future fleet wishing to move against England would be burnt in like manner."

It was then agreed upon between the two that a submarine should be built and tried out on the French fleet at Boulogne. Before this could be carried out, however, Pitt ran into strong opposition to the idea from his commanders in chief. Typical of the reaction from advocates of the existing naval system, British sea dog, Adm. Earl St. Vincent growled, "Pitt is the greatest fool that ever existed to encourage a mode of war which they who command the seas do not want, and which, if successful, will deprive them of it."

Pitt, himself, was soon doubtful of the honorable aspects of submarine warfare; yet he did not wish to totally absolve himself or England from its possible use in the event that the war went overwhelmingly against England. So while he pondered the ethics of the question, he set Fulton to work making "carcasses," gunpowder mines in copper cylinders that could be exploded by contact or clockwork mechanisms. When he figured his bombs were ready, he launched the promised attack on the French fleet at Boulogne, four long-boats dropping two of his bombs overboard at the mouth of the harbor. Joined by a seventy-foot line, the mines were supposed to drift in on the tide until the rope fouled a ship's anchor cable, swinging them in to destroy the vessel. But something went wrong, and the mines did not explode. Fulton figured it all out and corrected the problem, but the attempt was not repeated. Instead, in October 1805, he demonstrated the effectiveness of his reworked carcasses by blowing up the brig *Dorothea,* off Walmer Castle before Pitt and other dignitaries. But less than a week later all hopes of England using his submarine ideas were wiped out by a single resounding historical event: Admiral Nelson destroyed the combined French and Spanish fleet at Trafalgar. England no longer needed Fulton or his plans for submarine warfare.

All he could do now was try to lay claim to the monies which he felt were due him according to the terms of his contract with the British government. Repeatedly, he wrote various officials, asking, pleading, begging for a settlement. Twice he wrote Pres. Thomas Jefferson in an effort to sell his submarine to America. But neither Jefferson nor the British replied. With these cold rejections Fulton's windy diatribes were reduced to curt, angry demands for payment. Finally, a committee of arbiters met with him and fully agreed with his gripes. Still, he was paid no more money. In a burst of wrath Fulton threatened to return to America and publish all his submarine secrets in a "good Philosophical work" that would make his dreadful underseas mode of attack so commonplace that no navy in the world would ever again be safe. Pitt, invalided and close to death, was unable to respond. And Lord Grenville's government no longer cared to respond.

Completely frustrated, Fulton left England for America in October 1806. Before departing he deposited all his submarine drawings, descriptions and letters in a sealed container in care of the American consul with instructions that it not be opened unless he was lost at sea. "Should such an event happen," he wrote Joel Barlow, his faithful friend of early Paris days, "I have left you the means to publish these works, with engravings, in a handsome manner, and to which you will add your own ideas—showing how the liberty of the seas may be gained by such means."

We know, of course, that Fulton returned to America without difficulty and once again turned his attention to the development of the steamboat. With wealthy backer Robert Livingston he built the famous *Clermont,* and with the assistance of a steamboat monopoly it brought him the fame and fortune he had long sought elsewhere.

Never again did Fulton refer to either the *Nautilus* documents or his submarine efforts abroad. They comprised a chapter of his life which he apparently wished forgotten. Possibly he felt that if he could not bring the idea of submarine navigation to fruition then he preferred that his work on the subject be kept secret.

In retrospect it appears that Fulton's real love was the submarine but that the world was not yet ready for it. After acquiring wealth and renown with steamboats, he again went back to his first interest, building in New York, in 1815, an eighty-foot-long, twenty-two-foot-wide submarine named the *Mute.* Before it was completed, however, Fulton died at the age of fifty, and the *Mute* was junked.

Since the *Nautilus* documents did not come to light for 119 years, the extent of Fulton's work in the development of the submarine was generally unknown. In 1870, the papers were sold at auction and went into a private collection for fifty years.

In 1920, they were purchased by a Fulton biographer, William B. Parsons, who published their contents. The secret drawings and detailed explanations which Fulton left in London with the American consul in 1806 reveal that the underwater boat which he designed for the British government between his Brest experiments in 1801 and his British proposals in 1804 was a great improvement over the French *Nautilus.* His drawings show a seagoing submarine thirty-five feet long with a ten-foot beam capable of carrying a six-man crew and provisions for twenty days at sea. The boat was armed with thirty submarine bombs (mines) carried in individual deck compartments. The hull was designed more like a seagoing sloop with conventional sails which could be readily lowered with the mast for diving. Underwater propulsion was by the crew cranking a two-bladed propeller which Fulton had cleverly designed to be folded up out of water during surface operation to prevent drag, a feature not adopted by vessels until some fifty years later (1850). The underwater boat included two streamlined ventilation pipes for subsurface use and a remarkably modern-looking conning tower with direct-view glass ports. Such was the underwater boat Robert Fulton designed for a world not yet ready for anything quite so radical. And perhaps it was best that another century would elapse before such a craft came into being, for as the French commission decided after examining Fulton's first plunging machine: "The underwater boat invented by the citizen, Fulton, is a means of terrible destruction because it operates in secret in an almost unavoidable manner."

The world would learn soon enough the prophetic truth of that statement.

Feisty, dapper, Irish-American submarine inventor John P. Holland peers from the conning tower of the U.S.S. *Holland (SS-1)*. (Courtesy: U.S. Navy)

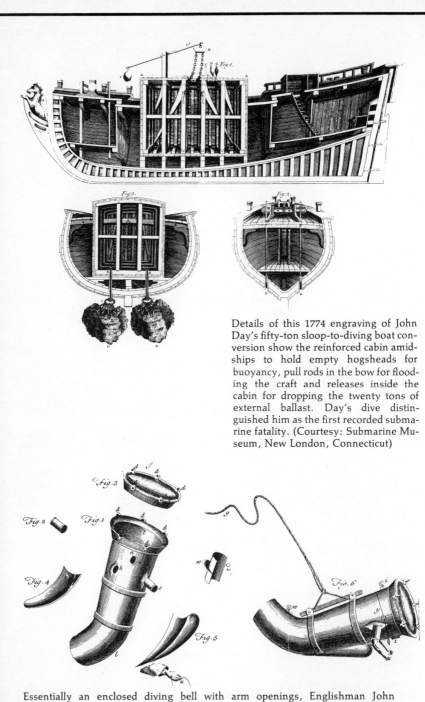

Details of this 1774 engraving of John Day's fifty-ton sloop-to-diving boat conversion show the reinforced cabin amidships to hold empty hogsheads for buoyancy, pull rods in the bow for flooding the craft and releases inside the cabin for dropping the twenty tons of external ballast. Day's dive distinguished him as the first recorded submarine fatality. (Courtesy: Submarine Museum, New London, Connecticut)

Essentially an enclosed diving bell with arm openings, Englishman John Lethbridge's "diving engine" of 1715 worked so well that he had great success in the treasure-salvage business. (Courtesy: Submarine Museum, New London, Connecticut)

An original engraving from the 1875 American edition of Jules Verne's *Twenty Thousand Leagues under the Sea*, a classic that enthralled generations of readers. While the book surely inspired future submarine inventors, at least twenty-five practical versions of the submarine were already in use before the book was written. (Courtesy: Submarine Museum, New London, Connecticut)

Early woodcut of Alexander the Great's supposed descent to the bottom of the sea in a device of his own manufacture. *"He looked to the bottom of the sea to show him the wonders there. He called for glassmakers and ordered that they make a glass barrel that would permit him to see clearly all things at great depths. . . ."* [Excerpted and translated from *La Vrai Histoire d'Alexandre*, a thirteenth-century manuscript in the collection of the Bibliothèque Royale, Brussels, Belgium.] (Courtesy: Submarine Museum, New London, Connecticut)

Below: "King Alexander's Submarine" titles this illustration from *The Romance of Alexander,* a manuscript written and illustrated in Flanders in 1340. (Courtesy: Submarine Museum, New London, Connecticut)

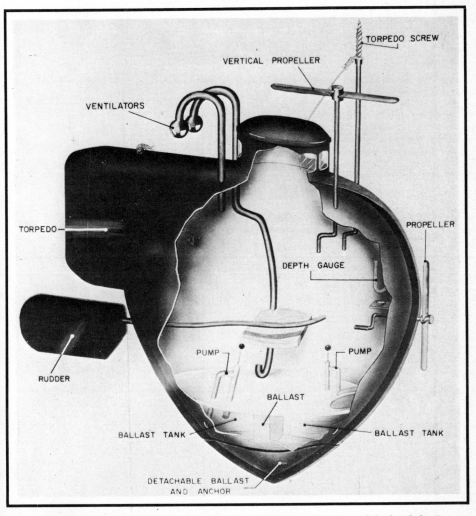

While this modern illustration of Bushnell's *Turtle* may make the craft look "slicker" than it was, it is essentially more accurate than most early illustrations of the boat. It shows, for example, the *Turtle*'s proper propellers, not *Archimède*'s screws. This model is at the Submarine Library, New London, Connecticut. (Courtesy: Submarine Museum, New London, Connecticut)

Part of the clockwork mechanism devised by David Bushnell to explode gunpowder charges underwater. It is the same as the one used by Sergeant Lee during his unsuccessful attack on the blockading British fleet with Bushnell's *Turtle*. (Courtesy: Submarine Museum, New London, Connecticut)

Engraving of an original Fulton painting depicting the destruction of the brig *Dorothea* by one of Fulton's underwater mines. The demonstration took place in England in the presence of William Pitt and others to prove the effectiveness of Fulton's "carcasses." (Courtesy: Submarine Museum, New London, Connecticut)

KEY

AB. Body of boat (ellipsoid).
CD. Metal keel.
EE. Pumps.
F. Metal conning tower.
G. Cross bulkhead.
H. Propeller.
I. Vertical rudder.
L. Horizontal rudder.
M. Fulcrum for L.
N. Gears for operation of L.
O. Horn of the Nautilus.
P. Torpedo.
Q. The bottom of a vessel.

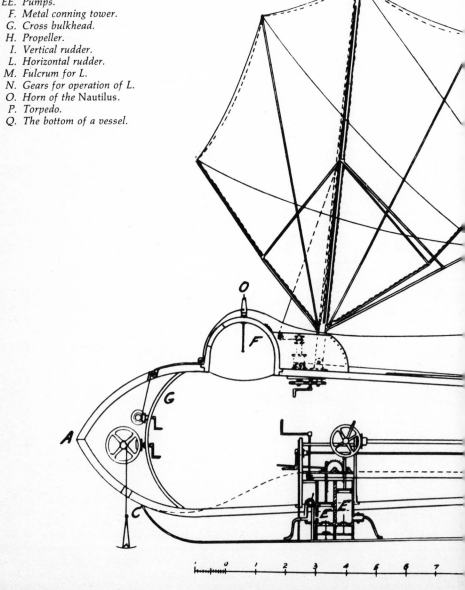

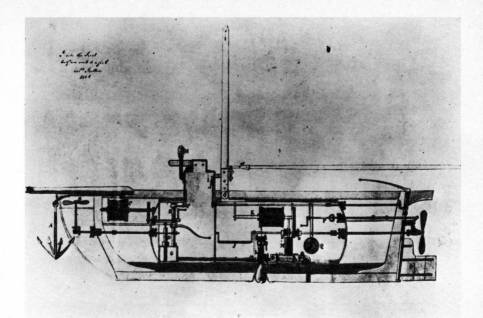

The improvements Fulton made over his first submarine are apparent in this sketch showing a more conventional boat hull, a vertical propeller in the bow and a folding one in the stern. The turret hatch is also equipped with a periscope. (Courtesy: U.S. Navy)

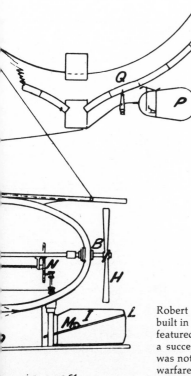

Robert Fulton's first diving boat, the twenty-foot-long *Nautilus*, built in France in 1798, was powered by hand-cranked propeller and featured a collapsable sail for the surface. While the submarine was a success, Fulton's efforts to get it accepted were not. The world was not yet ready for what many called "a coward's threat to proper warfare." (Courtesy: Submarine Museum, New London, Connecticut)

Fulton's illustration shows the final version of his submarine as it would appear when operated either above or below the surface. (Courtesy: Submarine Museum, New London, Connecticut)

Robert Fulton
1865

Bavarian ex-woodworker Wilhelm Bauer who in 1850 built a submarine boat so formidable that the mere sight of it routed the entire Danish fleet blockading Kiel Harbor. (Courtesy: Submarine Museum, New London, Connecticut)

This is not Wilhelm Bauer's *Brandtaucher*, as the engraving is incorrectly titled, but his *Le Diable-Marin*, the *Sea Devil*, built in Russia in 1855. And while the four-piece brass band seems to be serenading the crew at sea, in reality it played a concert on the bottom of a ship-packed harbor in honor of the coronation of Czar Alexander II. (Courtesy: Submarine Museum, New London, Connecticut)

Bauer's first submarine, the infamous *Brandtaucher* (*Sea Diver*) that panicked the Danish fleet in 1850. Following a near fatal disaster for its inventor, the boat spent thirty-six years on the bottom of Kiel Harbor before it was recovered and now rests at the Naval Museum in Berlin. (Courtesy: Submarine Museum, New London, Connecticut)

Above: A Civil War artist's rendering of the C.S.S. *Hunley* on the beach at Charleston, South Carolina, December 6, 1863. (Courtesy: U.S. Navy)

Left: A Confederate David, the generic name given to all such low-profile semi-submersibles in the Southern navy during the Civil War, moored off the U.S. Naval Academy, Annapolis, Maryland, in the late 1860s. (Courtesy: U.S. Navy)

Pioneer, the first ironclad underwater torpedo boat built by Horace Hunley in New Orleans in 1861. The little craft was scuttled in Lake Pontchartrain before it fell into the hands of Farragut's advancing fleet. Recovered years later it now rests in Jackson Square, Louisiana State Museum. (Courtesy: Submarine Museum, New London, Connecticut)

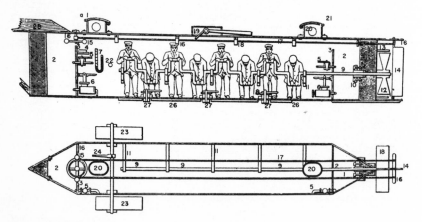

Longitudinal Elevation and Plan View of the Confederate Submarine Boat *Hunley* from sketches by W. A. Alexander. (*1*) Bow and stern castings. (*2*) Water-ballast tanks. (*3*) Tank bulkheads. (*4*) Compass. (*5*) Sea cocks. (*6*) Pumps. (*7*) Mercury gauge. (*8*) Keel ballast stuffing boxes. (*9*) Propeller shaft and cranks. (*10*) Stern bearing and gland. (*11*) Shaft braces. (*12*) Propeller. (*13*) Wrought ring around propeller. (*14*) Rudder. (*15*) Steering wheel. (*19*) Air box. (*20*) Hatchways. (*21*) Hatch covers. (*22*) Shaft of side fins. (*23*) Side fins. (*24*) Shift lever. (*25*) One of the crew turning shaft. (*26*) Cast-iron keel ballast. (*27*) Bolts. (*28*) Butt end of torpedo boom. (*31*) Keel ballast. (Courtesy: Submarine Museum, New London, Connecticut)

CHAPTER 4

The Resilient Sea Devil

 As the year 1847 came to a close, all Europe poised on the brink of revolution. Intellectual and political liberalism was on the move. By 1848, open revolts flared up in a half-dozen European countries. Amidst the furor for more liberties, new constitutions and broader reforms, an old and long-sensitive issue between Germany and Denmark caught fire. Before it could be extinguished, it broke out into a small but hotly contended three-year war between the two countries, thereby setting the scene for the second time in history that a submarine was used in warfare.

The trouble started in the 6,055-square-mile Schleswig-Holstein province bounded on the south by Germany and on the north by Denmark. Most of the German population within the province lived in the southernmost duchy of Holstein, the Danes in the northernmost Schleswig, and never the twain coexisted amiably. Nor, according to the old Charter of Ribe, could the two duchies be separated. So Germany claimed it all. But then so did Denmark. And therein lay the contention.

The strongly nationalistic German and Danes populating the province constantly argued over what nation they belonged to. The politicians were doing much the same thing in a slightly more diplomatic manner in Berlin. When the people of Schleswig-Holstein ran out of words, they took up arms to settle the question. An insurrection broke out in both duchies, Germany gave the nod, and Prussian troops swarmed in to take control of the entire province for Germany. Denmark reacted as could be expected, and the result was a three-year war waged intermittently between peace talks until the Treaty of Berlin in 1850 settled the dispute in favor of Denmark and things went back largely as they were.

During the hostilities, however, an ex-woodworker from Bavaria, turned corporal in the light-horse artillery, accomplished a stunning single-handed naval victory. Wilhelm Bauer was his name and he was probably considered by his comrades at arms the most unlikely artilleryman they had ever known. When he should have been busy with his cannons and carriages, the twenty-eight-year-old Bauer was studying boats and porpoises. And not just the ordinary run-of-the-mill boats but the kind that traveled underwater.

Corporal Bauer was part of the Prussian constabulary sent to quell the insurrections in Schleswig-Holstein. When things quieted, a provisionary military government took control and was headquartered in the seaport of Kiel on the Baltic. Danish ships soon blockaded Kiel Harbor and periodically raided the Prussians when conditions seemed favorable, so it was against this force that Corporal Bauer first turned his attention.

He would be glad, he told his superiors, to build a submarine that would raise havoc with the Danish fleet, if they cared to give him the opportunity.

The harassed staff officers in Kiel were more than glad to let the imaginative Corporal see what he could do. So Bauer found a local ironmonger, showed him his plans for the boat and said he hoped that she would have the lines of a porpoise. Since no one had ever duplicated the curves of a porpoise in sheet iron before, the result looked more like a flattened sausage-shaped boiler twenty-five feet long, six feet wide and nine feet deep. Four square windows adorned her sides, and she was powered by two men rapidly spinning two huge wheels attached to a four-bladed screw propeller. Side ballast tanks took on water to let the boat submerge. To angle her downward for a dive, Bauer slid a huge weight along a track running fore and aft down the middle of the boat, rather like a great cast-iron bowling ball rolling down the gutter. That arrangement should have told him something right from the beginning, but he was probably too dazzled by the easy way it made his boat tilt down in the water. He named his creation the *Brandtaucher,* or the "Sea Diver," and prepared to take on the whole Danish fleet in her, single-handed.

Accompanied by two crew members, Bauer pulled away from the Kiel wharf in his big strange-looking diving machine and navigated with his head sticking up out of the small midship hatch while his men cranked the ungainly vessel slowly out into the harbor. Instead of diving the boat and stealthily approaching from underwater, Bauer brazened himself out in full view of the enemy as fast as his crankers could go. What he intended to do once he met the opposition is anyone's guess, but that decision never came. The stalwart Danes took one look at the *Brandtaucher* and decided they wanted no part of whatever it was. Once certain that the thing creeping toward them was dead set on a collision course, every ship in the blockading fleet broke and ran. Sometime later they apprehensively regrouped and stood out at sea but only under doubled watches with all hands keeping a wary eye on the water.

Corporal Bauer and his men cheerfully cranked the *Brand-taucher* back to shore where the waiting men and officers hoisted the returning heroes to their shoulders and paraded them triumphantly through the streets of Kiel. They had indeed performed a military coup. Their mere presence, frightening as it must have been, had repulsed an entire fleet.

But sad to say for the beleaguered Prussian garrison, it was not enough. The blockading fleet warily kept its place and became more troublesome than ever. Meanwhile, Corporal Bauer was having troubles of another kind. A local physics professor named Karsten took it upon himself to publicly chastise the unschooled inventor for even daring to think that he could dabble in such profoundly academic matters as submarine navigation. Karsten called Bauer's boat the "Sea Devil" and ridiculed his ideas in pseudoscientific papers. Indeed, the professor did such a thorough job of proving that Bauer could not do what he had done that even the military began to wonder. After all, who could question the wisdom of a highly reputable physics professor? Surely he must be correct in saying that the woodturner from Dillingen would do better to see to his sawdust and shavings than involve himself in matters far beyond his abilities.

Of course this attitude made the young unschooled inventor all the more determined to go out and succeed in his *Brandtaucher.* Fortunately, Bauer was one of those people who could tread the thin line between success and failure without being too bruised by either. His successes were never complete, nor were his failures always total. But there was just enough smell of success to the latter to keep him bouncing back for more.

And so with Professor Karsten's derisive remarks ringing in his ears, the Corporal and two companions named Thomsen and Witt set out on another mission to confront the blockaders in the *Brandtaucher.* For safety's sake they charted their course over a relatively shallow part of the Kiel roadstead, stealthily approaching the enemy fleet silhouetted in the distance. Finally, to avoid detection, they decided to dive. Bauer's chart showed the same shallow depths beneath them when he opened the valves and took seawater into his ballast tanks. But as luck would have it, about the time he ordered seaman Witt to slide the big cast-iron weight forward for the proper downward dive angle, the *Brandtaucher* was passing over an uncharted hole sixty feet deep.

Down went the *Brandtaucher* in a steep glide, one that steepened considerably when Witt and Thomsen failed to slide back the heavy weight and let it crash full bore down to the far end of the track. Amid the clanging and screeching of pressure-squeezed iron plates the *Brandtaucher* dropped like a shot to the bottom of the hole and buried its nose in the mud.

As the three men unscrambled themselves, the submarine settled right side up. Water squirted from open seams, rivets popped like small-caliber gunfire, and the sheet-iron hull slowly buckled under the intense water pressure. The *Brandtaucher's* controls were demolished. As the men surveyed the damage in the dim light filtering through the ports, it was evident that the whole boat was close to collapsing around them.

Bauer frantically tried to blow the water out of the ballast tanks with compressed air but found the apparatus jammed. Gradually the shrieks and bangs of flexing hull plates diminished to intermittent squeals and groans as the wreckage quieted its death throes.

Witt and Thomsen were scared but cool. Bauer quickly assessed the damage and tried to figure out their next move. Surely someone on the surface had seen them dive and would sound the alarm when they failed to reappear. But help in that direction might be hours away. And what could the rescuers do? At the very most, maybe grapple them up. But by then it could be too late.

If they could open a hatch they might be able to swim to the surface. But at a depth of sixty feet—almost three atmospheres of pressure—there was little chance of even opening the two-foot-square hatch. It was being held closed by over 25,000 pounds of water pressure. Nothing short of a gunpowder charge would open it, unless . . .

Without a word Bauer crawled aft and started unscrewing a valve in the bilge. A fountain of water gushed up around his hands. With a yelp, Witt leaped on him like a wild man, bowling him over in the bilges. Thomsen scrambled after them, frantically shutting the valve and stopping the flow of water. Both men suspected that Bauer's mind had snapped; that he had opened one of the sea cocks to drown them all.

It was some time before they let him up but it was a lot longer before they thought he was rational. Bauer was talking the craziest nonsense they had ever heard from someone who moments before seemed sane. He told them about the outside water pressure holding the hatch closed so tight that the only way that they might be able to open it was to raise the air pressure inside the submarine. But to do that meant letting in water through the sea cock, actually flooding half the submarine until the air remaining inside became so compressed it would counteract the outside water pressure and enable them to open the hatch.

No matter how many times Bauer explained it to Witt and Thomsen, neither man grasped the idea of what he meant. All that was readily understood was that their crazy captain wanted them to let in the water so that they could drown like rats. Even when they scratched their heads and asked him how he knew that what he was saying would work, Bauer admitted that he was not sure it would. But he added that it was their only hope. Nothing else would budge that hatch even if they sat there until doomsday, which both Witt and Thomsen said they would rather do. And so they did, propped up in the wreckage, breathing up the air that was slowly getting warmer and stickier, using up their remaining energies arguing which was the better course of action to take.

They waited this way in the gloom of the half-drowned submarine for four long nerve-wracking hours until all three were dripping with sweat, gasping for breath and slightly out of their heads from breathing their own exhalations.

Suddenly a loud clattering echoed through the boat. Bauer thought her hull had finally collapsed. But when nothing more happened, he was baffled. Then it came again, only this time iron claws scraped loudly across one of the port windows.

A grapple hook! Someone above was trying to grapple up the boat!

The momentary surge of hope turned quickly to despair with another clanging jolt of iron hooks rasping along the iron hull plates inches away from a window. Now they feared that one of the grapples would break a window, trapping them instantly in the flooded hull.

Witt and Thomsen had taken as much as they could. They felt sure that Bauer was crazy and that this was the end of the rope. They were suffocating inside the boat, but with one unlucky blow from the grapple hook they would be taking that last big drink of water from outside. So, cursing weakly, they gave in and let Bauer have his way.

He crawled back to the sea cock and unscrewed the valve. The salt water poured in. It rose slowly up their legs to their waists. The air seemed to thicken and the pressure hurt their ears. More than ever they now risked passing out from breathing their own concentrated exhalations of carbon dioxide. The water was up to their chests when Bauer ordered Thomsen to open the hatch and go out first.

The seaman grasped the levers that dogged down the cover and tugged them aside easily. Then with a push he shoved open the hatch. As a torrent of seawater rushed in, Thomsen was sucked through the opening in a huge bubble of air, followed closely by Witt and Bauer. And to hear the inventor describe it later, he and the others soared to the surface in a welter of effervescence "like champagne corks," to be picked up by a wildly cheering crowd of rescuers.

The *Brandtaucher* lay in her watery grave for the next thirty-six years until she was fished up and put on display at the Naval School at Kiel in 1887. There she remained until 1906 when she was moved to the Naval Museum in Berlin.

Bauer and his men had made the first submarine escape in history, but despite the accident's happy ending, ensuing events went badly for him. Instead of praising him for his remarkable escape, his superiors decided that perhaps Professor Karsten was right and the wayward noncom from the light-horse artillery had better forget about such risky things as underwater boats. So when the Corporal asked for funds to build another submarine, he was promptly refused.

Bauer quickly decided he had had enough of both the service and the meddlesome Karsten. Leaving both behind he collected his severence pay and took his submarine plans to Austria. There, through the efforts of a lady of the court, he gained an audience with the Archduke Maximilian, who liked the young man's ideas for a submarine. A technical examining committee okayed his plans, 100,000 francs were allotted to build the boat, and everything looked rosy until the franc-pinching Austrian minister of finance cut off the appropriation.

Bauer packed his plans and went to England in 1853, when Great Britain, France, Turkey and Sardinia were about to embark on the Crimean War with Russia. What better environment to sell such a machine? On Bauer's first meeting with Prince Albert he mentioned his success in repelling the blockading Danish fleet with his *Brandtaucher* at Kiel. Duly impressed,the Consort put Bauer in touch with his engineering experts, Lord Palmerston, John Scott Russell, Isambard K. Brunel and Charles Fox. These gentlemen took the ex-corporal under their collective wing and before he knew it he was designing an improved version of the *Brandtaucher* for them and applying for a British patent on it. Unfortunately, however, too many of the "experts" wanted a hand in its creation, and before Bauer knew it, he and his invention were soon parted. His supposed friendly partners simply squeezed him out of business. Bauer left England convinced that they had stolen his work. In truth, his new submarine had been registered but never patented. During the Crimean War, Palmerston and Russell came out with a submarine of their own that incorporated some of Bauer's ideas. But it was so poorly conceived and badly built that on its first trial it sank and drowned all of its crew.

Meanwhile, the somewhat disillusioned but always optimistic Bauer offered his submarine invention to the United States government. It never replied.

Bauer now took stock of his situation. Thanks to Karsten and the common knowledge that the inventor was trying to make a deal with any government that would have him, Germany wanted nothing to do with him, the United States had been indifferent, and as far as he was concerned, Great Britain had tried to steal his efforts. That left one intriguing possibility. Now that the Crimean War was on, he would sell his submarine to England's enemy, Russia.

So off to St. Petersburg where he convinced the Grand Duke Constantine that he had the plans for the single most devastating naval weapon known to man, an underwater boat that Bauer was already calling by the name Karsten had coined—*Le Diable-Marin,* the "Sea Devil." Bauer hoped that somehow, somewhere, the professor who had started all this trouble for him would live to hear and remember that name with a certain amount of respect.

Immensely pleased with Bauer's designs, the Prince promptly arranged funds for the submarine's construction. Without a doubt the boat was Bauer's finest achievement. She was fifty-two feet long, twelve feet wide, eleven feet deep and, like the *Brandtaucher,* resembled a slightly flattened sausage of sheet iron. Her depth of dive was controlled by water ballast in her three big ten-foot-long by four-and-a-half-foot-wide cylinders operated by hand pumps. Her three-bladed propeller was driven by four men walking a treadmill. And if this sounds clever, consider the boat's mode of attack. The submarine carried a 500-pound bomb on her bow. To arm and deploy it a crewman stuck his arms into a pair of shoulder-length rubber gloves mounted through hull holes in the bow, released the bomb from the submarine, attached it to the hull of an enemy ship, then tripped the delayed-firing mechanism. Supposedly the *Sea Devil* would be well away by the time the bomb exploded. Nobody knows if the method was ever tried.

The *Sea Devil* was successfully launched and tested in 1855. From May until October 1856, Bauer and his thirteen-man crew made 134 dives in the boat, sometimes to depths of 150 feet. Russia kept the results secret, but we can assume that they had no serious difficulties. On one of the early tests the boat returned late with the crew singing lustily as they tromped the treadmill. Hearing the commotion in the darkness, a guard on the mole challenged them. When from out of the gloom Bauer appeared as if astride a whale and replied with the correct password, the sentry dropped his rifle and fled. At each barrier passed by the *Sea Devil* on her way into Port Imperial the scene was repeated, the crew delighting in playing the game of Panic the Sentry.

On another occasion Bauer sat the *Sea Devil* on the floor of the harbor where he wrote letters to the Grand Duke Constantine, King Ludwig Maximilian II of Bavaria and to his mother. And in honor of the coronation of Czar Alexander II, Bauer took a four-man brass band to the bottom where they played the Russian National Hymn accompanied by the singing of Bauer's thirteen-man crew. The world's first underwater concert lasted four hours and was said to have been heard by people in boats 600 feet away.

Such feats may have endeared the cheerful Bavarian to the Russian people, but he had few friends in the Russian navy. As far as the officers of the Imperial Navy were concerned, there was something badly wrong with anyone who preferred to travel *under* the water instead of on it. So jealous were they of his successes that, whenever Bauer and his *Sea Devil* excelled in anything, the naval hierarchy took it as a direct affront. Consequently, everyone from the admirals on down was out to bump Bauer from royal favor one way or another. An opportunity that seemed made to order came after all the tests when Bauer felt it time to demonstrate to the navy what a capable boat it had at its disposal. On this special show-and-tell day Bauer was to demonstrate how easily the *Sea Devil* could sneak up under an enemy ship and attach one of its mines without being detected.

Not only prominent naval and army officials turned up at Kronstadt for the affair, there was also an impressive gathering of royalty. While the band struck up a military march, Bauer and his crew nervously checked and rechecked the *Sea Devil* to be sure it was ready. Meanwhile the navy was setting up for the test. The target ship was towed into position before the reviewing stands on shore. But what Bauer and most of the reviewers did not know was that the boat had been placed purposely over a drop-off so that directly below its hull was nothing but shallow water and a weed-covered mud bank.

At a given signal the *Sea Devil* left her berth and proceeded up the waterway, running semisubmerged with just her upper works out. Bauer passed in review of the stands, turned and sighted his target. The *Sea Devil* submerged and swept in to attack. Everything was running smoothly and Bauer saw the hull of the target ship loom up dimly through the forward hatch ports. Then suddenly he saw the mudbank!

Too late to avoid it, the *Sea Devil* plowed into the soft embankment. While the four sweaty seamen tried to run in reverse on their treadmill, Bauer ordered the forward ballast tanks pumped. The treadmillers got nowhere, the propeller was already heavily entangled in weeds. But gradually by expelling water forward, the bows rose. Dropping the main keel weights angled the boat steeply upward. Bauer tried to raise the stern, but it was hopelessly ensnarled.

When the submarine's bows broke water Bauer ordered his men out to safety. He stayed behind to see if there was anything he could do to save the boat. Water began sloshing in the forward open hatch. Bauer climbed the steeply angled deck to close it, but with his weight forward, the hatch coaming dipped underwater and a flood poured through the opening. His only chance was to fight his way out through the torrent and let his boat swamp. Smirking sailors pulled him and his men into rescue boats, but the accident had just the opposite effect that it was intended to have. At least a few royal observers understood what had happened and backed Bauer's efforts despite objections from the navy. Unfortunately, however, his submarine service, unique as it was, was still considered part of the navy. And this was Bauer's ultimate undoing.

It took Bauer and his men four weeks of hard work to raise the sunken submarine. Then after refurbishing her, the *Sea Devil* met her final fate somewhere in the deep water off Ochda where she went down for the last time and never came up. Details are vague, but one account says that under orders from the Russian Admiralty, the navy gained control of the submarine, took her to sea and purposely scuttled her far from land.

It was a terrible blow to Bauer but it did not finish him. The resilient Bavarian came back with a design for a radically new submarine that was to be bigger and better than the *Sea Devil*. How the Imperial admirals must have gnashed their teeth when he laid out his plans for a boat armed with twenty-four cannon that operated on the surface with a steam engine, then tooled along underwater on a compressed-air motor.

Right from the beginning the navy was dead set against her. Was this a reaction against the non-Russian Bauer? Or was it again the more understandable antagonism of surface sailors against the invention of a machine that ultimately threatened the very existence of all surface sailors?

Whichever the reason, Bauer began building his new boat in 1858, assisted financially by whoever controlled the governmental purse strings. The navy contributed with criticism and so many demands for alterations that the project became a nightmare. Bauer fought the lone battle as long as he could, but when he learned that the navy was moving the construction site of the submarine to Siberia and suggested that he go along, Bauer took the hint and left Russia.

Next he appeared in France, the only country still left open for him to try. Napoleon III listened sympathetically to Bauer's offer to build submarines for France but turned him down. As the dejected inventor left, Napoleon gave him a gift of 150 francs.

In the next few years the often virtually penniless Bauer drifted from France to Switzerland and back to his native land. In 1861, he tried to form a company to finance the construction of a new and novel submarine, but when he was unable to raise the money, the project failed.

This was Wilhelm Bauer's last venture in the submarine field. Thoroughly beaten and disappointed he finally went home to Munich. But for the brave, clever, ex-woodturner who had taught himself enough engineering to design successful submarines, the battle was not yet over. As an undeserved finale to his life, Bauer contracted tuberculosis of the spine and lay bedridden for seven years before he died in 1875.

CHAPTER 5

The Davids and the Goliaths

On the moonless night of October 5, 1863, blacked-out Federal gunboats blockading Charleston Harbor were barely discernible against the quiet harbor waters. But there was no mistaking the huge angular silhouette of the large ship on station near Morris Island, squarely in the middle of the Union fleet. She was the *New Ironsides,* one of the early offspring of the U.S.S. *Monitor,* a formidably armed, three-masted, wooden-hulled Goliath. Twenty heavy Dahlgren cannon and several lighter Parrott-rifled cannon protected her steep-sloped flanks, scaled like some prehistoric monster with four-inch iron plates.

Besides making an imposing spectacle of herself, the awesome ironclad made an inviting target, one not easily overlooked by the beleaguered Confederate forces ashore. Indeed, that very night a handful of stalwart Johnny Rebs had slipped past half the blockading Yankee fleet to sneak up on the armor-plated giant with a smaller, unorthodox vessel they appropriately named a "David."* This forty-foot-long, wooden, cigar-shaped half boat–half submarine was so heavily ballasted that little more than her barrel-sized observation turret and her smokestack showed above water. She was

---

*A generic name given to all such low-profile semisubmersible boats used by the Southern navy during the Civil War to attack the blockading fleet of northern "Goliaths."

light, maneuverable and looked virtually unarmed. But despite appearances, she was about as harmless as a ticking time bomb. An eighteen-foot pine spar protruded from her pointed bow, and tied to its end was a forty-pound keg of gunpowder. The idea was to stick this lethal charge on the enemy's hull, retreat a discreet distance, then jerk a rope to explode the bomb and sink the ship.

Such were the intentions of the resolute handful of sweaty volunteers huddled inside the David as she chugged through the black night spewing a trail of steam and sparks in her wake. In the observation turret, young Lieut. William T. Glassel stared intently at the gradually growing silhouette of their target and prayed that they would get close enough to be under the ironclad's guns before she could deliver a broadside.

But at that very moment, aboard the *New Ironsides,* Ens. Charles Howard was staring just as intently at the barrel-sized object moving toward him faster than any flotsam he had ever seen. Howard had no idea what he was looking at, but since it kept coming, sparking and smoking, he lost no time shouting an alarm.

A bugle blew, drums rolled, sleepy sailors hit the deck, and gunports banged open. By then some of the marines were taking potshots at the small, rapidly approaching target. Gunners cussed their cannon, trying desperately to depress their muzzles, but by then it was already too late. The onrushing object swept in below them and suddenly, with an ear-shattering explosion, a huge chunk of the bay shot into the air beside the *New Ironsides.* With the concussion the mighty ironclad heaved almost halfway onto her beam ends, then down again in a great whooshing roar that pushed out a colossal wave.

Screams, shouts, shots and sheer bedlam broke out on board. Certain that they had been dealt a deathblow, officers and men abandoned ship in wholesale lots, hurling themselves over the side without benefit of lifeboats. Adding to the confusion, several marines, electing to stay and fight, fired their Maynard carbines in wild abandon, the weapons going off with resounding bangs and foot-long tongues of flame.

Aboard the Confederate David things were no better. In his eagerness to get at the ironclad, Glassel had jerked the bomb's lanyard too soon, and the result had caught both vessels unaware. The David was lifted high out of the water and hurled backward by the explosion. Seconds later the ironclad's wave rolled entirely over her, sending a torrent of water down through the hatch to sputter into clouds of steam when it hit the hot boiler. First man over the side and into the briny was the boat's commander, Lieutenant Glassel. Right behind him came most of the others. Only the fact that he lacked a life preserver stayed the pilot, Walker Cannon, from following his commander and the rest of the crew. But he was not alone. A wild-eyed, half-drowned engineer named James Tombs crawled out of the David and tried to surrender to the *New Ironsides,* but there was so much shooting and shouting going on that nobody heard him. Finally, somewhat sheepishly, Tombs realized that the David was not sinking. As she drifted away from the confusion, he and Cannon picked up a few of their shipmates, managed to rekindle the boat's fires and limped off into the darkness. Glassel and the others were taken prisoner by various blockaders. Neither ship suffered serious damage, but the encounter did establish a historical first. The dutiful *New Ironsides'* ensign, Lieut. Charles Howard, who saw it all coming, earned the dubious distinction of being the first fatality of submarine warfare.

His contribution was just the beginning. In an all-out effort to break the stranglehold of Federal blockades that had halted all Southern shipping, the Confederacy was grabbing any ideas that came along no matter how strange or bizarre they seemed. And to some people's way of thinking, the Davids being built along the coast as a kind of last-ditch countermeasure were about as bizarre as you could get. But always there was the tantalizing possibility that the sinister things might work. So the cigar boats were born, first as planked-over, heavily ballasted, conventional gunboats that steamed along at the water's level with their uncluttered decks almost awash. Then came the more sophisticated cylindrical semi-submersibles such as Glassel had used against the *New Ironsides*. Even as this encounter took place, Charleston harbored another David that had gained such a reputation as a jinx ship that it was getting hard to find anyone to volunteer for duty on her, so few had survived. Thanks to a couple of unfortunate events that did away with her prototypes, the real history of this particular boat starts even before she was built.

In the port city of New Orleans in 1863, two Confederate naval officers named Hunley and McClintock teamed up with civilian engineer, Baxter Watson, to build a Confederate-financed blockade buster of McClintock's design. Before the submersible was completed, however, Capt. David Farragut swept in with his imposing Federal fleet of forty-six ships armed with 286 guns and took the town. The sixty-year-old leathery-faced, salty-mannered, Union naval officer had several ironclads in his contingent but he was not overly fond of them. "When a shell makes its way into one of those damn teakettles," he snorted, "it can't get out again. It sputters around inside doing all kinds of mischief."

Hunley and McClintock would have been pleased to have added to this kind of mischief with their fledgling David. But to prevent it's falling into Yankee hands they scuttled the boat, rolled up their plans and hurried off to Mobile, Alabama, to start over again.

Their second effort slid down the ways a couple months later. She was an oblong iron boat twenty-five feet long, five feet wide and six feet deep with tapered bow and stern. They were towing her to Fort Morgan from which she was to attack the blockading fleet in Mobile Bay, but rough weather hit and in the heavy seas the boat sank with no loss of life. A plan for another McClintock boat was proposed to the Confederate government, but in view of the two previous costly losses the offer was politely declined. Hunley came up with a design of his own which he generously agreed to build with his own funds. In that event the project was readily sanctioned.

Hunley, McClintock and Watson retired to the Mobile

machine shops of Park and Lyons where they started anew with builder-engineer, W. A. Alexander. This time they selected a twenty-five-foot-long, four-foot-wide cylinder boiler they had on hand and cut it in two lengthways, riveting an iron strip between the two halves to give it more depth. With the addition of bulkheads at each end to serve as ballast tanks and shaped bow and stern castings, the boat now measured thirty feet long, four feet wide and five feet deep. Considering that these dimensions were intended to provide space for an officer and his eight-man crew the vessel already had all the characteristics of an iron coffin. In addition to the water tanks the boat was to be ballasted by cast-iron weights bolted to the outside bottom of the hull and fitted to be released from inside if the need arose.

The superstructure was an oval hatchway sixteen inches long, twelve inches wide and eight inches high at each end of the boat. The rubber-gasketed, hinged hatch covers could be bolted from inside. In the raised coamings of each hatchway were fitted four glass observation ports. Midway between the two conning towers was a four-foot length of one-and-a-half-inch hinged pipe which could be raised from inside for air.

The craft was to be powered by eight men sitting in a row along one side turning a large camshaft whose end was attached through the stern to a three-foot-wide propeller encircled by an iron guard.

In actual operation when everything worked as it should, a dive in this David, named the *Hunley*, must have called for nerves of steel. The major responsibilities lay with the first officer who stood with his head in the forward hatchway and his hands on the steering controls. The second officer stood in the aft hatchway when he was not working the aft ballast controls or cranking. In any event, each stood in the hatch through which he entered, since the boat was so crowded it was impossible for anyone to move from one hatch to the other once they were inside. The only man left standing at all times was the first officer who simultaneously assumed all the duties of pilot, navigator, helmsman, diving controller and gunnery officer.

To the order "Forward at half-speed!" the row of men sitting along the port side in the tight confines behind him commenced cranking their camshaft at a leisurely but noisy rate. If they were to remain on the surface for awhile, hatches were usually left open and the boat rode low but level in the water. Upon the order "Prepare to dive!" hatch covers were closed and fastened tightly, the air pipe was lowered, and a candle was lighted. Then came the order "Dive!"

The first and second officers opened valves letting seawater into the fore and aft ballast tanks. If one tank got more water than another, there was instant trouble. Too much in the stern sent the boat down backward; too much in the bow and she nosedived. Equal amounts fore and aft and the boat remained level underwater. As the camshaft crew continued their cranking, the first officer returned to his duties of helmsman, his eyes firmly fixed on a mercury gauge in front of him that told their depth underwater, and an adjusted compass to determine direction.

Since it was the commander who had to see what he was doing most of the time, he held the boat's only candle in his left hand. With his right he turned a wheel located on the starboard side which manipulated a stern rudder, steering the boat in any direction on a horizontal plane. Raising or lowering a lever in front of him changed the angle on the forward dive planes outside the hull, steering the boat up or down. If the boat was not underway it was necessary for the first and second officers to laboriously operate force pumps by hand which slowly ejected the seawater from the fore and aft ballast tanks, allowing the boat to rise. In an emergency when it might be desirable to rise immediately, the outside bottom ballast had to be dropped. This maneuver required three of the camshaft crew to reach down and turn three separate wrenches which loosened the tee-headed bolts that dropped the extra ballast. If one of the three was in too much of a hurry and his bolt was not turned quite far enough, the ballast would not drop.

Originally, Hunley's planned method of doing away with enemy ships was the same as that used by Fulton. The charge or "torpedo" as it was then called was a copper cylinder containing 90 pounds of gunpowder with a percussion and friction primer mechanism set off by triggers protruding from the outside of the device. It was intended to float the torpedo on the water's surface. Towing it on a 200-foot line, the boat would then dive under the vessel to be attacked. As the charge was dragged up against the ship's hull, one of the triggers would touch, exploding the charge. Both in theory and in experiments on flatboats on the calm waters of the Mobile River the plan was successful. But when the *Hunley* tried it in rough waters, the torpedo came too near the wrong boat. So, before they blew themselves up, the crewmen dropped the idea and returned to the torpedo-on-a-spar method. They rigged a tapering, twenty-two-foot, yellow-pine boom to the bow of the boat, banding and guying it on each side. A socket on the torpedo secured it to the boom. All that remained was to attach the charge to an enemy ship and set it off. With her weapon in place and some of her idiosyncrasies corrected the *Hunley* was now ready to do battle.

Since authorities at Mobile thought she could be more useful against the monitors and blockaders in South Carolina, General Maury had her sent by rail to General Beauregard at Charleston. That was the beginning of the *Hunley's* troubles.

A Lieutenant John Payne, and eight other courageous members of the Confederate navy volunteered to take the boat out on a trial run. As they were moving along the surface with the hatches open, the wake of a passing paddle wheeler swamped them. Payne, who was standing in the forward hatch, was the only man to escape; the eight crewmen drowned.

The *Hunley* was raised, dried out and refitted. The determined Lieutenant Payne and a new eight-man crew volunteered to take her out again, no doubt basing their action on the old time-honored logic about lightning not striking twice in the same place. But it did. The boat swamped in a storm. Payne and two others escaped; six men drowned. After that the lucky Lieutenant Payne volunteered for duty elsewhere.

In desperation General Beauregard sent for the boat's

creator, Captain Hunley, to see if he could get the jinx out of his deadly contraption. Hunley arrived with his practiced Mobile crew including Thomas Parks from the firm of Parks and Lyons in whose shop the boat had been built. Parks was so eager to participate in the adventure that on the eve of the crew's departure from Mobile he had talked one of the regulars, engineer W. A. Alexander, out of going, so that he could take his place.

Right from the beginning the *Hunley* responded to the familiar touch of her old crewmates with nothing but perfect ladylike behavior. The "Hunley and Parks Crew" as it came to be known was often seen practicing diving and rising the boat along the waterfront, and the scene never failed to draw an interested crowd of spectators. Then, one evening, in front of a wharf full of people, she dove and remained down for the next three days, thereby drowning all nine members of her old crew. This brought the *Hunley*'s total number of fatalities to twenty-three men. As one Rebel wag put it, she had killed more Southern gentlemen than the whole Yankee navy put together.

Normally the powers that be would have hurriedly scrapped the *Hunley* and turned her into a cannon or something less destructive to their side. But the memory of how close Glassel had come to wiping out the *New Ironsides* with his David was far too fresh on everyone's mind. If there was even the slightest chance that any of the ten or twelve Davids operating along the Southern coasts could break up the Yankee blockade, then it was worth the effort. It was not the time or place to consider the cost.

But in light of the misfortunes showered upon the *Hunley,* the Confederacy felt that it could do without the particularly deadly David and was more than willing to let it rest in peace on the bottom of the bay. One may well wonder why so many men volunteered for duty on the boat with such obviously good odds that they would meet disaster. Was it pure patriotism that drove them to take such chances? Probably not. More likely it was the lure of substantial rewards being offered by wealthy Southern businessmen for the sinking of Union vessels. For example, it was well known that one such firm, the John Frazier Company of Charleston, was offering rewards of $30,000 for the sinking of any monitor-type vessel and $100,000 for dispatching the Union frigate *Wabash*. With such incentives, who cared about the odds of survival? Each new crew to inherit the *Hunley* figured it could beat the odds.

Without a doubt the unfortunate *Hunley* would have been promptly forgotten but for the stubborn insistence of a Lieut. George E. Dixon, an army officer from the Twenty-first Alabama, who pleaded with the military to resurrect the *Hunley* and give him her command. Why an army rather than a navy man? And why such a suicidal choice as the *Hunley?* Well, primarily because Dixon was no stranger to this David. He had watched with interest while she was built and tested on the Mobile River. In fact, he would have been one of the Hunley and Parks Crew had there been a vacancy. And now that there was definitely a vacancy, he volunteered for the position. Accompanying him was the faithful engineer, W. A. Alexander, the crew member who had let the anxious Parks talk him out of going on the last trip so that he could take his place. Now Alexander wanted to contribute his all to the next effort.

Everyone was intensely interested to know what had happened aboard the *Hunley* to cause her fatal disappearance. Certainly she had not swamped, because her hatches were closed. The crew was highly experienced, the boat was in good shape, and no one was more qualified to handle her than Hunley himself. What then could have conceivably gone wrong?

Dixon and Alexander must have asked themselves that question a hundred times as they journeyed from Mobile to Charleston to report to General Jordan, chief of staff. Before long they had their answer.

The boat was found resting at a thirty-five-degree angle on the bottom with her bow buried deep in the mud. The bolts holding down the hatch covers had been removed. When the covers were lifted considerable air and gas escaped. Captain Hunley's body was found in the forward hatch with his right hand raised over his head as if he had been trying to open the hatch cover. In his left hand was the candle that had never been lighted. The sea cock on the forward ballast tank at Hunley's end was wide open, the cock wrench not on the plug but lying on the bottom of the boat. Park's body was found in the after hatchway, his right hand above his head. He also had been trying to raise his hatch cover, but the pressure was too great. The sea cock to his tank was properly closed, and the tank was nearly empty. The other bodies were floating in the water. Hunley and Parks undoubtedly suffocated; the others drowned. The bolts holding the iron keel ballast had been partly turned, but not enough to release it.

Since Alexander was completely familiar with Hunley's normal operating procedure aboard the boat, he pieced together what most likely happened in those critical moments just after the submersible slipped beneath the surface:

> Captain Hunley's practice with the boat had made him quite familiar and expert in handling her and this familiarity produced at this time forgetfulness, [wrote Alexander]. It was found in practice to be easy on the crew to come to the surface by giving the pumps a few strokes and ejecting some of the water ballast than by the momentum of the boat operated on the elevated fins. At this time the boat was underway lighted through the deck lights in the hatchways. He (Hunley) partly turned the fins to go down but thought no doubt that he needed more ballast and opened his sea cock.
>
> Immediately the boat was in total darkness. He then undertook to light the candle. While trying to do this the tank (open at the top) quietly flooded and under great pressure the boat sank very fast and the tank soon overflowed and the first intimation they would have of anything being wrong was the water rising fast but noiselessly about their feet in the bottom of the boat. They tried to release the iron keel ballast but did not turn the keys quite far enough, therefore failed. The water soon forced the air to the top of the boat and into the hatchways where Captain Hunley and Parks were found. Parks had pumped his ballast tank and no doubt Captain Hunley had exhausted himself on his pump, but he had forgotten that he had not closed the sea cock.

The eager young Lieutenant Dixon and engineer Alexander soon had the boat dried out, refitted and working as good as ever. They reported to General Jordan that the *Hunley* was ready for service and all they needed now was for him to send them a crew. In all good conscience, General Jordan simply could not bring himself to ask seven more young men to volunteer for a duty he considered nothing less than suicidal. To Dixon and Alexander's amazement, he turned down their request. They kept asking. After many refusals and discussions, General Beauregard finally consented to let the two eager iron-coffin sailors go aboard the C.S.N. *Indian Chief,* then lying in the river, and ask for volunteers. The only strict provision was that the volunteers be told the entire history of the *Hunley,* of its having been lost three times and drowning twenty-three men in Charleston, and a full explanation of the hazardous service required of them.

Dixon and Alexander complied. It would be interesting to know what persuasion they used to counterbalance the grim story they had to tell. Possibly they emphasized patriotic duty or stressed the substantial financial rewards that awaited them at the end of a successful mission. Whichever it was, they had no trouble getting a new crew.

After making a few practice dives in the river, the boat was ordered to moor off Battery Marshall on Sullivan's Island, the crew to be quartered at Mount Pleasant, seven miles away.

Although the *Hunley* had been within easy reach of the Federal ironclads and monitors in Charleston Harbor, these ships were not as vulnerable as they once were. They were now encircled with chain booms to protect them against attack. So the *Hunley* was forced to turn her attention to the fleet outside. The nearest Union ship, believed to be the U.S. frigate *Wabash,* was twelve miles off. She became the boat's primary target.

In comparatively smooth water and light current the *Hunley* could make four miles an hour, but in rough water her speed was much slower. It was necessary to go out with the ebb and come in with the flood tide, which meant at least a laborious six hours of cranking the camshaft to reach their objective and return. Moreover, the mission also called for a fair wind and a dark night since the boat could not run underwater the entire way. From experience the crew had found it necessary to surface and lift the after hatch slightly to let in fresh air. On several such occasions when they were on the surface they heard men in the Federal picketboats talking and singing.

As winter came on, the *Hunley* tried repeatedly to reach her target, but something always went wrong. The usual daily routine consisted of the crew leaving Mount Pleasant about 1 P.M., walking the seven miles along the beach to Battery Marshall and practicing with the boat for two hours in the back bay. Then Dixon and Alexander would stretch out on the beach with the compass between them and get the bearing of the nearest vessel as she took her position for the night.

After dark, with her torpedo on her boom, the *Hunley* would head for the target ship and keep going until the condition of the men, sea, tide, moon or daylight compelled them to give up and return to the dock. Disappointed but not discouraged they would unship the torpedo, leave it under guard at Battery Marshall, then walk the beach back to their quarters at Mount Pleasant to cook breakfast.

For more than three months from November 1863 to the early part of February 1864, a strong contrary wind made it difficult for the *Hunley,* with her limited power, to make much headway. Yet during this time the men went out on an average of four nights a week, trying to cross the twelve miles separating them from their target, and each time being beaten back. Often they would be out six or seven miles when they would have to return because of the weather or the men's physical condition. Sometimes the return trip was so exhausting that it took every ounce of strength to keep them from drifting out to sea, daylight often breaking while they were still on the surface in range of enemy guns.

This latter experience and the desire to know what to expect in an emergency prompted the crew to experiment during one of their practices to see how long it was possible for them to stay underwater without surfacing for air.

Alexander described the experience:

It was agreed to by all hands to sink and let the boat rest on the bottom in the back bay off Battery Marshall, each man to make equal physical exertion in turning the propeller. It was also agreed that if anyone in the crew felt he must come to the surface for air and he gave the word "Up," we would at once bring the boat to the surface.

It was usual when practicing near the bay that the banks would be lined with soldiers. One evening after alternately diving and rising many times, Dixon and myself and several of the crew compared watches, noted the time and sank for the test. In twenty-five minutes after I had closed the after manhead and excluded the outer air, the candle would not burn. Dixon forward and myself aft turned on the propeller cranks as hard as we could. In comparing our individual experiences afterwards, the experience of one was found to be the experience of all. Each man had determined that he would not be the first man to say "Up." Not a word was said except an occasional "How is it?" between Dixon and myself until the "Up!" came from all nine.

We started the pumps. Dixon's worked all right but mine was not throwing. From experience I guessed the cause of the failure, took off the cap of the pump, looked at the valve and drew out some chunks of seaweed that had choked it.

In the time that it took to do this the boat was considerably by the stern. Thick darkness prevailed. All hands had already endured what they felt was the utmost limit. Some of the crew almost lost control of themselves. It was a terrible few minutes, better imagined than described.

We soon had the boat to the surface and the manhead opened. What an experience! While the sun was shining when we went down and the beach lined with soldiers, it was not quite dark with one solitary soldier gazing on the spot where he had seen the boat before going down the last time. He did not see the boat until he saw me standing on the hatch coaming calling for him to stand by to take the line.

The line was struck and the time taken. We had been on the bottom two hours and thirty-five minutes. The candle ceased to burn twenty-five minutes after we went down showing that we had remained on the bottom two hours and ten minutes after the candle went out. The soldier informed us that we had been given up for lost and that a message had been sent to General Beauregard that a torpedo boat had been lost off Battery Marshall with all hands.

Early the next morning the *Hunley*'s crew squelched all rumors of its demise when it reported in a body to General Beauregard in Charleston. While everyone was glad to see them, some of General Beauregard's staff officers doubted that the men had stayed underwater as long as they reported. Although the crew was not eager to try it again the men offered to put on a diving demonstration for any doubting Thomases who would come over to Sullivan's Island and watch. They had no takers.

Whenever the weather permitted, the *Hunley* continued trying to reach the nearest blockade ship twelve miles offshore, each time taking greater risks of not returning. Finally, on the last of January, Dixon and Alexander interviewed the Charleston pilots again and they felt the wind would hold in the same quarter for several weeks. Then, on February 5, Alexander was ordered to report to the chief of staff, General Jordan in Mobile, to build a breech-loading repeating gun. This was a terrible blow both to Dixon and Alexander since they had been through so much together for so long. Moreover it was a blow to the entire crew since they were now a smoothly operating team and the loss of one team member would be felt by all. Even though General Jordan told Dixon that he could get two men as replacements for Alexander from the German artillery, the Lieutenant was discouraged with this new turn of events. He decided not to tell the crew about it until after Alexander had left.

Shortly after reaching Mobile several days later, Alexander received two notes from Dixon. One mentioned that the wind still held in the same quarter and the other told of the crew's regrets over his leaving and the men's feelings for him.

Soon afterward he received another note from Dixon saying that for two days the wind had changed to fair and he intended to try to get out that night.

Next came the news that on February 17 the submarine torpedo boat *Hunley* had sunk the U.S. sloop of war *Housatonic* outside Charleston Harbor. Alexander was both elated over the *Hunley's* success and disappointed that he had not been there to taste the victory with his shipmates. Then he realized with growing alarm that in every account he read there was no mention of the *Hunley's* safe return.

He immediately wired General Jordan asking her whereabouts. The reply he received was the same answer he would get to his daily wires for the next week: "No news of torpedo boat."

What had happened to the *Hunley*? Why had she picked the *Housatonic* instead of their original target the *Wabash*? Was there a failure of the boat, or of the crew? These questions bothered Alexander. After much thought he concluded that Dixon had been unable to work his way back against wind and tide and that the boat and crew had been carried out to sea.

But did it really happen that way? The plan was to take the bearing of the ships as they took position for the night. Fully armed with her warhead in place, the *Hunley* would steer for the nearest target, keeping about six feet underwater and coming occasionally to the surface for air and observation. As she approached the target she would surface for a final bearing on it before diving and moving forward to strike the ship if possible, just under her counter. That much Alexander knew for a certainty. He learned more after reading an account in the *Army Navy Journal* by one of the officers from the *Housatonic*: "It occurred February 17, 1864 at 8:45 P.M. about 2½ miles off Charleston bar. It was moonlight with little wind or sea. The lookout observed something moving in the water. The chain was slipped and the engines backed when the crash came, the ship sinking in three minutes after being struck."

Not until the close of the war did Alexander or anyone else know with absolute certainty what had happened to the *Hunley*. Then, while the government was working with the wreckage of the *Housatonic,* they found the twisted wreckage of the *Hunley* entangled with it.

And with this final bit of information, Alexander, the only surviving member of the *Hunley*'s last ill-fated crew, pieced together exactly what had happened!

The 1,264-ton, thirteen-gun corvette *Housatonic* was a new vessel on a station that anchored closer in than the *Wabash* and the others. On that night the wind had lulled with but little sea on. Although there was moonlight, Dixon, who had been waiting so long for a change of wind, took the risk of being seen and went out. The lookout aboard the ship spotted the boat when Dixon surfaced for a last look at his target. Dixon, of course, did not know that the ship had slipped her chain and was dropping back on him when he submerged and steered to plant the charge just under her counter.

With the unexpected collision of the two vessels, the *Housatonic's* stern was blown entirely off, instantly killing five of her men and sending the ship to the bottom in minutes. Caught in the wreckage from which Dixon and his men could not extricate themselves, the *Hunley* sank with the *Housatonic,* taking another nine men to their deaths.

Never again would the South use another David. The *Hunley* alone had cost the Confederacy thirty-two lives—a high price to pay for her single most notable achievement: to go down in history as the first submarine to sink an enemy ship in warfare.

CHAPTER 6

The Indomitable
Fenian Ram

 On a sunny afternoon in May 1878, millworkers
hurrying home from the silk factories and locomo-
tive shops in Paterson, New Jersey, were stopped
in their tracks by something they saw from the Spruce Street
bridge above the falls overlooking the Upper Passaic River. A
crowd gathered. People craned their necks for a better view
of the strange scene unfolding below them. There, on the
right bank of the river beside John Lister's boathouse, eight
pairs of stallions were being coaxed to back a long wagon to
the water's edge. Sitting astride the wagon was a big, black,
lozenger-shaped mass of iron topped off with a turret.
Standing some distance away from the men working with the
team was a short, thin bespectacled man in a black coat and
bowler hat. The more knowledgeable among the workers
pointed him out as the "professor" who had conceived the
contraption on the wagon. "Well," sang out one of the
spectators, "I see that the professor has built himself an iron
coffin!"

A burst of laughter broke out over the sound of the falls.
The horses whinnied and stomped their hooves in the
hard-packed mud. The wagon backed into the water at a
sharp angle. The men momentarily fidgeted with fastenings,
then the two-and-a-quarter-ton iron object slowly slid off the
wagon and splashed into the waters of the Upper Passaic.

As it surfaced and came to rest at the end of its towline, the
spectators cheered. Then there was a moment of hushed

silence that gradually turned to laughter as the iron object slowly settled on its tail and sank from sight.

Workmen hurriedly tugged on the towline until the glistening hump-backed shape reappeared in shallow water and grounded ingloriously in the mud.

The crowd dispersed, the workers talking animatedly. As far as they were concerned, the professor's test was a complete success. His "iron coffin" did exactly what anyone with any sense knew it would do when pushed into the water—it sank.

"Down among the Fishes," headlined a Paterson, New Jersey, newspaper the next day, describing the "success" of the launching of what it termed a "wrecking boat," which "went immediately to the bottom; and this without even the assistance of the captain."

Such was the public's reaction to the launching of teacher-inventor John P. Holland's first submarine. If it bothered the quietly reserved little man it was not evident. He was too busy asking himself what went wrong. Had he miscalculated the vessel's buoyancy? No, the Upper Passaic was fresh, not salt, water. Had he failed to dog down the turret hatch securely? Unlikely. The ship sank stern first. What about the valves controlling the two intake plugs in the bottom of the central compartment—could they have been inadvertently left open? That was a possibility. It was also possible that the craft had simply sprung her seams from some piece of faulty workmanship. Whatever the reason, Holland could not afford the failure. He had come too far to chance losing the opportunity of a lifetime to prove his ideas. If the unfortunate launching of his *Holland I* resulted in his supporters withdrawing their financial assistance, he knew the kind of future that awaited him. One doesn't build submarines on a teacher's salary. If it ever came to that, he couldn't be much worse off if he went back to Ireland.

And that was far from a happy thought. He remembered his native Ireland as the not-so-emerald isle. Lush green hardly characterized those agonizing gray-with-hunger years of the mid-nineteenth century. John Philip Holland was born in the village of Liscannor, County Clare, Ireland, on January

25, 1841. Before he was ten years old he knew famine and death, having lost a brother and two uncles to cholera. Crop failure, starvation and civil strife were a few of the horrors which he associated with those years. Like many Irishmen, he grew up believing that Ireland's miseries were England's fault and the only salvation was Irish independence. While some of his countrymen fought for their freedom with open rebellion, others, like Holland, chose to keep their strong feelings to themselves and await a more propitious moment. At twenty-one he was a schoolteacher whose health was so poor that he was forced to take a two-year leave of absence from the Christian Brothers school in County Cork. It was the second year of America's Civil War, and the news story that swept Ireland in that spring of 1862 was read by Holland with more than passing interest. It told how the Confederate navy had recovered a scuttled wooden Federal ship named the *Merrimac,* sheathed her in iron plates, renamed her the *Virginia,* and on March 8, sent her out to do battle with the blockading fleet of wooden Federal ships at Hampton Roads, Virginia. As solid shot rattled off her plates, the *Merrimac* sent one ship to the bottom with her iron ram and destroyed another with her shells. Every ship that tried to stop her felt the fiery wrath of the ungainly metal monster. It was a sad day for the U.S. Navy. But only temporarily nonplussed, the North rushed a surprise of its own to Hampton Roads.

The next day, when the giant *Merrimac* lumbered out to duplicate her victories, she was met by a small Federal ironclad named the *Monitor.* The two vessels were in striking contrast to one another—the big Confederate *Merrimac* so heavily armored that she was hardly manageable, and the small Union *Monitor* built so low and sparse that little more than her revolving gun turret showed above water. Then began the historic first battle of the ironclads. For over three hours, both armored vessels threw everything they had at each other. But in the end, it was a standoff; neither ship had damaged the other. The *Monitor,* who some observers said resembled a tin can on a shingle or a cheesebox on a raft, merely bounced cannonballs off her hulking antagonist who in turn was unable to ram or land a lethal blow to her more nimble foe. Finally, by common consent, both vessels retired from the field of battle, and the era of the ironclads began.

To Holland, the *Monitor-Merrimac* encounter meant more than a stalemated battle between two armored ships. It made him realize that the day of the wooden warship was over. And with it could pass British supremacy of the sea. What a delightful thought that was! With a little help the day might be hastened by such cunningly designed vessels as John Ericsson's "cheesebox on a raft." "What a devilishly elusive target we would make," thought Holland, imagining himself at the controls of such a vessel as he single-handedly bottled up the entire British fleet in Cork Harbour.

Although the idea lingered provocatively on the fringes of his imagination, Holland's interest in a semisubmersible craft that would spell the end of the British navy was generally forgotten while he concerned himself more with the mystery of flight. Living on the coast he had ample opportunity to observe the airborne antics of a multitude of sea birds. For their size and energy he marveled at the formidable tasks they performed. "What keeps them aloft?" he wondered, then puzzled over it with pencil and paper, mathematically trying to solve the complicated problems of flight. He calculated that the force needed to propel birds through the air was nine times their weight. He filled notebooks with his computations until gradually he gleaned an understanding of the principles of aerodynamics that was far ahead of his time.

With improved health, Holland returned to teaching. In the spring of 1864, his attention once again focused on nautical matters, for he had read and was duly impressed by accounts from America of the Confederate submarine *Hunley* sinking the Federal blockade ship, *Housatonic*. Now it was no longer an ironclad *Monitor* he thought about but a full-fledged underwater boat, a submarine. Again, however, his will-o'-the-wisp interest shifted elsewhere, and in 1865 he was transferred to a school in the seaport town of Drogheda just north of Dublin. This was the beginning of a renewed period of Irish-British friction resulting in an outbreak of riots in several Irish cities. The British retaliated swiftly and mercilessly, arresting, among others, two leaders of the Irish revolutionary movement—John Devoy and Jeremiah O'Donovan Rossa. Both men drew heavy prison sentences, and although Holland knew neither one personally, they were destined to play an important role in his future.

Four years later Holland was moved to a post in Dundalk where he taught music and for the first time began seriously thinking about submarines. Local legend has it that while he was in Dundalk he made and experimented with a clockwork model submarine in a wooden tub of water. During this period others were experimenting too. While he may have been inspired by the *Hunley* during the American Civil War, one can imagine how he felt when he read in the newspapers of 1870 that England had built two semisubmersibles named the *Abyssinia* and the *Magdala.* With only their gun turrets visible these vessels were supposedly intended for use in the defense of Bombay Harbor. Nor were the British alone in their efforts. In 1872, in Newark, New Jersey, Oliver Halstead designed and had built a twenty-six-foot-long by nine-foot-wide underwater vessel called the *Intelligent Whale.* Unfortunately this wide-waisted iron blimp, powered by thirteen crewmen cranking a propeller shaft, failed to live up to its expectations. Following a spectacular initial demonstration which prompted its purchase by the United States government, the *Intelligent Whale* subsequently drowned thirty-nine crewmen in various tests before it was finally put to rest in the Brooklyn Navy Yard where it could cause no more trouble.

If it had been a bad year for Halstead's *Whale,* it was an equally bad one for Holland. His health worsened. His weight fell to 140 pounds. He no longer had the energy nor the inclination to ponder the problems of his submersible-boat ideas. His face took on new lines, his hair was receding, and there was no longer any twinkle in the eyes behind his thick rimless glasses. In general, he looked and felt much older than his thirty years. Then, in the spring of 1872, his family left Ireland and immigrated to America. This severing of family ties filled him with mixed emotions. He was relieved to have his family leave the tense and uncertain political environment in Ireland and "escape" to the "Land of the Free" as so many of his countrymen were doing, but he disliked the inevitable separation.

Holland stayed with his teaching job through the long difficult winter. But by the following spring he was weaker than ever. Finally he applied for and received a special dispensation for another leave of absence from the Irish Christian Brotherhood on account of his health. Gathering his few belongings and meager savings, Holland followed his family across the Atlantic to Boston. At the age of thirty-two, this move marked the end of his Irish years and the ebb tide of his life.

Not long after arriving in America, Holland's health improved, and he soon found a job teaching in a parochial school in Paterson, New Jersey. One day, a student he was tutoring happened to see some of the early sketches of his submarine and told his father about it. The boy's parent was a friend of Navy Secretary George M. Robeson, and he suggested that the schoolteacher submit his idea to the government.

Holland was flattered that anyone would think his early efforts to design a submarine were good enough to offer to the United States government. But it was far too ambitious an idea to even think about. Or was it? "Why not try it?" his younger brother Michael urged. "They bought Halstead's *Whale*, didn't they?"

In the end, John Holland was persuaded that perhaps the idea wasn't so far-fetched after all. He *had* thought out the principles of submarine navigation and he believed his theories were right, that the submarine he had sketched would work. So why not let Washington decide?

Holland gathered up his long-forgotten figures and sketches but instead of reviewing them he started from the beginning again, confronting himself with the old problems to see if there was some way he might improve them.

When he finished and then compared his early work with that he had just completed, Holland was delighted to find that there was no real difference. His present approach to solving the problems of submarine navigation was the same as his original conception. This was the kind of logic that he understood. Concluding that he was on the right track, he wasted no time drawing a slightly refined version of his original submarine. The drawing showed a stiletto-shaped vessel fifteen and a half feet long being foot-treadled by a semireclining operator in diving gear. Fore and aft compartments of the craft contained air reservoirs in oiled silk bags, and the vessel was armed with two torpedoes. From its bubble-dome cockpit to its superstreamlined silhouette, Holland's idealized drawing closely resembled a picture of a pilot in the cockpit of a twentieth-century jet aircraft. While the drawing showed some of the functional details of his submarine, Holland purposely left certain things out because he felt that government personnel would have no real regard for his wish to keep some of his plans a secret. As it turned out, he was right.

Holland submitted his papers to the Navy Department in February 1875. They were returned later with an observation by a Captain Simpson of the Torpedo Station that since the craft offered no means to visually determine a course, navigating the vessel underwater would be as bad as steering in a perpetual fog. Therefore the whole scheme was impractical.

"Faith and begorra!" roared Holland. "Hasn't the man ever heard of a compass!"

Once he bridled his Irish temper, Holland wrote Captain Simpson a letter in which he drily commented that quite obviously the officer was unfamiliar with navigating a submersible by compass underwater.

Captain Simpson replied to the effect that no one with any sense would go underwater in such a contraption in the first place, that the inventor was wasting his time and should forget the entire matter because "to put anything through in Washington was uphill work."

Holland was to learn the truth in Captain Simpson's last remark. But for the moment the naval officer's opinion of his submarine only spurred the schoolteacher into more fervent thoughts on the subject. Many nights after school was out, he stayed in the classroom drawing and redrawing details of his submarine on the blackboard. When he was finally satisfied, the improvements were then transferred to paper.

On these occasions he was often joined by William Dunkerly, an engineer who checked his calculations and offered the kind of moral support that was needed at the moment.

One must marvel at Holland's courage to continue planning despite a probably gloomy future for his hypothetical diving machine already rejected by Washington. So who would be interested now? Who cared? Why continue shadowboxing with the idea of a submarine when there was no one to build it? A lesser man would have quit. But not John P. Holland, stubborn Irish schoolteacher from County Cork.

A little over a year from the time he submitted his submarine plans to Washington and had them turned down, events occurred which were to bring Holland assistance from a totally unsuspected quarter—from his own expatriated countrymen.

Irish political refugees had been immigrating to America even before the Civil War. Their sympathies, however, still lay with Ireland's struggle for independence. As citizens of another country they backed organizations working for Ireland's freedom. The American counterpart of the Irish Revolutionary Brotherhood was the Fenian Brotherhood established in this country in the 1860s. While John Holland was not a member of this radical organization, his younger brother, Michael, was. So it was Michael who first broached the idea to his fellow Fenians that was to affect John Holland's future in the submarine business.

Michael proposed that the Fenians build and use his brother's submarine to further their fight against England.

As absurd as the scheme seemed, it tickled the Fenians' fancy. Some members were willing to try anything to strike even a remote blow against the British. For example, the United Irishmen, a particularly militant group that had split from the Brotherhood, went so far as to twice attack Canada. Both raids were unsuccessful, but the United States had to intervene to put an end to the affair. As far as the United Irishmen were concerned, this was but a temporary respite. When new leaders arrived from Ireland, however, some of the dissident factions returned to the fold, and the Brotherhood became stronger and more unified than ever. All it lacked now was a worthy patriotic project, and Michael Holland felt his brother could provide that.

Letters of introduction went out. John Holland met influential members of the Fenian movement and he talked to their leaders, Jeremiah O'Donovan Rossa, Jerome Collins, John Devoy and John J. Breslin. Although both Devoy and Rossa had drawn long prison terms in Ireland while Holland was teaching in Drogheda, instead of prison the agitators were exiled to America where they consolidated and strengthened the revolutionary organization.

Holland's idea appealed to them. In his usual direct but reserved manner, the professor from Paterson wasted no words explaining exactly how important it would be to their cause to build his submarine and put it to use against the British fleet. Meanwhile, Devoy quickly and accurately sized up the Irish professor. He reported that "Holland is well informed of Irish affairs and is anti-English . . . with clear and definite ideas of the proper method of fighting England. He is cool, good-natured and talked to us as a schoolmaster to his children."

Less than six months after Holland made his proposal, it was an accomplished fact. Money came from the Fenians' "Skirmishing Fund" made up of the pennies, nickels and dimes contributed by clan members. An arrangement was made with a New York City ironworks, and the construction of Holland's boat No. 1 began under a general cloak of secrecy.

But the building of a strange new underwater boat is not the easiest thing to hide. The public was told only what the Fenians wanted it to know. Local papers reported that the submarine was being financed by a wealthy friend of Holland's. This "friend" was supposedly a Jacobs Senior of Jacobs and Company. These were cover names for Rossa and the Skirmishing Fund. When Breslin, another of the clan leaders, appeared frequently on the scene, he became Jacob Junior. The submarine was built for about $4,000 and, on May 22, 1878, this was the "iron coffin" that millworkers saw launched with such unfortunate results in the Upper Passaic River. While it may have been the first launching of its kind that they had ever witnessed, it was assuredly not the last.

Several days later the *Holland I* was readied for another test. Again she almost sank. A speedy rescue and close investigation revealed that the boat was taking water through some faulty riveting. Repairs were made. Another test followed. This time to guarantee that the boat would not sink unexpectedly, she went to sea slung between two rowboats and finally floated on an even keel.

Despite this seemingly minor and rather hollow success, Holland was pleased. At least his creation floated upright instead of plummeting to the bottom like an anchor. But to further avoid any prying eyes or spectators' jibes, the boat was towed upriver into a less public area for more intense tests. Ballast was shifted to give the boat better balance. Holland labored over the boat's cantankerous two-cylinder Brayton gasoline engine which occupied a prominent position in the central compartment. Unfortunately, no amount of coaxing would induce the engine to combust gasoline. Holland fussed and fidgeted over it until most men would have thrown down their tools in despair, jerked the infernal thing loose from its bed and called for a pair of oars. But this was not Holland's way. He stubbornly assessed all the problems and concluded that the engine was fully capable of functioning providing it had the proper power to do so. Since it did not take to gasoline, Holland decided perhaps it would work on another source of power. Ingeniously he ran a hose from the Brayton pressure chamber out of the turret through a waterproof hole and connected the other end to the boiler of the steamboat towing the submarine. Hot steam was then "piped" into the submarine's engine, and lo and behold it ran, tethered though it was to the accompanying steamboat. Once reasonably certain that he could satisfactorily demonstrate the boat's potentials, Holland arranged for another test before prominent Fenian leaders.

When the day arrived, the steam launch, loaded with O'Donovan Rossa and others, chugged up the Passaic with the *Holland I* in tow. Then the steam hose was attached.

Holland climbed into the narrow confines of his boat and put her through her paces. As those on the launch payed out the hose, the *Holland I* submerged to her turret, then dipped her nose down and disappeared in a gurgle of bubbles.

Those tending her lines reported that the boat reached a depth of twelve feet, and then she rose to the surface, her hatch opened, and a jubilant John Holland emerged grinning from his "iron coffin."

The test was a complete success, and to prove that it was not just luck Holland repeated the performance that afternoon. This time, however, he performed so dramatically that he gave the Fenians a scare. Holland submerged, but instead of returning smartly to the surface as before, he took the boat to the bottom and lay there for one hour before surfacing once more victorious before the worried onlookers. Holland was undoubtedly as pleased and impressed at the boat's performance as were they. Magnanimously he offered to let any of the Irish clan leaders "take her down" who cared to. It is recorded that no one took him up on his offer.

Only one thing marred the otherwise flawless demonstration. A suspicious character on shore was seen to be leaning against a rock and surreptitiously watching the events through field glasses. The Fenians immediately suspected a British spy. One in particular had been troubling the clan's activities ever since someone had tipped off the Canadians to the Fenians' second raid there in 1870. O'Donovan Rossa felt sure it was the notorious Henri LeCaron, alias Thomas Beach of Braidwood, Illinois. No one was positive of the arch spy's presence during the test, but the suspicious figure on shore left the Fenians feeling uneasy. So far as anyone knew, however, nothing came of it.

Holland had proved to the Fenians the feasibility of his boat. Now it was decided that he should build them a larger one. To keep his prototype from falling into someone else's hands, he pulled out the engine and scuttled his first effort in fourteen feet of water near the Spruce Street bridge.* Soon

---

*Almost fifty years later, enterprising students recovered the submarine and presented it to the Paterson Museum, where it is now exhibited.

he wished he had found deeper water when local citizens tried to grapple it up for its scrap iron. All they managed to do, however, was tear off the boat's turret with their grappling hooks and cause enough damage to the bridge in the process that the authorities swiftly curtailed their salvage activities—much to the relief of Holland and the Fenians.

The little Irish schoolteacher-turned-inventor learned a lot from his first serious plunge into submarine designing. He found, for example, that there was considerable merit in a boat having positive buoyancy while employing a low center of gravity for maximum stability. His test revealed that it was better to move the lateral hydroplanes from their original position near the boat's center of buoyancy to a more effective position on the boat's stern, perpendicular to the rudder. This would increase the boat's speed and maneuverability, particularly since Holland favored a porpoising or bow down, stern up, attitude for diving rather than taking on water ballast and gradually submerging the boat in a forward moving but horizontal attitude. Most importantly, he changed his mind about having the vessel's operator wear a self-contained diving suit similar to the Rouquayrol-Denayrouze equipment introduced in 1865. The primary reason for this elaborate getup was to enable the operator to leave his submarine to blow up an enemy surface vessel. Holland envisioned it this way: the operator would build up the submarine's internal air pressure until it equaled the outside water pressure. He would then open his hatch, emerge and attach a deadeye to the bottom of the target ship. Through this he would run a long line attached to an explosive charge. When the line was pulled, the bomb would strike the ship's hull detonating the device and sinking the vessel. While the idea seemed feasible, common sense told Holland that if it succeeded there was a good chance that the operator and his boat would be blown to kingdom come along with his target. So, wisely, he discarded the idea, along with the necessity of demonstrating to the Fenians how adroitly his submarine could sink a ship. On his next model, however, he determined to incorporate a gun or cannon to do the job.

Holland's dream of a bigger and better submarine sounded so good to the Fenians that they rallied behind him with all the enthusiasm and financial assistance the clan could muster. Everything looked favorable, even the long-range prospects. The uneasy political situation fermenting between England and Russia added fuel to their fervor. The Fenians watched these developments with high hopes. If England and Russia went to war, it was all the excuse they needed to whip out their secret weapon—Holland's new submarine—and strike a blow for Irish independence by doing battle with the British fleet wherever they encountered it.

So in this fertile environment, John Holland came to a major turning point in his life. He knew now that there was no turning back from the promising future the zealous Fenians had so graciously prepared for him. So, after eighteen years of teaching, the thirty-seven-year-old Holland reluctantly told his students good-bye, layed down his chalk and textbooks and turned to a new career. From that moment on, he was John Holland, inventor.

Now, more than ever, this new endeavor—the designing and building of a larger, more formidable war machine—called for utmost secrecy. Even among themselves the Fenian leaders made no direct mention of the project, referring to it only as the "salt water enterprise," while clan members warned each other about loose "barroom palaver."

Holland spent long hours at his drawing board quietly working out the many problems which were his alone to wrestle with. For months he laboriously struggled with the intricacies of designing a diving machine that would not only perform as he visualized it but which would merit all the time, money and trust lavished upon the project by the Irish Brotherhood.

If he had moments of doubt about his ability to measure up to the task, no one was ever aware of them. He was single-mindedly determined to succeed and in that spirit he finally completed his plans and sought out an old and reliable New York firm to build the boat for him.

Officials of the Delamater Iron Works on West Thirteenth

Street looked at his plans and raised skeptical eyebrows. One might imagine the ensuing conversation:

"Well, now, this is a most remarkable boat, Mr. Holland, but what does it do?"

"I'm sorry, I'm not at liberty to tell you that."

"Well . . . ah . . . What firm are you with? Whom do you represent in this matter?"

"Sorry, I'm not at liberty to divulge that either."

"Hmmmm. . . . How then, sir, do you propose that we be paid for our work?"

"I'll pay you," said Holland, "in good sound American currency. All I ask is that you give me an estimate."

"Well, yes, ummmm." The officials bent over the unrolled plans and scrutinized the cigar-shaped iron boat that carried three operators and buried three quarters of its bulk underwater like an iceberg. In conclusion they decided that the monstrosity would probably sink upon launching, but if this mad Irishman was willing to pay cold cash for its construction, then who were they to say nay? They told Holland that they would build his boat for him at a cost of no more than $20,000.

Almost as soon as work began on the new submarine, Holland had trouble with the Delamater employees. They openly criticized his plans, doubting that they were any good. They argued that the boat could not be built to such strange specifications; moreover, if it were, and by sheer good fortune the whole thing held together long enough to launch, then it would surely go straight to the bottom.

Holland controlled his temper as best he could. He told them quietly that as long as he was paying for the job, they would build the boat according to his specifications. If they couldn't, then he would get someone who could.

That quieted them for a while, but the wrangling continued periodically through the boat's entire construction. Privately Holland reconciled the workmen's antagonism by noting with typical Irish humor that almost to a man they were of English, Welsh or Scottish descent.

Despite the aura of mystery surrounding the project, a steady stream of German, Swedish, Italian, Russian and

Turkish envoys managed to visit the ironworks sometime during the two years it took to build the boat. The Turkish sultan even asked that Holland build one for him; however, the inventor put him off by saying his boats were still only in the experimental stage. One wonders if among all those visiting dignitaries there might not have been one aide or private secretary taking notes for the arch spy, LeCaron, who surely was concerned about what Holland and the Fenians were doing at the expense of the Skirmishing Fund.

How interested he was became apparent not long after the successful May 1, 1881, launching of Holland's second submarine. That month the Brotherhood held its convention. Circulars broadly listing the clan's financial affairs were distributed to members. One item showed that $90,453 had been contributed to the Skirmishing Fund at the rate of about $2,000 a month. There was no mention of how much had been paid out for the "salt water enterprise," but Holland revealed later that the Delamater Iron Works did the job for $18,000. This did not include the cost and installation of the submarine's machinery, so as nearly as possible it appears that of the Fund's $90,453, Holland's submarine projects gobbled up about $60,000 worth. Fortunately enough for the clan members' peace of mind these figures were not common knowledge, but there was one person who would have liked to have made them so—the infamous LeCaron. One of his agents masquerading as a loyal Fenian at the convention gave the master spy a full report of all the financial statements available. LeCaron used them in turn to provoke Irishmen into demanding to know where their donations were going when they left the Skirmishing Fund.

This tactic caused enough bickering among clan members for Devoy to complain that "England always gets her dirty work done among Irishmen by ardent 'patriots' who want value for their money and ten cents' worth of revolution every week. . . ."

Now that the new submarine had survived her launching, Holland spent several weeks readying her for her first test dive. For an ex-schoolteacher not overly experienced in such matters, he had designed a remarkably fine boat. She resembled a streamlined cigar thirty-one feet long and six feet wide. Her nineteen-ton displacement hull of $^{11}/_{16}$-inch-thick flange iron drew seven feet four inches of water. Her single screw was powered by an improved fifteen-to seventeen-horse, two-cylinder Brayton gasoline engine built to Holland's specifications and mounted directly under the helmsman's seat just aft of amidships. Bow and stern sealed compartments contained compressed air that assured the boat of a positive buoyancy. Between these reservoirs and the crew's compartment were fore and aft ballast tanks for taking on or expelling water to make the boat rise or submerge. Passing lengthways through the center of the bow compartments was an eleven-foot-long pneumatic gun with a nine-inch bore. The breech could be opened in the control compartment and the gun loaded with a six-foot-long projectile which was "fired" out through the bow with a 400-pound blast of compressed air.

Holland had designed his boat to be operated by a three-man crew: the helmsman who sat in a bucket seat over the engine and controlled the boat with two vertical levers, one connected to the rudder, the other to the diving planes; an engineer to read the gauges and manipulate the valves that filled or emptied the ballast tanks, and a gunner who did the necessary things to arm and fire the boat's pneumatic gun.

Outwardly the low-profile boat exhibited clean lines. Nothing cluttered her decks. Not even the turret distracted from her hydrodynamic shape, a quality characteristic of all Holland submarines.

By June 1881, everything was ready for her first test dive. As usual, the professor was the first to try her out, accompanied by his engineer George M. Richards. The two men climbed through the boat's narrow hatch, and Holland closed it behind them, dogging it down tightly. From then on they would breathe compressed air.

In the semidarkness they waited a few minutes. Feeling no ill-effects, Holland decided to submerge. He turned two little iron levers on either side of his head, operating the Kingston valves that let water into the ballast tanks. The boat immediately began settling, giving the men the impression of going down in an elevator. Through the turret ports Holland saw the bow disappear and water rise until it was inches from the glass. Seconds later the boat darkened. A dark green blur showed at the ports.

Then, with a slight jar, the boat settled on the bottom in fourteen feet of water. There was no light except the greenish glow from the ports, barely enough to read the gauges. In the future, the men would carry a lantern to see to make adjustments; otherwise it would not be used, because it would consume too much oxygen.

Richards checked for leaks but found the boat sound. Holland then opened the valve admitting compressed air into the ballast tanks. The air hissed as it drove out the water and the boat began to rise. The green blur in the ports grew lighter until bright daylight suddenly burst through the glass, dazzling them. Holland opened the hatch and stood on his seat so that his head and shoulders protruded from the conning tower. A cheer rose from a crowd of spectators on the dock.

He now knew that the boat was tight, satisfactorily ballasted and that the compressed air was breathable. The next day the two men took her down for an hour and a half, until onlookers grew so worried that they were grappling for the submarine when she surfaced.

Other questions had yet to be answered. Would the boat's Brayton engine run underwater? Would it "breathe" and exhaust the way Holland had designed it or would it fill the boat with deadly fumes, killing the crew before they could surface? If the engine did not asphyxiate them, would the submarine dive, maneuver and rise under its own power? Holland had to have the answers to these questions.

Days later the tests continued. The boat was sealed for diving. Holland started the Brayton engine and released the clutch. Onlookers saw the submarine move out across the water, then slope forward and slowly sink from view. Three hundred yards from where she went down she reappeared, still moving swiftly under her own power. Holland found that the boat was capable of surface speeds up to nine miles an hour and suspected that she could travel equally as fast underwater; however, he had no means of checking this.

In all, he was overjoyed with her performance. The engine worked exactly as he had planned, "breathing" air from the boat's interior and exhausting the noxious fumes out through a hull valve. The exchange would always take place providing the boat's air pressure equaled that of the surrounding water.

"If the boat dives deep, we merely increase the air pressure," Holland confided to friends. But since too much air pressure would be uncomfortable to the crew, he was already planning a ventilating system to eliminate the problem.

Now that the mystery boat was out in the open being tested, newsmen hounded Holland for interviews, but he skillfully avoided them. Blakely Hall, an enterprising reporter for the *New York Sun* kept after him, pleading to be allowed to see inside the boat by emphasizing how helpful publicity had been for some of Holland's foreign competition who were also designing submarines. But Holland kept his word to the Fenians and politely refused.

Hall wrote his story anyway. When it appeared in the *New York Sun* it not only named and popularized the mystery boat but Hall's assumptions were remarkably astute. He called the boat the "Fenian Ram," which immediately identified the boat's sponsor and its intended function. Further, Hall speculated that the *Ram* could fit in a railroad boxcar or could be loaded aboard a ship and sent to England to prey on British shipping. He couldn't have come closer to the truth if master spy LeCaron had been briefing him.

While Holland may have expressed displeasure over the article with the Fenians, he was secretly amused and pleased with the story. It saved his having to name his boat which from then on was always called the *Fenian Ram*.

Next to be tested was the *Ram*'s pneumatic gun. This device was designed to fire a six-foot-long cylindrical missile with an explosive warhead, but Holland had not taken the time to build or obtain ammunition for it. His machinist was seriously considering using an empty nail keg for a dummy projectile when help came from a most unexpected quarter.

Holland's long-time hero and early inspiration, Capt. John Ericsson, skipper of the famous *Monitor,* was having a boat built for him at Delamater Iron Works. When someone told him about Holland's submarine and his need for ammunition, Ericsson graciously sent a note to the professor offering him some dummy projectiles of his own design.

Holland was enormously pleased with the offer of assistance from this famous man whom he so highly esteemed. He immediately wrote his acceptance, and two of Captain Ericsson's missiles were placed at his disposal. The tests that followed were indeed spectacular, but if LeCaron had been watching he probably would have folded his file on the *Fenian Ram* and told the British to forget that he had ever mentioned the subject.

Under the usual cloak of secrecy, Holland cranked up the *Fenian Ram* early on the morning of her gunnery test, and the boat slid away from her berth out into the Morris Canal Basin. Loaded in the breech of her eleven-foot-long pneumatic gun was one of Captain Ericsson's six-foot dummy projectiles. Neither Holland nor his engineer were sure what would happen when they fired the weapon, so they decided to be cautious. Instead of using the gun's full firing power, they chose to try it at a conservative 300 pounds. Then, if the thing worked the way it was supposed to, they would avoid torpedoing a floating dry dock some distance down range.

Valves were opened, and the *Ram's* water-ballast tanks began to fill. The boat settled. When the gun's bow cap was three feet underwater, Holland held the boat steady.

"Make ready to fire," he ordered.

"Ready, sir," his engineer replied.

"Then fire!"

Three hundred pounds of compressed air sent Captain Ericsson's dummy projectile hurtling down the gun barrel and out the bow of the submarine. Ten feet from its muzzle the projectile shot out of the water, soared eighty feet in the air, then plummeted down again, burying itself forever in the muddy bottom of the Basin.

"Good Lord," grumbled Holland. "Fool thing thinks it's a mortar!"

Another projectile was slid into the gun's breech. This time Holland purposely pointed the *Ram*'s bow down five degrees. "Fire!" he commanded.

The projectile whooshed out its tube, traveled twenty feet underwater, then rocketed into the air on a high arcing flight that cleared not only the dry dock but also the Basin before crashing into a piling on the breakwater.

"Ericsson needs more work on his projectiles," Holland commented drily.

So much for the gunnery tests.

Although the public had read about the *Fenian Ram* in the newspapers, nothing compared to an actual confrontation. One day the ferryboat *St. Johns* was plodding serenely across the narrows off Stapleton when a glistening metal monster suddenly surfaced in a welter of foam off her bows. While passengers and crew watched wide eyed, the thing churned its tail and dived quickly out of sight.

The captain of the *St. Johns* promptly put his ferryboat in reverse and broke all records steaming back to port.

Later when the *Ram* returned, Holland wondered why men on the docks were jumping around as if they had lost their minds.

"What's wrong?" he asked the boatyard owner.

"Seems you just scared the devil out of the *St. Johns.*"

"By golly, I *knew* I heard paddle wheels," said Holland. "Thought we were about to have a collision so I took her down to twenty feet to be safe. When we surfaced a few minutes later there wasn't a big boat in sight."

Another time during a trial run in the summer of 1883, Holland looked out the turret's forward port and wondered why his view of Staten Island was framed by two brown rags. Thinking that trash had caught on the turret, he prepared to dive. Suddenly he heard scuffling overhead. He turned the boat to run with the waves and opened the hatch. Sitting astride the *Ram*'s turret, clutching it with his hands and knees, was a black boy.

"Where in tarnation did you come from?" Holland asked.

The boy was too frightened to answer.

"All right, at least come inside out of the wet," Holland insisted.

The youngster shook his head. He wanted no part of it.

The ex-schoolteacher gave the boy a quick dissertation on the principles of submarine navigation, explaining that the boat was made to travel underwater. "Now, lad. Come inside."

"T-that's all right," the boy assured Holland. "I'll hang on."

It was too late to argue, the sun was already setting. All Holland could do was head for the nearby unfamiliar Brooklyn shore at slow speed.

As the *Ram* with her reluctant passenger riding her like a bareback pony neared the wharfs, she was intercepted by two boys in a rowboat.

"What's that thing?" they called.

Holland stopped the submarine and told them, hoping perhaps that the newcomers would relieve him of his stowaway.

"Want to come aboard and look her over?" he asked. They needed no urging. After a quick inspection tour of the *Ram's* interior they climbed into their rowboat. Since it was growing too late for Holland to attempt a safe crossing to the New York shore, he asked if the boys knew a place to berth the submarine for the night.

Assuring him that they did, the youngsters tied their painter to the *Ram's* bow ring and set off for the Bergen boatyard, not entirely unaware of the spectacle they were creating. Not a soul on the waterfront failed to stare at the strange procession of two boys in a rowboat towing a humpbacked iron whale astride which rode a black boy and a little man wearing a bowler hat and a walrus mustache.

Even while Holland was conducting experiments with the *Fenian Ram*, he was having a third submarine built. This was another small boat, similar to the *Holland I* which he had scuttled in the Upper Passaic River. But there was a difference. The new boat was to be a sixteen-foot working model incorporating major design improvements over the *Fenian*

Ram. It was a natural progression, the next step in Holland's development of the submarine. However, some members of the Fenian movement were far from pleased with the project's current state of affairs.

"Where will it end?" they asked. "How much money must be spent before we can taste the fruits of victory? Are we building Mr. Holland a fleet of pleasure boats or are we going to stop these expenditures and use his invention the way it was intended?"

Such were the rantings of those who "wanted their ten cents' worth of revolution every week." Holland understood their impatience but he resented their implying that he was personally benefiting from the project. The truth of the matter was that during the submarine trials he received no salary. Forced to board with his cousin in Newark, he often did not even have carfare to get to New York. But there was no appeasing the discontented. Once it began, the situation grew worse. Arguments and accusations followed. In the fall of 1883, while Holland was outwardly delighted about successfully taking the *Ram* down to sixty feet without mishap, he was inwardly distressed about the dissention riddling the Brotherhood. Members accused each other of pilfering from the Skirmishing Fund. The Mulcahy case then before the New York Supreme Court sought an injunction against Trustees of the Fund, preventing them from using any money in the treasury without the court's jurisdiction.

Then the unexpected happened. On a cold, bleak November night in 1883, a group of radical Fenians bearing a pass with Holland's signature forged on it entered the dock area where the *Ram* was berthed. Considering how much secrecy shrouded the project, the night watchman suspected nothing when the men tied the *Fenian Ram* and Holland's sixteen-foot submarine behind a tugboat and steamed off into the darkness of New York Harbor. The leader of the group was John J. Breslin, who at an earlier date had been code-named "Jacob Junior," one of the project's managers. He and Holland had had a minor altercation which might explain why he failed to include the inventor in his plans. At any rate, Breslin felt that the court was about to act in the

Mulcahy case and would impound the clan's submarines. Rather than let that happen, he and several other stalwarts took matters into their own hands and absconded with the property in question. But misfortune was hard on their trail.

Late at night the pirates cleared Manhattan and were towing their ill-gotten gains up the East River when they were struck by high winds off Long Island Sound. As the ungainly flotilla wallowed through the choppy waves, the little submarine took on water through her improperly closed hatch. Settling stern first behind the *Fenian Ram,* she finally snapped her towline and sank in 110 feet of water. The tug chugged on through the Sound with the *Ram* still in tow. The next day Breslin and the others reached New Haven, where the submarine was hidden at a brass foundry on Mill River.

One can well imagine John P. Holland's feelings when he learned of the abductions. He immediately protested Breslin's actions in a letter to Devoy, but the Fenian leader was either unwilling or unable to help. And not surprisingly, that was as far as Holland pursued the matter. After all, he had only designed the submarines. They belonged to the Brotherhood. "I have no intentions of advancing any excuses for the incident, as no official explanation was ever made to me concerning it," he wrote. "As a result, I never bothered again with my backers, nor they with me."

Such was the sad, if not perhaps inevitable, culmination of a remarkable association. Although Holland was no longer a part of this Irish drama, he still had the last laugh. He was the only one who could operate the submarine. Engineer Richards thought he could, but the attempt ended in disaster. Once, when Holland was absent from the dock, Richards took out the *Ram* and swamped it in the wake of a tug. As the sub sank stern first, she belched the engineer out through the hatchway with a blast of escaping air. It cost the Fenians $3,000 to raise and rehabilitate the *Ram.* So Holland knew that Breslin had a white elephant on his hands. And as far as he was concerned, he could keep it until it rotted.

Since ignorance is bliss, however, Breslin and his cohorts somehow managed to operate the submarine well enough to sally forth on various nautical excursions without either losing the vessel or drowning themselves. That is not to say that they did not cause some damage; and it appears that they were afraid to take the submarine underwater. But it is reliably reported that the irresponsible Irishmen were seen hot-rodding the submarine around New Haven Harbor, sinking imaginary British boats and almost doing in a few real ones. Things got so bad that the local harbor master declared the submarine a menace to navigation and halted the shenanigans before someone really got hurt.

So the last surviving member of the Irish Underwater Fleet was put in mothballs. The *Ram* was hauled into a lumber shed on Mill River where her Brayton engine was removed to operate a forge in the foundry and there she sat ingloriously turning to rust.

Five years later Mulcahy was still trying to claim her for part of the debt he felt was owed him. But Devoy refused to give up the boat. Not for sentimental reasons but because he still thought she could be sold. It was later rumored that the *Ram* was offered to Russia, but if this is true, nothing came of it.

While it seemed that this unique boat was destined to end her days in obscurity, this was not to be. She still had one last patriotic duty to perform for the cause of Irish independence. In 1916, the hull was brought to New York City's Madison Square Garden where the *Fenian Ram* was exhibited at a bazaar to raise money for victims of the Irish uprising that year. The next time the *Fenian Ram* appeared in public, she was in full retirement, having been purchased by Edward A. Browne of Paterson and put on permanent display at the West Side Park in Paterson, New Jersey. And there she still may be seen.

After the *Fenian Ram* affair, John Holland did not involve himself with another submarine for the next five years. Then he tried to sell the navy some of his ideas. Oddly enough the navy referred him to the army where in 1886 at Fort Hamilton, New York, he teamed up with an artillery officer, Lieut. Edward Zalinski, in the construction of what was later called the "Zalinski boat." Since the Lieutenant was a gun inventor, he loaded the boat with heavy ordnance, one of the contributing factors in her premature demise. As the ponderous submarine was being launched, the ways collapsed; she split her seams and went to the bottom where she stayed.

Back to the drawing board went Holland. His next venture was to enter a government-sponsored competition with the top submarine designers of the day. When his design won, he was awarded a $150,000 navy contract to build a boat, so he founded the Holland Torpedo Boat Company and set to work. Unfortunately, the navy had its own ideas of how the submarine should be built, and they differed radically from Holland's. The conglomerate result was the *Plunger,* an eighty-five-foot-long, eleven-and-a-half-foot-diameter iron monstrosity displacing 168 tons, armed with five Whitehead torpedoes and powered by one 300-horsepower and two 600-horsepower engines. Her altered specifications gave the boat so many quirks and flaws that during trial runs Holland could not even make her hold a straight course. In the end, as he had predicted, the venture was a colossal "technical and financial failure." The navy never accepted the boat.

Even before the *Plunger* was completed, Holland had drawn plans for another submarine, one which he knew would work if he could avoid government interference. He offered to build this boat for the navy at his own expense if he could do it the way he wanted. The navy acquiesed, so Holland's company, assisted financially by a private backer, built the innovative and successful *Holland.* This boat was fifty-three feet ten inches long, ten feet three inches in diameter and displaced under seventy-five tons. On the surface she was powered by a gasoline engine; submerged, she ran on storage batteries. The boat had a fifty-mile range before the batteries required charging. A pendulum linked to the diving planes kept her level fore and aft; another device took her automatically to any predetermined depth. Since the boat lacked a periscope because that instrument had not yet been invented, she was supposed to attack surface vessels by porpoising out of water for a quick sight at the target, then submerge to avoid enemy fire. Again she would porpoise out of water, fire one of her three torpedoes, then dive out of sight. A rather complicated procedure in light of later methods but one which was "modern" for its time.

Like all Holland submarines the boat was partially buoyant even with her ballast tanks flooded. If her pumps or motor failed, this inherent safety factor enabled her to float to the surface. Only when under power with diving planes angled down would she dive. This mode of operation was the main difference between Holland's submarines and those of his contemporaries which were designed to dive and rise on an even keel, the boat remaining horizontal at all times.

The costly effort of building the *Holland* almost bankrupted the Holland Boat Company. But the boat so impressed the firm supplying Holland with storage batteries that it agreed to financially back any new projects. Thus the Holland Boat Company became the Electric Boat Company and it has done well ever since. In 1955, Electric Boat Company launched the first atomic submarine, *Nautilus.*

On April 11, 1900, following a month of trials, the navy accepted the *Holland.* The next year the Irish inventor designed a bigger boat, the *Fulton.* While it was an improved version of the *Holland,* the navy felt that it had all the submarines it cared to buy for the moment.

Meanwhile, Russia and Japan were about to go to war and both countries were interested in Holland's latest effort. Finally, when he was certain that the American government was not going to take the *Fulton,* Holland sold her to Russia. Delivery was made clandestinely when the *Fulton* went to sea, was hoisted aboard a freighter in international waters and deposited along with her crew in Russia. Five similar boats were later sold to Japan, but there are no records that any of the submarines figured in the Russo-Japanese War of 1904–1905.

The U.S. Navy finally got into the act in 1903 when Holland was commissioned to build six new boats—the *Addler, Grampus, Moccasin, Porpoise, Pike* and *Shark.* Once the *Plunger* was rebuilt and added to the group, these seven boats comprised the first United States Submarine Service.

At last, after forty years of fighting, the ice was broken for

Holland. Foreign powers began eyeing each other's small but growing submarine fleets. Britain still felt that the answer to supremacy at sea lay with surface ships, but when she learned that France was busy building a fledgling submarine force, she quickly ordered plans for five submarines. From whom? Why, from John P. Holland.

The first British submarine built from Holland's plans turned turtle in the water! Seems there was a slight discrepancy in the plans. When it was corrected, the British boats floated upright. But Irish eyes were smiling.

Then, in 1906, his 105-foot-long, 14-foot-beam, 270-ton *Octopus* slid down the ways to become one of Holland's crowning achievements. This submarine with a surface speed of eleven knots and a submerged speed of almost ten, carried a fifteen-man crew and was designed to withstand depths of 200 feet. She was successfully test-submerged empty at 205 feet for ten minutes with some 15,000 tons of water squeezing her sturdy hull. The submarine later figured in a much-publicized competition with the *Lake,* the boat of Holland's closest competitor, Simon Lake. In the ten-day performance duel between the *Octopus* and the *Lake,* the navy judged the *Octopus* the winner.

But this, not unlike other small personal victories that kindled his own knowledge of what he had accomplished, had a hollow ring. Events in the later years were not overly kind to John P. Holland. While he had been occupied with designing and engineering his boats, better business minds than his had left him little more than a figurehead in the underwater boat company he had begun. Litigation was of no use because the skullduggery had all been done neatly and legally and others were to reap the profits of his inventions. Although he still received some money from a few early patents that he held, the injustices that were done him left the once peppery little Irishman a bit debilitated and discouraged with it all. When his health fell off with his enthusiasm for the troublesome business of underwater boats, he renewed his interest in flying and wrote *How to Fly as a Bird.* Few people understood John P. Holland, because they did not understand his submarines. His neighbors in East

Orange, New Jersey, remember him as a small, stooping, nearsighted man who was "a kind of inventor."

He never lived to fulfill his youthful dream of overthrowing the British at sea with one of his marvelous diving machines for he died in Newark on August 12, 1914, five days after the beginning of World War I. But the old Fenian would have been pleased to know that Holland submarines fought valiantly in that war—even though some of them were on the side of the British Royal Navy.

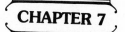

CHAPTER 7

Marching to a Different Drummer

 For every submarine ever built, many never got beyond the drawing board. Some, however, progressed to the model stage and a few were even patented. No story of submarines would be complete without mention of the more bizarre boats and their sometimes equally bizarre creators. Once we know what the competition was like, it is easier to understand why such men as Fulton, Bauer, Holland and others had such a hard time getting their projects accepted when they were surrounded by crackpot inventors striving for the same acceptance for their highly imaginative ideas.

Consider, for instance, this 1822 French version which seems originally intended to be an improvement over Robert Fulton's submarine. Named *L'Invisible,* she was designed to be a cast-iron underwater battleship 112 feet long, 28 feet wide and 16 feet deep. Along with her conventional surface-craft shape went a pair of folding masts for sails when traveling above water. Her superstructure was a domed conning tower three feet above the deck. Tower, deck and bulwarks were six-inch-thick armor plating. In addition to sails the boat was powered by oars and paddle wheels, the latter driven by an engine that used gunpowder explosions to make it go. While the inventor was remarkably vague on exactly how this worked, he was much more specific about the submarine's ambitious armament. In addition to eight short-barreled cannon on her upper deck, *L'Invisible* carried four underwater cannon called "colombiads" that would supposedly fire through special waterproof stoppered ports, one hundred torpedoes, a ram and, last but not least, a kind of huge syringe that squirted an explosive mixture of naphtha and nitrate of potash on any vessel foolhardy enough to come within reach of this floating incendiary bomb. Needless to say, *L'Invisible* remained exactly that.

Five years later, in 1827, Fulton's submarine inspired a gentleman named Castèra to draw up and apparently patent the plans for an underwater boat employing some avant-garde ideas antedating both Bauer and future submarine inventor Simon Lake. Castèra's submarine was supposed to roll along the bottom on four wheels and would employ an air lock to allow a diver to come and go as did Lake's *Argonaut* sixty-eight years later. And dangling from the bow of the boat was a pair of long leather gloves to be used for grasping things by a man inside the submarine, as was designed by Wilhelm Bauer on his *Sea Devil,* twenty-eight years later. Despite the innovations on Castèra's boat, he was not taking any chances that the thing might fail him while he was on the bottom and leave him there. He therefore suspended his submarine by two ropes and a flexible air hose from a giant float that always remained on the surface. That way he could crank himself up or down like an elevator whenever it pleased him. Safe as it seemed, Castèra's creation never reached the construction stage.

Next, in 1856, a man with the unlikely name of Althabegöi-ty designed and built a model of an equally unlikely diving machine he called a "hydroscaphe." It was shaped like a wooden lemon eighty-two feet long and forty feet wide with a propeller at each end. A third propeller stuck up out of the top like the rotor on a helicopter. Mounted beside it was an air tube to the surface with a ladder inside for hasty exits. Althabegöity took one look at his model and wisely scrapped the whole thing.

The last idea Wilhelm Bauer had for a submarine in 1861 might have been conceived as a direct result of his feelings for the Russian navy. Bauer called it a *Brûleur des Côtes,* ("side burner" or "coast burner") which was to be "in the form of a whale . . . its hull . . . of iron, and provided with engines of 100 h.p. which will enable it to travel and maneuver at great speed at the surface of the water until it arrives within cannon-shot of the enemy's ships; thenceforward it dives to the depth of about 30 feet and then approaches them either on the bow or broadsides, being careful to avoid touching the enemy's ship to whom it should not give the least indication of its presence. . . ." At this point Bauer would bring into use the submarine's formidable weapon—a mortar protruding from its bow like a giant pipebowl. Supposedly, its vertical blast blows a two-foot hole in the ship's bottom, then the submarine swiftly surfaces, runs alongside with its gunports open and gives the confounded vessel a scathing broadside. The Russian admirals would have sent Bauer to the salt mines for that one.

In 1857, Hubault of Amiens, France, patented a kind of underwater boat that also carried its own safety float on the surface as did Castèra's. However, this machine had two tubes to the surface, one for bringing in fresh air; the other for expelling the bad. It also sported through-the-hull gloves, four pairs of them, and some special contrivance for the crew to stick their heads out underwater if they so wished. In addition, the hand-cranked machine was crowned by a spotlight, but there was no explanation as to what powered it. Lightning bugs perhaps.

By 1889, a Russian named Apostoloff came up with a real winner—a submarine he claimed could overcome the frictional resistance of water and therefore cross the Atlantic Ocean in twenty-eight hours! And how was this wondrous machine to perform this miracle? Why by literally screwing itself through the water. Apostoloff's proposed boat was shaped like a huge World War II blockbuster bomb, tail fins and all. But the body of the device was grooved like an auger. Moreover, it spun around a central axis, thereby "screwing" itself through the water. The interior hull, of course, remained still. Sticking up near the stern was a tall conning tower which also remained static. Just aft of this were the vessel's tail fins which could be raised or lowered as a unit swiveling on a kind of universal joint. It was said that one reason Apostoloff's "screw-marine" never caught on was because passengers feared that the outer revolving hull might jam its machinery and spin the inside lounge and everyone in it around like an eggbeater.

Another novel diving machine was patented by Silas and George Rogers in England in 1898. These clever inventors knew that a submarine would sink or rise by increasing or decreasing its displacement. So they designed an underwater boat that did this by telescoping the last third of its cylindrical body into the first two-thirds section, thereby obtaining the desired results. In addition, the forward conning tower was really a self-contained boat which, in an emergency, could be detached to carry the crew to the surface and safety. Roger's twin-screw piggyback boat-submarine was powered by electricity. But as plausible as it was, the idea never caught on and the boat was never built.

In 1876, Donati Tomassi, an Italian engineer, came up with a kind of underwater boat-observation platform called a "hemi-plongeur" that was neither "fish nor fowl." It was a conical-shaped submarine that sprouted two tall hollow columns supporting above the water's surface a window-encircled platform with an air vent, chimney and observation platform on its roof. The underwater part of the machine moved the platform to any desired location, and passengers could pass freely between the two sections on ladders in the hollow legs. Furthermore, the legs telescoped so that according to the inventor the submarine could sink into safer depths to avoid the worst of the wave action. Surely Tomassi's "hemi-plongeur" would have filled some kind of need until someone started thinking about the reliability of those two hollow legs. If a big storm wave caught the contraption just right, the "half-diver" might provide its passengers with more diving thrills than its name implied. So that was the end of that.

Near Toulon, a French dockworker named Jacquemin suggested a similar semisubmersible in 1884. Powered by a stern-drive propeller, the cigar-shaped hull had a rather high conning tower for taking in air and providing an easy means of egress. All very conventional. But then Jacquemin lined the hull with numerous pairs of shoulder-length leather gloves and helmets so that passengers could stick their heads out and see what their hands were doing. This feature should have appealed to the budding marine scientists of the day, but it did not.

And then there was the proposal in 1887, by a San Francisco man named Gerber, for such a preposterous diving machine that newspapers were reluctant to describe it in detail for fear readers would think it was the product of a deranged mind. What particularly annoyed everyone in that advanced age of steam and electricity was that Gerber insisted on powering his creation with hand-turned paddles and a rubber-band motor. But when he announced his intentions to build the boat to look for the pharaoh's chariot wheels at the bottom of the Red Sea, some readers suspected that he might be putting them on.

Brazilian Virissimo Barboza de Souza pondered a jungle lizard one day in 1891 and gave birth to a truly ingenious idea for an underwater boat. It was cone-shaped at both ends and powered by whatever source was available. This minor detail did not bother Barboza. He probably would have even used Gerber's rubber bands had they been available. What was more important was the manner in which the submarine got itself out of trouble. It could shuck its bow or its stern or both appendages at once like a lizard's tail while its midsection went on safely without them. Unfortunately, nobody could have cared less, so the boat was never built.

As it was with Gerber's brainstorm, words failed writers trying to describe the underwater monstrosity dreamed up by an inventor named Möller in 1898. One chronicler said it was shaped vaguely like "an ovoid bent askew." Möller's diagram seems to represent a kind of brick-walled underwater factory with a large window, but it could be something else. Whatever it is, it is powered by a big engine with a flywheel. Wearing full diving dress, the "boat's" commander stands in a kind of sentry box which may be raised or lowered mechanically from the rear of the structure. Möller shows him facing aft about to release a floating bomb from beside him. One hopes that it is set for self-destruct.

By the turn of the century some inventors were engrossed not merely in designing a particular kind of submarine but in refining what was already in use, such as submarine propulsion, for example. In 1901, a man named Ponthus said he had devised a way to improve the efficiency of his submarine propeller to such a degree that his boat would break all speed records. Ponthus' submarine was shaped like a stubby cigar with three propellers, one each on the bow and stern and another amidships underneath the boat. When these propellers were working at top speed, Ponthus reasoned that they created a kind of vacuum around themselves in the water and lost much of their effect. To counter this he was prepared to blow water back into the screws with jets of compressed air. According to the inventor, this would allow his submarine to travel at the astonishing speed of forty miles an hour. Apparently that was faster than anyone cared to go underwater, because the Frenchman's pipe dream never materialized.

Ponthus was not the last of the long line of "inventors" who marched to a different drummer, but their heyday was over. Despite a plethora of crank ideas, the submarine of the future was already launched and well on its way.

John P. Holland's first submarine, a three-foot model of the *Holland I*, presently on display at the Paterson Museum, Paterson, New Jersey. (Courtesy, Submarine Museum, New London, Connecticut)

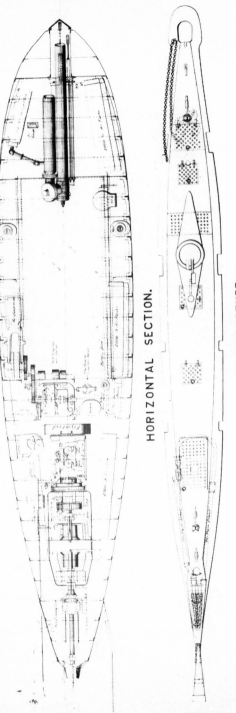

HORIZONTAL SECTION.

PLAN OF SUPERSTRUCTURE.

Above and below: Plans of Holland's *Holland (SS-1)* built at the turn of the century at a cost that almost bankrupted the Holland Boat Company. Like all Holland-designed submarines, the boat had positive buoyancy, floating rather than sinking if her pumps or motor failed. (Courtesy: Submarine Museum, New London, Connecticut)

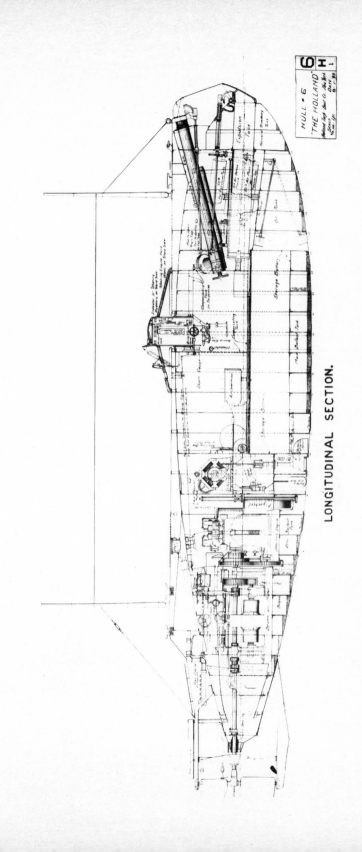

LONGITUDINAL SECTION.

STEEL FISH WITH REVOLVING TAIL THAT WILL PROTECT OUR HARBOR AGAINST ANY FLEET.
The Holland Submarine Terror, the Newest Wonder of Naval Science, Which Dives and Swims Under Water and Noiselessly and Unseen Creeps Up Under an Enemy's Side, Hurling Into It Thunderbolts of Dynamite from Its Torpedo Guns.

FIRST DETAILED INTERIOR VIEW OF THE MYSTERIOUS HOLLAND TORPEDO BOAT, SHOWING INVENTOR HOLLAND AND HIS EXPERTS AT THEIR STATIONS.

John P. Holland's innovative and successful *Holland (SS-1)* moves smartly up the Passaic River on a trial run. The fifty-three-foot boat was powered on the surface by a gasoline engine; submerged she ran on storage batteries that gave her a fifty-mile underwater cruising range. The U.S. Navy quickly bought her. (Courtesy: Submarine Museum, New London, Connecticut)

THE HOLLAND BOAT'S RIVAL.

A *New York Herald* political cartoon of the period pokes fun at some of Holland's antisubmarine opponents. (Courtesy: Submarine Museum, New London, Connecticut)

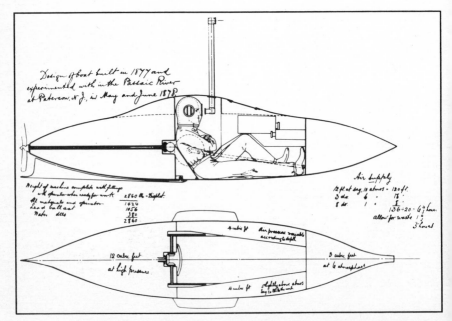

For a boat designed and built almost 100 years ago, Holland's first submarine looked modern. Originally intended to be pedal-powered by an operator in diving gear, Holland added a two-cylinder gasoline engine and eliminated the diving dress. (Courtesy: Submarine Museum, New London, Connecticut)

Early engraving depicting Wilhelm Bauer's last theoretical submarine, *"Bruleur des Cotes."* The mortar projecting from the vessel's bow like a giant pipebowl could supposedly fire vertically, blasting a hole in an enemy ship's bottom. The idea, however, never got beyond the drawing board. (Courtesy: Submarine Museum, New London, Connecticut)

Apostoloff's fanciful submarine was supposed to be auger shaped, thereby screwing itself through the water so effortlessly that the would-be inventor envisioned transatlantic crossings in twenty-eight hours. (Courtesy: Submarine Museum, New London, Connecticut)

Although Templo's idea for a pedal-operated underwater boat was probably thought too laughable to be practical, similar craft are in use today by scuba divers employing the same means of propulsion. (Courtesy: Submarine Museum, New London, Connecticut)

The novelty of Englishman George W. Garrett's 1879 submarine *Resurgam* was its steam-engine propulsion above or below the surface. For submerged running a full head of steam was raised and the
fires put out. The heat stored in the hot-water tanks then generated enough steam to run the sub ten
miles underwater at two to three knots. (Courtesy: Submarine Museum, New London, Connecticut)

The first practical electrically driven submarine, the eleven-ton *Goubet I*, launched in 1881, is about to
be tested by the French inventor Goubet. (Courtesy: Submarine Museum, New London, Connecticut)

Simon Lake envisioned submarines being used for something more important than waging war. Here his remarkable wheeled *Argonaut* is depicted on a salvage operation. Not surprisingly the vessel resembled some of our modern-day submersibles. (Courtesy: Submarine Museum, New London, Connecticut)

Years later with the beached and rotting hulk of Lake's *Argonaut Junior* passing into obscurity, Lake had already gone on to build its successor, *Argonaut I*, in 1897 with ten-foot-high wheels and an iron dirigible-shaped, thirty-six-foot-long hull that made submarine history. (Courtesy: Submarine Museum, New London, Connecticut)

Simon Lake's first youthful attempt to build a submarine may have looked comical with its flatiron-shaped hull of wood and canvas mounted on wheels, but it worked. Moreover, the *Argonaut Junior* featured a unique air lock that enabled a diver to leave or enter the boat underwater. (Courtesy: Submarine Museum, New London, Connecticut)

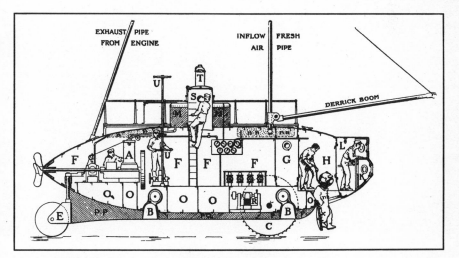

"Whoever heard of a boat on wheels?" people asked when they saw Simon Lake's 1897 *Argonaut I.* But Lake believed the real future for submarines was in the field of scientific underwater research, hence the innovative wheels and diver lockout. Note too the boat's mastlike snorkels. (Courtesy: Submarine Museum, New London, Connecticut)

Once a controversial issue in an Irish-American Revolutionary Movement plot to sink the British fleet on sight, Holland's *Fenian Ram* is now on permanent display at the West Side Park, Paterson, New Jersey. (Courtesy: Submarine Museum, New London, Connecticut)

Below: Dr. William Beebe crawls through the small hatch of the bathysphere prior to its descent, while an NBC radioman prepares to document the historic dive; February 1933. (Courtesy: U.S. Information Agency)

Right: Dr. William Beebe at the bathysphere's narrow hatch before it was closed and the steel ball descended into the ocean's depths where the scientist observed strange marine life a mile below the surface. (Courtesy: U.S. Information Agency)

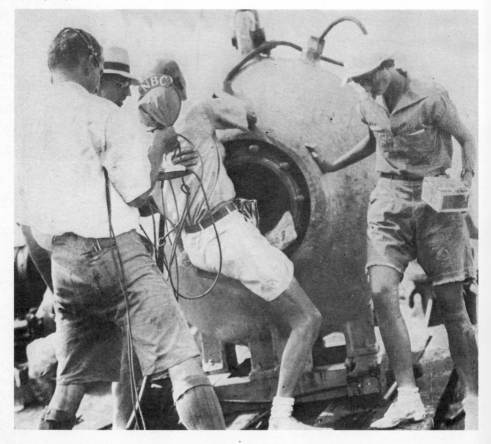

CHAPTER 8

Accolade for an Argonaut

 At dusk on a chilly mid-December evening in 1897, two seamen aboard a small schooner out of Baltimore Harbor saw something strange float to the surface of Maryland's Patapsco River. Its black flanks glistened wetly. Tendrils of weed trailed from its sides. Three sightless eyes gleamed dully from a hump in the middle of its rounded back. The seamen stared, puzzled but not particularly frightened by what they thought was the bloated carcass of a large sea creature floating in on the tide. As they cautiously approached for a closer look, the creature's "hump" suddenly opened and a ghostly figure emerged bathed in an eerie yellow light. The men promptly ran their schooner ashore, swarmed over her bowsprit and fled up the country road, certain that they had seen the devil riding a sea monster. But they were not quite correct. The "monster" was a thirty-six-foot-long, cigar-shaped, iron diving machine the likes of which few people had ever seen before. And despite a certain gleam in his eye, the "devil" was Simon Lake, the submarine's stocky, red-bearded inventor wearing a rumpled Panama hat and an equally rumpled business suit as he climbed out of the submarine's conning tower in the yellow glow of the vessel's cabin lights.

Simon Lake, the man who had scared the bejabbers out of the boatmen, may have been born with an angelic disposition but he mislaid it somewhere early in his childhood. By his own admission he began life as a bad boy, the kind that experts of another century would call a "problem child." Simon was that and more. And perhaps there was cause. His mother died when he was three. His father left him with a stern, authoritarian stepgrandmother, and went West. In addition the little boy had belligerent red hair, his face was one big freckle, and during his first year at school his stepgrandmother made him wear a pair of his grandfather's old trousers whacked off at the knee but not shaped to fit his small frame. The pants themselves were an open invitation to a fight. The boys pulled his hair and the girls chanted a rhyme he well remembered sixty-four years later when he was still going strong at the age of seventy-one:

> Simon, Simon sucks eggs—
> Sold his wife for duck's eggs.

In those early 1860 school days Simon Lake literally did not have a friend to his name. Nor did he try to make one. The feisty freckle-faced, red-haired boy with a perpetual chip on his shoulder was much fonder of the devilment he could cause. Most of the time if he was not directly involved in trouble, he was encouraging it among others. One example of an altercation with a teacher named Rogers should suffice to show the extent of Simon Lake's creative mischief during this period. While it was sparked off most unspectacularly, the incident quickly got hotter than a four-alarm fire. The boy had misbehaved in school, and Rogers mildly reprimanded him by telling him to stand beside his desk.

Nothing could have pleased the young exhibitionist more. Suddenly the center of attention, he made faces and pantomimed behind the teacher's back. Rogers was not quick enough to catch the act but he had no trouble reading the audience's reaction. He ordered the boy front and center and told him to climb up on his desk and stand there until told to get down.

Simon obeyed, standing at rapt attention, a picture of angelic innocence. Even if someone had watched his southern extremities it is doubtful that they would have seen his feet move. But move they did, sliding sideways fractions of an inch at a time.

Suddenly a large bottle of ink toppled off the teacher's desk and shattered on the floor in a great black puddle.

Pupils screamed. Rogers slapped the boy hard from behind. Simon's heel caught the teacher in a tender spot. Rogers swept the boy off the desk, trussed him up with a girl's scarf and hung him crucifixion fashion from a large nail usually reserved for hanging a map of the United States during the geography class. The pupils stared in stunned fascination. Simon swung his leg and kicked out a window.

Red-faced with rage and muttering indistinguishable words, Rogers snatched the boy off the nail, dragged him out of the room and locked him in a broom closet under the stairs.

Investigating these new surroundings, Simon found a way to trip the old lock and crack open the door to admit light. In due course he found a pot of lampblack, so he crept out and blacked the banisters down which the children slid at recess. Then he discovered the teacher's lunch in the closet and ate it. After that he locked the door upon himself and sat back to await developments.

The lunch hour was almost over when Rogers opened the door and told him, "You won't have time to go home to lunch. Here's a nickel. Get something to eat at the store across the street."

Simon vanished from the scene of his crimes.

Instead of buying lunch, however, he spent the nickel on a large bag of red-pepper candy drops which he liberally passed out by the handful to each girl coming back to school from lunch. By the time the bell rang, the red-hot confection had produced the desired reaction—all the girls were crying with burned tongues.

"Lake, stand up!" ordered Rogers. He did, for the rest of the afternoon.

When school was out, Rogers, a tall man, lifted Lake by the tip of his left ear and danced him along on his tiptoes for the next mile and a half to Simon's stepgrandmother's house. The boy never forgot that frog's march and years later Lake often laughed about the incident as he pensively touched the dislocated cartilage of his left ear. Rogers never mentioned his missing lunch or the lampblacked banisters. All considered, Lake figured everyone got what they deserved.

No matter what city the family moved to or what new school he attended, the boy's antisocial attitudes remained unchanged. He so completely cut himself off from normal relationships with other children that he had to find other interests. Simon's talent for thinking up diabolical new ways to unhinge people was no accident. Inventiveness ran strong in the Lake blood. His share of the family trait simply needed rechanneling. When he discovered at an early age what he could do with his father's tools, this was part of it. He got more pleasure from playing with tools than he did with children his own age. Before he was nine years old, he completely dismantled his stepmother's sewing machine, then put everything back together and made it run better than before. The family was amazed. When he was ten years old he found a box of spare watch parts on his father's worktable and built himself a watch. Years later it was still running, but only as long as it was always on its back. Young Simon had been forced to install the wrong size balance wheel. Finally when he reached the advanced age of eleven, the boy read *Twenty Thousand Leagues under the Sea,* and from that moment on, Jules Verne was the director-general of Simon Lake's life.

Nothing ever fired his imagination so intensely as the gripping adventures of Captain Nemo and his fabulous submarine, *Nautilus.* Simon read and reread the book, memorizing favorite passages, fascinated with the idea of a vessel that could probe the mysterious unknown regions of the underwater world. He daydreamed himself into superb subaquatic voyages replete with harrowing adventures and personal discoveries of vast sunken treasures. He studied Verne's descriptions of the *Nautilus* so closely that they left indelible impressions in his mind. In fact he soon felt he knew the submarine so well that he began making mental improvements in the design of Verne's vessel. If there was one moment that could be called the turning point in Simon Lake's life, this was it.

The family moved to Philadelphia. The red-haired,

freckled-face boy with the bad reputation was confronted with a new school, new teacher and new schoolmates. Then a miracle happened. Simon suddenly changed his ways! For the first time in his life he experienced a real thirst for knowledge. He took pride in his personal appearance. Now, instead of warring with teachers' pets, he became one. Scholastically he did so well that he soon rose to the head of the class. And to what could be attributed this incredible metamorphosis? He had fallen in love with his new schoolteacher, a pretty young girl who suspected that behind all those freckles and bluff belligerence was a boy studiously trying to conceal more than a few good qualities. After she made it her business to bring them out, Simon was never the same again.

Another move brought the family to Toms River, New Jersey, in 1881 where he now lived the kind of idyllic life he had only dreamed about. Each day he sailed his boat, built things with his father's tools and worked on plans he was drawing up for a homemade submarine. With this grand project in mind he read everything he could get his hands on that concerned the problems he had to solve. Since he had always liked the idea of a diving compartment in which divers could enter or leave a submarine underwater as described by Jules Verne, Simon determined to have one like it on his submarine. He read up on the use of air locks in driving caissons and was convinced that the principle would work on his proposed submarine. He experimented with such matters as how long he could breathe the air of a small enclosure no larger than an overturned canoe; and how to make his air lock work. The canoe experiment was upset when a spectator, fearing the boy had drowned, righted the boat before Simon had finished. And the air-lock problem solved itself when the youngster noted the mechanics of a simple device that automatically shut off the flow of gunpowder from a powder horn when the charger was full.

Despite his hunger for learning about the things that appealed to him, Simon found formal education more than he could bear. He dropped out of school at seventeen and went to work in his father's foundry. Certainly, thought his friends, this steady hard work would do away with Simon's crazy idea of building a submarine. But it didn't. It simply postponed it while Simon's imaginative curiosity moved off in other directions—all highly inventive.

Two years after leaving school he invented and patented a unique steering gear for high-wheeled bicycles. Next he invented improved winding gear for oyster fishermen, then a new capping machine for the canning industry. It was ten years since his canoe and air-lock experiments that the idea of building a submarine came back to him as something more than just a project for the future. He learned that the Navy Department was advertising for bids on a submarine. And Simon Lake knew that he had the best plans around. With high spirits he rolled them up, tucked them under his arm and headed for Washington.

Ushered into the office of the secretary of the navy, crowded with senators, congressmen, lawyers, bankers and other obviously important figures, the twenty-seven-year-old Lake felt like a fish out of water. But there were only two other inventors submitting samples of their work, a George Baker of Chicago, and a John P. Holland who had already built a submarine named the *Fenian Ram.* When his turn came, Simon submitted his plans and was told that he would be informed of the Department's decision.

Sometime later he learned that Holland had been given the contract. Simon was understandably disappointed but not discouraged. He felt certain that the officials had not even bothered to look at his plans, because if they had they would have seen that he had incorporated workable features in his boat that were not only superior to anything anyone else had previously done but were entirely unique. The rejection of all these splendid ideas served one good purpose: It aroused the old Simon Lake wrath to the point that when the steam cleared he had settled down to an "I'll-show-them" attitude and set out to build his own submarine.

The first stumbling block was finances. He had none, and little hope of getting any. But he knew where they were, so he headed for New York bent on canvasing the entire financial district until he found a backer.

The effort was a depressing failure. Bankers, financial wizards, influential people who knew absolutely nothing about the unique features of the submarine he proposed to build, criticized and ridiculed these very things which he felt made his boat superior to all others.

So broke he hardly had enough money for carfare home, Simon returned to his rented apartment and his young wife in Atlantic Highlands, New Jersey. He did not know how he would manage it, but he was determined to build his submarine. The plans for the full-scale submarine, which he had named the *Argonaut* but could not get financed, were layed aside for the time being while Lake drew up the plans for a much smaller, simpler boat he now named the *Argonaut Junior.* It was designed so that he could build it himself inexpensively, yet, it would have all the features which were so important to him. And for the same reason that he had designed his larger *Argonaut,* this one was not to be a submarine of war. It would be for peaceful purposes; for such things as underwater photography, salvage work or scientific explorations. To Simon Lake, these goals were far more important than building an underwater boat for the destructive purposes of warfare.

Just when it seemed that he could not possibly get even the small amount of money for the raw materials to build the *Argonaut Junior,* the Lake family came to his aid. His aunt and her husband advanced him what he needed, and with the help of his cousin, Bart Champion, Simon set to work. The following year the boat was finished.

It was very small, about fourteen feet long and wedge-shaped like an old flatiron. The flat-sided waterproof hull was made of canvas sandwiched between inner and outer layers of caulked yellow-pine planks. The conning tower hatch amidships was a wooden box with fore and aft portholes. There were also two 6-inch glass ports in the bows and one midway down the hull along the port and starboard sides. One of the most unusual features which strongly appealed to Simon and which the New York moneymen had found terribly funny was the boat's wheels! Two large wheels were mounted forward on a strong axle and a smaller third wheel was mounted at the stern. "Whoever heard of wheels on a submarine?" chortled the would-be investors.

Nobody had, but Simon saw a practical use for them, and by george, there they were!

And so too was his cherished air lock, a separate compartment within the boat that could be pressurized by air from a compressed-air tank Simon had liberated from a bankrupt soda fountain. A plumber's hand pump compressed the air to 100 pounds per square inch. The boat was powered manually by turning a propeller crank. The front wheels revolved on a crank connected to a bicycle chain and pedals. What more could one ask for?

The day for the moment of truth arrived. Simon and Bart wheeled their machine to the edge of the water. It was a very informal occasion. Nobody broke a bottle of anything over the bow for fear of caving in the boat's wooden walls.

Instead they just shoved her into the water and climbed aboard with Bart's cheerful remark, "Well, here's to the bottom of the sea!"

They paddled the *Argonaut Junior* along the Shrewsbury River until they came to an old fishing hole they knew was about sixteen feet deep and there they tested her.

Simon closed the hatch tightly against its rubber gasket. "Okay, open the valve, Bart."

His cousin turned a small wheel, and water gurgled into the ballast compartment.

The boat sank beautifully with but one minor mishap. Just as the conning tower went under, a finger-sized jet of river water from a bolt hole Simon had drilled and forgotten to plug hit Bart in the back of the neck.

"Yeow!" he yelled. "Let's get out of here!" He lunged toward the bow.

Simon grabbed a small piece of wood and jammed it into the offending bolt hole, then he looked at his cousin.

"Where were you going in that direction?" he asked.

"Out, I guess," said Bart somewhat sheepishly.

"Through those six-inch portholes?" Simon grinned.

The test was a complete success. The boat was ballasted

just heavy enough to stay on the bottom, and when they cranked the wheels it crawled along the bottom.

Simon and Bart had a lot of fun with the *Argonaut Junior* that summer. They prowled around the bottom of New York Bay picking up oysters and even occasionally spearing a fish from the door of their air lock. All that had to be done was to step into the tiny compartment, release enough compressed air so that the pressure inside equaled the water pressure outside, then a trapdoor could be opened on the bottom of the boat and the water would not enter. Simon even built his own diving helmet so that he could climb through the door with sash weights tied onto his arms and legs and prowl around for a short while outside.

Finally they decided they needed a larger submarine. First, however, Simon's uncle suggested that they put on a public demonstration to show what the *Argonaut Junior* could do. Invitations went out, and almost everyone in town showed up at the river to see the performance.

Bart and Simon climbed aboard the boat and put her through her paces. The spectators were not too impressed by the clamshells and rusty tin cans the boys brought up from the bottom; some thought it was a trick. But then Simon's uncle suggested a more impressive test.

"Let's have the mayor and a few of the town officials sign their names on a wooden shingle," said his uncle. "Then we'll tie it to a sash weight, throw it in the river and see if Simon and Bart can find it with their submarine. If they can, then that should prove that their boat is everything they say it is."

The crowd thought that was fair enough. A shingle was found and signed, then weighted and tossed out into sixteen feet of water where it sank to the bottom.

Simon and Bart paddled the *Argonaut Junior* over the place and submerged. Moments later the submarine reappeared, the hatch flew open, and Simon waved the shingle at the cheering crowd.

It was years later that the inventor revealed how he and Bart had accomplished the feat so quickly. As the submarine sank, Simon opened the bottom door to the air lock and waved a boat hook around under the boat until he caught the string from which floated the wooden shingle.

After the immediate success of his miniature submarine, Simon Lake could not wait to get started on his full-scale *Argonaut I*. From past experience, however, he knew there was no use trying further to interest the big-money people in his proposed project. Instead, he hit upon another idea. He formed a company and sold stock to people who might not be able to afford to invest heavily but would be willing to invest modestly. Shares were sold to neighbors, friends and relatives, and when the Lake Submarine Company had accumulated $2,500, it was time to find a boatyard to build the *Argonaut I*. Fortunately Simon not only sold stock to the yard owner but arranged a pay-as-he-built proposition. If the company was flush, the work progressed. If stock sales fell off, so did the work.

In this on-again-off-again manner the *Argonaut I* was built and launched in 1897. She was shaped like an iron dirigible thirty-six feet nine inches long topped off by a rather tall, skinny conning tower replete with four circular ports. The submersible was powered by a gasoline engine. Two hollow masts designed to stick up out of the water when the boat was just below the surface allowed for air intake and engine exhaust. But perhaps the most startling thing about the *Argonaut* was its wheels. Two ten-foot-high, solid cast-iron disks toothed like giant cogwheels were mounted under the hull a third of the way back from the bow. A smaller, pivotal tail wheel stuck down from the stern. These terrestrial appendages probably created more unfavorable feelings for the early Lake submarines than anything else he could have put on them. But he simply had a thing about putting wheels on underwater boats no matter how absurd some people thought they were. Even navy officers often asked him, "What would happen if your submarine came to a precipice, Mr. Lake? Would it fall over the edge?"

The obvious answer, of course, was that Lake's submarine had just enough negative buoyancy to keep her on the bottom. If she went off a precipice, she would simply float slowly downward. If, however, the helmsman wished to rise, he pumped out some of his water ballast, and the boat would become more buoyant. Despite this explanation people still could not get used to the idea of wheels on a boat, even one that rolled along on the bottom of the ocean.

Interestingly, Lake's *Argonaut I* was built in the same shipyard and at the same time as John Holland's *Plunger,* the submarine that had been given the navy contract. Either intentionally or by chance both boats were launched in August 1819. Thanks to multiple government specifications and design changes, the *Plunger* did much as Holland had anticipated. It turned turtle at dockside. On the other hand, Lake's *Argonaut I* was launched and test-dived successfully beside the dock. This triumph must have titillated Lake's sense of one-upmanship until he remembered that for better or worse the government was backing Holland's efforts, not his.

Despite Lake's initial success with the launching of his submarine, the *Argonaut I* was not entirely without its faults, as Lake and his co-workers were to learn a few days later.

Simon and two others took the *Argonaut* out into Baltimore Harbor for an open-water test run. They submerged and were cruising around for about two hours when everyone developed splitting headaches. Lake surfaced immediately and opened the hatch. As soon as the fresh air hit them, one of the men passed out and the other two were overcome by nausea. No one had any idea what was wrong, but the next day on a dive, the same thing happened. The men almost passed out on their feet before they could reach the surface. Simon returned to shut off the engine, and when he did it backfired. He knew then what was wrong. The engine was leaking deadly carbon-monoxide fumes into the boat. It was a wonder that they were not overcome by fumes before they discovered the trouble. Simon built an intermediate tank to catch the backfire fumes and never had that trouble again.

When he had fully tested the boat to his satisfaction and had vanquished all her bugs, he felt it was time to have a press party for the *Argonaut.* Invitations were sent, and the affair came off remarkably well. He packed two dozen New

York reporters aboard and showed them the bottom of New York Harbor from his air lock. They poked around in the mud, picked up a stray tin can, scratched up some oysters and quaffed a bottle of champagne in honor of the successful voyage. The readers loved the story, but navy brass were unimpressed. They felt that if only half the claims of what the *Argonaut* could do were true she was still too much of a toy to consider. One only had to look at those absurd wheels. . . .

Nor were scientists any more interested in Lake's invention. Often Lake took the *Argonaut* to the bottom and explored there most of the day. Once he saw a fish staring at one of the glass ports. Out of curiosity Lake waited to see how long he stayed. The fish stuck it out for ten hours, leading Lake to comment that he showed more interest in his submarine than did most admirals and professors.

Through the submarine's portholes Lake took some excellent photographs of fish which were published in *McLure's* magazine in 1899. Unknowingly he almost became the first man in the world to make underwater photographs; but in fact he was the second. The first was French diving scientist Louis Boutan, in 1897.

There was enough theatrical flair in Simon Lake that whatever he did made good newspaper copy. But despite the publicity, it was not selling submarines. And Lake was not in the business of building them for his own amusement. No matter what politician or high-ranking government official he talked to, the answer was always the same: the Navy Department was simply not interested in his submarine. It had Holland under contract and felt that one submarine designer was all it cared to handle at that time.

After these repeated failures, Lake felt that his only hope lay in attracting commercial interests to his submarine—salvage companies, transportation people, scientific groups—but all he could do was wait until they made the first move to contact him.

Just before the turn of the century, while Cuba was struggling for her independence from Spain, Lake got a call from a New York publisher who wanted him to meet a group interested in the *Argonaut I.* Lake hurried to New York where he was introduced to members of the revolutionary Cuban junta. Would he, they wanted to know, be available with his submarine to lay some mines for them in Cuban waters?

Since the United States was still neutral, Lake wanted no part of it. Would he then, they asked, be willing to sell them the boat? Lake agreed to this but said that if they bought it he did not care to know what they intended to do with it.

A price of $3 million was settled upon, the amount to be paid providing the *Argonaut* could be demonstrated satisfactorily to one of their members. Lake was more than ready.

Liaison man between Lake and the junta was the New York publisher's swashbuckling star reporter, Karl Decker, who as a correspondent covering the Cuban revolution often made the news he wrote about.

On the day of the demonstration, Decker arrived with the junta's most important representative, a tall, sinister, black-bearded man wearing a cape and known only as the Admiral. The man seemed almost haughty as Lake explained details of the submarine to him while Decker translated. Finally, Lake closed the hatch and took the *Argonaut* down.

Suddenly the Admiral became very talkative, glaring at Decker and firing questions.

Lake heard the reporter answering but he had no idea what it was all about. He was too busy operating the submarine.

Once on the bottom, Lake ushered them into the air lock for a demonstration. When he closed the door on the three of them in the tiny compartment, the Admiral began to twitch nervously. When Lake switched on the compressed air to pressurize the lock, the Admiral came completely unhinged. Over the hissing of the air he screeched like a parrot.

Decker tried to calm him but he started waving his arms and screaming something at Lake that sounded like *"Assassin! Assassin!"*

Lake did not understand what else he said but from the tone of his voice he suspected he was being cursed.

Decker tried to pacify the man, but it was hopeless. "It's no use," he said. "He's lost his nerve completely. We'll have to go up."

Lake surfaced and took them back to the dock. As soon as the Admiral's feet touched ground, he was off and running, the cape standing out straight behind him. That was the last Simon Lake ever heard from the junta. The submarine deal was definitely off.

On February 15, 1898, the U.S.S. *Maine* was sunk in Havana Harbor, and the United States went to war with Spain. Lake offered the services of his submarine, but the government turned him down. He then decided that maybe he could shake up the navy by dramatizing how valuable the boat could be. As a defense measure, the navy had mined Hampton Roads, a channel in southeastern Virginia connecting the James and Elizabeth rivers with Chesapeake Bay. The minefield was, they declared, impenetrable. That was all the challenge Lake needed. He and the *Argonaut* headed for Hampton Roads. He launched the submarine near the minefield, submerged and wheeled his way along the bottom into the impenetrable forest of cables and mines, cautiously noting where each was and observing that he could just as easily have approached and done whatever he had wished to several nearby naval vessels.

After that he told the navy exactly what he had done, pointing out that a submarine not only could lay mines but could disarm them as well. The navy never bothered to respond.

Miffed, Lake took his tale to the army. The army reacted by telling him that what he said he had done was impossible and that they did not believe a word of it. But if they were to catch him doing it, they would lock him up.

Lake was both angered and mystified by the indifference of the army and navy. Surely they understood the point he was trying to make; but if they did, they failed to acknowledge it. And in the years to come, Lake was to learn the reason why: Right or wrong, no one wanted to rock the boat. No one wanted the responsibility of accepting something that might fail. It was far easier to say no to everything new, radical or unproven. It had happened before to American inventors, and there was no reason to believe that it could not happen again. The usual solution was for the inventor to sell his wares elsewhere. Before Lake reached that decision, however, the *Argonaut* received an accolade of the highest order that could not have pleased Simon Lake more.

The incident occurred while Lake was bringing the *Argonaut* back from Hampton Roads by the outside or open-ocean route, one of the first open-ocean voyages of any submarine. A disastrous storm struck the coast, taking some one hundred ships to the bottom. Ice, sleet and towering waves were so bad that Lake had to lash himself topside and direct the boat's navigation from outside while it wallowed through the holocaust, but the *Argonaut* and its two-man crew made it.

Newspapers around the world praised the feat, but what touched the inventor most was a cable of congratulations from the man who had been responsible for his first interest in submarines—Jules Verne. Lake so respected Verne's genius as a visionary scientist and writer that he considered this accolade one of the high points of his life.

Despite its hardships the voyage taught Lake that the *Argonaut* was not long enough to handle well in the open ocean. Major modifications began as soon as he found the money. A twenty-foot midsection and a more streamlined superstructure of light iron plates were added to the hull.

After adequate tests, Lake decided it was again time to advertise the submarine in his inimitable way, by having another party aboard. This time he invited twenty-eight of the socially prominent citizens of Bridgeport, Connecticut, and while the crowds cheered and the bands played, Lake took Bridgeport's best to the bottom of the river with the intention of returning by 2 P.M. When the voyagers had not returned by three o'clock, a rescue tug hurried to the spot where the top of the *Argonaut*'s fifty-foot-long air pipe protruded above water. Repeated raps on the pipe failed to get any response. The rescuers were certain that all had drowned. By the time they sent to New York for a derrick to dredge up the tomb, all Bridgeport had heard of the tragedy. Silent crowds gathered on shore to mourn the loss of Bridgeport's mayor, the heads of the telephone and railroad companies, several bankers, merchants and other prominent community leaders. And then, at four o'clock, before their startled eyes, the missing *Argonaut* arose from the depths with its gay crowd of social celebrities singing "Down Went McGinty to the Bottom of the Sea."

The relieved but somewhat peeved bunch of Bridgeport ex-mourners welcomed the return of their community's leading lights but they were not too impressed with Lake's reason for their delay. It seems that since only two people could enter the air lock at a time, the dive took longer than the inventor had anticipated. Besides, they had raked up a bunch of clams and oysters and cooked a shellfish dinner. The rapping of the would-be rescuers went unheard over the sounds of their merrymaking.

Despite Bridgeport's momentary shock at the thought of losing all its leaders in the hands of Simon Lake, it was Bridgeport money that built the inventor-showman's next submarine.

By now he had learned his lesson. There were no wheels on this new creation: its design was more in line with what would soon be considered the conventional form of the future submarine. Named the *Protector* and launched in 1902, the sixty-five-foot, 130-ton submarine ran with gasoline engines on the surface and battery power underwater. In some respects she was similar to the *Holland* submarine, but the two boats submerged differently. The *Holland* dove by angling downward and being thrust under by the force of her propeller and the angle of her diving planes, executing a rolling or "porpoising" maneuver which Lake said made her occupants cling on with the tenacity of barnacles. On the other hand, Lake's submarines all dived or surfaced while remaining level, the same method used today in all modern submarines. In addition, Lake was the first to mount a small gun on his boat's foredeck and to equip his boat with a practical periscope, an instrument which he designed and called an "omniscope." The *Protector* was also adept at crashing her way through shallow surface ice, a characteristic which could have been used a bit more shrewdly at her first military trials. For it was a cold wintery day when the examining Naval Board was chugging for Newport to see the sub in action. Halfway across the bay, the examiners' steam-boat got stuck in the ice. Instead of crashing through and dramatically rescuing the officials, thereby impressing all concerned with the resourcefulness of his crew and the capabilities of his boat, Lake unintentionally did just the opposite. He took his submarine out to the trapped boat and ran circles around it, chewing up the ice as he went. Then he and his men returned to the dock "as chesty as pigeons," certain that they had put on a fine demonstration for the Board.

They had, but it created the wrong effect. When the half-frozen, red-eyed officials finally reached shore, they could only mumble something about the weather being too bad for a trial and that they would have to wait until spring.

Once more Lake's hope of selling his submarine to the navy was dashed. So he turned now to the navy's traditional rival, the army. Before a board of army examiners, the *Protector* was put through her paces in ice-clogged Narragansett Bay and was warmly endorsed. The army agreed to take five submarines like the *Protector* for mining channels in fixed minefields. But after a barrage of lobbying from navy-Holland interests, the bill for appropriations was killed in Congress.

Lake and his stockholders were right back where they started—without a customer. Since funds were fast dwindling away, something drastic had to be done. The only hope that Lake had was the war between Russia and Japan which was then going full blast.

Earlier, when both nations made offers for the submarine, Lake turned them down. But now that his own government was no longer interested, he was open for negotiation. Although his feelings were neutral toward the Japanese and the Russians, both sides had their spies and front men working on him. Finally he agreed to sell the *Protector* to Russia and build them five more. The next morning the first downpayment of $125,000 went into his account. Now he had to fulfill his part of the bargain.

The transaction was kept secret to prevent Japanese interference. But how was he going to make delivery of a 130-ton submarine to Russia without alerting the Japanese or having the U.S. government confiscate the boat as contraband?

Lake finally hit upon a plan which required the assistance of international wheeler-dealer, promotor and arms procurer, Charles Flint.

While the still uninformed Russian and Japanese agents shadowed each other, Flint chartered the S.S. *Fortuna* in Norfolk, Virginia, to haul a load of coal to Russia. In New York a floating derrick was hired for an unspecified job off Sandy Hook. Meanwhile, Simon Lake told his usual following of curious reporters that he was taking the *Protector* on a trial run to check her surface engines and he might be gone for a week. Even his crew suspected nothing different.

The *Protector* left Bridgeport in a late Saturday afternoon fog. She crossed the Sound and waited until dark, then headed for Prince's Bay near Sandy Hook. There, at midnight, she rendezvoused with the floating derrick. A while later the S.S. *Fortuna* arrived and dropped anchor. Only then did the derrick operators learn what they were to do. They hoisted the 130-ton *Protector* into a deck cradle aboard the *Fortuna*, and the ship steamed off for Russia.

Lake apologized for not being able to tell his technicians what was happening in advance, but now he revealed that the *Protector* had been sold and was being delivered to her new owner. He could not tell them who that was or where the submarine was going, but he said that he would like them to go along. To a man they elected to go. Lake later revealed that he did not know what he would have done if someone had wanted to stay. To keep their secret he probably would have had to have gone anyway.

For appearances, Lake returned to Bridgeport to make excuses for some of the wild guesses that began circulating when it was learned that the *Protector* had disappeared. A steamer captain had reported seeing a strange bulky cargo on the deck of the S.S. *Fortuna* while at sea. Since the *Fortuna* failed to acknowledge his radio message, there was considerable newspaper speculation as to the nature of that cargo.

Meanwhile, Lake managed to lose his following of Russo-Japanese spies and reporters long enough to catch a ship for Cherbourg, France. There, under the assumed name of Elwood Simon, he received a Russian passport and made his way overland to join his men and the *Protector* aboard the S.S. *Fortuna* in the port of Kronstadt, Russia.

Not long after their arrival they were treated to a taste of the Russian sense of humor. Lake and his crew, accompanied by a high-ranking Russian naval officer, took the *Protector* on a trial run in the Gulf of Finland. Preparing to dive, Lake had trimmed the boat until her decks were several feet under water and only about eighteen inches of her conning tower was above the surface. Momentarily he left the controls to stick his head out of the hatch and look at a school of fish they were passing. Suddenly the submarine dove, and Lake ducked inside pulling the hatch closed behind him a split second before the water rushed in to swamp them. The Russian laughed so hard there were tears in his eyes. He had pushed the hydroplanes into the dive position as a joke. Lake wiped his brow and smiled weakly. He knew nothing could be done about this highly placed jackass who, he said later, went on to become an admiral of the fleet.

Lake and his technicians stayed in Russia for the next seven years, overseeing the building of his five submarines for the czarist navy and training the Russians in their operation. As a whole he liked the people but found their morals a little lacking. He was appalled to learn that young girls were sold through newspaper classified ads. And when one of the Russian engineers offered to sell him his wife for seven dollars, Lake promptly sent for his family. It seems that throughout their entire stay the Lakes were constantly in a state of shock over Russian manners and morals.

None of the Lake submarines ever saw action in the Russo-Japanese War, but business was booming. The Russians wanted Lake to set up an entire underwater fleet for them, but he chose to move on. He built Austria's first two submarines, then set up business in Berlin, where he entered into a contract with the Krupps for his submarines. He gave

the company his plans but made the mistake of not register-
ing his patents in Germany. As a result, they built Lake-type
submarines and simply overlooked paying him any royalties.

Having supplied foreign nations with his submarines, Lake
wanted to save the best of his work for the United States.
Therefore he instructed the Lake Torpedo Boat Company to
build the *Simon Lake X,* a boat that was the last word in
submarine design. But somewhere along the way Lake had
incurred governmental wrath. The navy refused to watch a
test of his new boat. Angered and disgusted, Lake went back
to Europe and sold *number X* to a country that was pleased to
get it. Russia now owned eleven Lake submarines.

Not until the United States took the business of buying
submarines out of the hands of the navy and gave it to
Congress did Simon Lake ever sell his country a submarine.
But then how could it resist this kind of offer:

> The Lake Company will build at its own expense a submarine
> which will be:
> Faster on the surface or under it than any boat now building,
> either in the United States or abroad.
> It will have a greater radius of action, more powerful
> armament, eight torpedo tubes, safety features by which a man
> can escape when the boat is submerged, and facilities for
> planting mines and cutting cables.
> It will do more than the United States Government has ever
> asked that any submarine do. If it does not do all that is
> claimed for it the United States Government need never pay us
> a cent of money.

Simon Lake's supersubmarine *Seal* did all that he claimed it
would and more. With a surface displacement of 400 tons, a
length of 161 feet and a beam of 13 feet, she was the largest
submarine ever built up to that time. She was armed with six
torpedoes and carried a compliment of twenty-four men. The
navy accepted the *Seal* without a whimper, and she was
commissioned on October 28, 1912. Jules Verne's greatest
fan, the incorrigibly honest Simon Lake of the crumpled felt
hat, unruly red hair and perpetual optimism, who had to go
to Europe to prove that his invention was more than a toy,
had finally come home.

CHAPTER 9

Swing Low Deadly Chariot

 World War I had almost run its course. On the Italian front the Allies had successfully repulsed the Austrian thrust across the Piave River in June 1918. By mid-October three Allied armies were massed to open a second major offensive along the Piave. The main attack was to push through to the northern town of Vittorio Veneto, splitting the Austrians in the Adriatic Plain from those in the mountains, and bring about Austria's downfall. One concern, however, was the Austrian fleet holed up in the heavily fortified Adriatic port of Pola. Three dreadnaughts and a squadron of battleships had sat out the war there. But now the Allies were worried that they might break out and go on a rampage.

How to prevent it? The fleet was virtually untouchable. As the principle naval port and arsenal of the Austro-Hungarian monarchy, Pola's commodious harbor was nearly land-locked. The hills surrounding the harbor were studded with gun batteries commanding the whole area. Steel-mesh anti-submarine nets barricaded the bay into the harbor. In 1914, the Allies had tried before to break into Pola without any luck. The French submarine *Curie* was lost in the attempt. But now it was a matter of utmost urgency that the fleet be put out of action. Two seemingly sober young officers named Raffaele Rossetti and Raffaele Paolucci volunteered for the job. Once it was positively ascertained that neither man was motivated by the wrong kind of spirits, the staff granted them a few minutes to tell how they could pull off a coup that had baffled the best military minds for the last four years. The more the men talked, the longer the commanders listened. When they finished explaining their fantastic plan, not a staff officer there believed it could be done. But they were all willing to support the attempt.

One reason why what they said carried so much weight was because Major Rossetti and Surgeon Lieutenant Paolucci were both specially trained underwater saboteurs, experts in a profession so new that Italy was the only country up to then that had schooled men in the art of underwater demolition. If anyone could breech the barriers of Pola Harbor and do the job on the Austrian fleet, Rossetti and Paolucci felt they were the ones. All they needed, they said, was a chariot and a couple charges of TNT.

The parts were provided them, and they built the chariot, a twenty-three-foot-long miniature submarine with external controls so that the operators could ride astride it. Powered by a compressed-air engine capable of a top speed of two knots, the boat was essentially a streamlined bomb. Its two detachable warheads were 350-pound charges of TNT. Rossetti and Paolucci proposed to ride their "guided missile" through the obstacle course blocking Pola Harbor. Once inside, they would pick out the biggest ship they could find and blow it up, then ride their chariot back the same way they had come. Theoretically it sounded good, but would it work?

On a moonless night in late October, a blacked-out torpedo boat slowed to a stop a quarter mile off the Austrian Peninsula opposite the Bay of Pola. The heavy steel chariot was eased overboard, its ballast tanks trimmed, then the two Raffaeles straddled the machine and moved off into the darkness.

Paolucci navigated from the forward saddle; Rossetti steered from the rear. Both men wore waterproof suits with built-in buoyancy compartments. With the chariot properly trimmed, only their heads would be above water, so they had wrapped shiny cloth around them in the hope that if they were seen, they would be mistaken for floating Chianti bottles.

Before long the men reached their first barrier, a steel-mesh net suspended from the surface by floating cables. The heavy steel strands were too thick to cut and too close together for a submarine to pass through. So the men lifted their chariot over the net, climbed back on and continued.

As they neared the mouth of the harbor they heard a patrol boat approaching. Rossetti shut off their motor and put his hand on the detonator of their bomb. If they were to be caught, they intended to blow themselves up to keep the chariot and their method of attack a secret.

The patrol boat drew closer. The two saboteurs hugged their chariot and held their breath. Abruptly the harbor lights blacked out as the prowling boat passed between them and the harbor. They waited until the sound of its quietly chugging engines disappeared in the night before they started their own motor and eased forward.

Instead of heading straight toward the mouth of the harbor they decided to approach it by staying close to the breakwater. When they reached it, they found a wall of rock. If it was vertical, they could move along it without difficulty. But if it was built on a sloping pile of boulders that would block their boat, they would have to stay further away from it, exposing themselves to sentries.

While Rossetti kept the chariot still, Paolucci slipped off and dived down the face of the wall, feeling it out underwater. Returning, he signaled his findings to Rossetti. It was safe to proceed; it was a vertical wall.

Carefully they made their way along it, hugging the sheer wet stone along their starboard flank. Suddenly Paolucci motioned for his companion to kill the motor. Rossetti obliged. Over the lapping of the water he heard what Paolucci must have barely sensed—muffled voices coming from the steep stone parapet above.

Again they crouched low over their deadly chariot, with everything submerged except their heads. As Rossetti lay with his face turned sideways in the water so he could breathe, he glanced upward to the top of the wall. His heart lurched. Dimly outlined against the glow of the starlit sky was the unmistakable silhouette of a sentry who appeared to be looking down at him.

Mustering every ounce of courage he had, Rossetti slowly rolled his head, hoping that he was simulating the movement of a bobbing bottle.

Apparently he succeeded, because in a moment the sentry turned and walked away. The two perspiring saboteurs heaved a sigh of relief as they moved on.

Finally they reached the narrow opening into the harbor. There, beside a net, they found another obstacle they had not counted on. A 180-foot log boom bristling with 3-foot-long steel spikes. Once in the past the Italians had used an amphibian with tractor treads to crawl over the nets in an attempt to get at the fleet. Although the effort failed, from then on the Austrians reinforced the net with a log boom.

Rossetti and Paolucci hung on the spikes and tried to figure a way around the obstacle. It was 1 A.M. They were to have negotiated their last barrier by 3 A.M. Dawn was due at 5:15. By then they had to have completed their mission and been well away before the harbor came to life and they were spotted.

Earlier, as they had moved in closer to the harbor, they realized that the tide was starting to run out. Now it was flowing swiftly enough that as they whispered over their predicament the chariot suddenly got caught sideways by the tide and slipped away from them.

Paolucci immediately plunged after it, forgetting that his vigorous swimming was churning up so much phosphorescence in the water around him that he looked as if he was caught in the beam of a bluish-green searchlight. He dived down, caught the submarine and brought it back to the surface. It started raining as the two of them hauled the boat back to the boom. There was no more time to delay. They had to chance being seen. Hoping that the light rain would drive any sentries into cover, they climbed up on the log boom and laboriously dragged the heavy submarine over the long spikes onto the other side.

Minutes later they were confronted with three rows of steel-mesh torpedo nets. Coolly, patiently, they negotiated each of these obstacles, hauling the chariot over them. Hardly had they started again when they found their way blocked by three more rows of steel nets. Paolucci could not believe it. He felt sure they had somehow got turned around in the dark and were back at the first nets. But Rossetti insisted that they had not changed course, that these were a second set of nets.

By now the tide was running out at a good clip. They were nearly exhausted from fighting it. The chariot once again broke away from them, and they had a harrowing moment catching up to it and driving it back to the net. Rossetti saw that the tide was almost too strong for the chariot to run against, so he tied a line on the bow of the submarine and swam underwater to the sixth net. Bracing himself on the steel mesh he pulled the boat and his companion to him. As they were dragging the chariot over the top, it flipped over and sank. They dived to retrieve it.

After crossing the last net, they had negotiated eight barriers into the harbor. But before them, its silhouette only dimly visible through the cold October rain, was the Austrian fleet lined up under Pola's protective guns. The Italians checked their time. Their mission was already far behind schedule and half the compressed air powering their chariot was gone. By now they should have been making their way back through the nets to rendezvous with the torpedo boat. But they had not accomplished what they had come to do. And their orders were to push the attack at all costs. If either man wondered how they were going to do that and still escape before dawn, neither mentioned it. Their main goal was to do what they had come to do.

Two hours of darkness remained. They decided to attack the largest ship in the fleet, the huge dreadnought *Viribus Unitis*. Air reconnaissance photos had shown the ship to be the sixth in line. To reach her the saboteurs would have to pass by five other warships without being seen by their deck watches. As they headed for their target, the rain turned to hail.

Silently they slipped past the first five ships in line. There was no mistaking their target, but they were surprised by what they saw. The superdreadnought was ablaze with lights; some kind of celebration was going on. So much the better, thought Major Rossetti; the diversion will keep their attention. But now there was no protective cover of darkness around the ship. They had to be more careful than ever of being seen.

They edged past the big ship to see if the tide would help them approach without using their motor. Abruptly the stern of the chariot sank, taking Rossetti underwater. Paolucci turned to help, and the whole boat went under. They dived down after it, fumbled with the ballast controls, and it bobbed to the surface again. Of all their difficulties, this was one of the worst. Here they were about to attack, and their machine acted up practically under the very noses of the enemy. But their luck still held; nobody aboard ship saw their fumbling attempts to trim the submarine and climb aboard for another try. Now they motored a hundred yards past the *Viribus Unitis* and cut their motor. The tide took them away from their target. They moved to another angle and tried again. This time the chariot drifted silently down to the flared bow of the vessel.

From the decks above they heard the sound of loud talking and laughing. Both men later recalled that at the time this seemed strange to them but they were so intent in their mission that they thought no more about it. As it was they had their hands full trying to detach one of the heavy warheads and work it down under the hull where its magnets would hold it to the ship's plates. Paolucci attempted it while Rossetti held the chariot. It was an incredibly difficult job, and they took turns helping each other. The charge was finally placed and the timers set when Paolucci and the chariot were swept away by the tide. Rossetti had no idea where he was. In the darkness beyond the light of the ship he could not see him, and over the sound of the powerful tidewaters he could not hear him. All the Lieutenant could do was to try and keep himself afloat beside the slippery side of the ship where he pondered what to do next.

The tide was running so swiftly that Paolucci was twenty-five minutes fighting his way back to the ship to get Rossetti. By then it was 5:15, dawn. They detached their second warhead, set its timer to detonate at 6:30 and let it drift off on the tide toward the string of other ships.

There was no longer any place to hide. They were caught by daylight. Still they were trying to slip away unnoticed when a lookout in a liberty launch spotted them and sounded the alarm. The two Italians were quickly picked up and taken prisoners aboard the very ship that they had rigged to blow up in thirty-five minutes.

They immediately identified themselves as Italian officers but were surprised to learn that their captors were not Austrians but Yugoslavians. Brought before the ship's commander, Captain Vukovitch of the Yugoslav National Council, they were astounded to learn that they were among friends. Ironically, all their efforts had been for nothing. On the night that they had set out on their mission, the Austrian-Hungarian Empire had collapsed. Revolutionary Yugoslavs had taken over the warships just hours before the Italians mined the *Viribus Unitis.* It was their victory celebration the two had heard.

Without delay Rossetti told Captain Vukovitch that his war prize was in danger of sinking and that he and his men should abandon ship at once. Without being told the details, the captain guessed that the Italians had attached a bomb to the bottom of the dreadnought. He ordered the ship abandoned and told the two Italian saboteurs to look after themselves. Along with almost everyone else, Paolucci and Rossetti promptly leaped overboard. Already weary from the night's ordeal, Paolucci almost drowned trying to get ashore. Rossetti helped him. As they swam, they were overtaken by a boatload of angry sailors who thought the Italians had lied to save their lives. The Yugoslavs fished the two bedraggled saboteurs out of the bay and hustled them back to the *Viribus Unitis.* The two stunned charioteers sullenly went from the frying pan back into the fire.

Back aboard the doomed ship, the sailors stripped them of their rubber suits, searching for more concrete evidence. A chocolate bar fell out of Rossetti's suit, and the sailors jumped back from it as if they were confronted by the bomb itself. Regaining their courage they picked it up and examined it minutely. On the cabin clock Paolucci saw it was 6:27.

"Take them below," roared one of the sailors. "We'll see if they're telling the truth or not!"

Three minutes later the ship's bell struck 6:30. There was no explosion. The Italians were both relieved and mystified. Now that the moment of oblivion had passed, the highly incensed sailors were more certain than ever that they were the brunt of some kind of Italian joke. They did not like it in the least and they spent the next fourteen minutes arguing among themselves about what to do with the practical jokesters.

At that moment Paolucci and Rossetti heard a deep, dull roar inside the ship followed by a tall soaring column of water that erupted beside it. Except for themselves the cabin was instantly vacated. To the sound of sailors jumping overboard, Rossetti picked up the chocolate and bit into it. He was famished.

In the companionway they met Captain Vukovitch strapping on his life preserver. He shook hands with them and pointed to a line hanging over the side that they could use to abandon ship.

Paolucci and Rossetti did not stay to gloat over their handiwork. They slid down the rope, climbed into a boat and pulled away. From a safe distance they saw the huge dreadnought sink bow first. The big turret guns snapped off like toys as the *Viribus Unitis* keeled over and turned turtle. Then her dripping stern rose high in the air, and the men were horrified to see Captain Vukovitch clinging to her keel and crawling toward the ship's propeller cage.

Just as he reached it, the dreadnought slid beneath the waves, and he was sucked down in the swirling waters that engulfed the ship. Moments later he reappeared, swimming hard to avoid the suction, but a timber caught in the whirlpool and struck him on the head, killing him.

A few days later, Paolucci and Rossetti went home to a hero's welcome. In recognition of their deed the Italian government awarded them the highest medals for bravery and gave them 650,000 lire. The two men accepted the medals but they gave the money to the widows of the men who had gone down with the *Viribus Unitis*. And one in particular they would never forget. "While I live," said Rossetti, "the image of that gallant captain will remain."

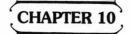

CHAPTER 10

To the Ultimate Floor

 One day in the early 1930s, Dr. William Beebe, a tall, lean, athletic man who had already established himself as a noted naturalist, explorer, author and photographer of wildlife in South America, Borneo and the Himalayas, looked across a frontier so totally unknown that until then it was a place where none but dead men had gone.

Wearing a copper diving helmet, Beebe was poised on the edge of a precipice sixty-three feet underwater, peering down into the flickering blue depths of an unknown abyss. "I realized that I was looking toward a world almost as unknown as that of Mars or Venus," he later wrote, "a world in which up to the present time, our efforts at capturing the inhabitants have been pitifully trivial."

Beebe had dredged the deep with nets, bringing up strange fish from two miles below the ocean surface. These feeble attempts to sample the life there only whetted his appetite to actually penetrate the watery abyss, to see whatever sights might await him there. Several years earlier, while he was discussing deep-ocean diving with Teddy Roosevelt, Beebe had sketched a cylinder which he thought might be capable of carrying a diver to these extreme depths. Roosevelt, however, drew a sphere, pointing out that it would be stronger. Beebe acknowledged that there was nothing like a ball to evenly distribute the pressure but he still favored a shape that would more comfortably accommodate a diver.

By 1929, Beebe was still pondering the pros and cons of the cylinder over the sphere when he was contacted by an ambitious young geologist-engineer from New Jersey, named Otis Barton, who had designed such a ball. In fact, Barton wrote Beebe many letters explaining his diving device in which he planned to descend two miles. Beebe, however, remained strangely aloof and cool to the idea. He had already been showered by so many crank ideas that Barton's proposal simply got lost in the shuffle. Eventually, however, the two men got together, and the rest is underwater history.

Barton built the ball with his own funds. The first steel-sphere casting weighed five tons. Since it was too heavy for any of the winches procurable in the proposed diving area, it had to be smashed and another made. This one was four feet nine inches in diameter with walls an inch and a half thick and it weighed 5,000 pounds. The circular door covering the fifteen-inch-wide entry hatch weighed 500 pounds alone. It attached to ten studs surrounding the opening and was closed tight by screwing down outside nuts. A four-inch-wide, wing-nut plug in the center of the door could be quickly unscrewed in the event of an emergency. The vessel's two viewports were eight-inch-diameter, fused quartz cylinders three inches thick made by General Electric Company. Each cost $500 and their mortality rate had been high. The first was chipped in fitting and had to be discarded; the second exploded in its socket during an internal pressure test of 1,250 pounds per square inch, and the third cracked when frame bolts were tightened unevenly. Two ports were finally made, seated and pressure-tested without further mishap. For outside illumination a 250-watt bulb was mounted on a projection beside the windows. It would be powered by a surface generator. Since two men were to be hermetically sealed inside the sphere for long periods of time, a special air purification apparatus was installed. It consisted of two cylinders of oxygen and trays of chemicals for removing the moisture and carbon dioxide from the divers' exhalations. To ensure adequate circulation and proper functioning of the apparatus, the men were to be furnished palm fans.

Lifting gear for the sphere was a large-spool, seven-ton

winch accommodating the 3,500 feet of special thumb-thick, steel-cored, nontwisting cable on which the steel ball would be suspended. Attached to the cable at intervals was an inch-thick rubber hose containing light and intercom wires. It passed through a double-gland stuffing box into the diving chamber. Beebe named the ball a "bathysphere," a coined Greek word meaning "deep sphere." An old but reputable vessel named the *Ready* was found, and once the diving ball was safely ensconced aboard ship, Beebe and Barton with a few assistants set off for Nonsuch Island near Bermuda to establish a base camp.

On June 3, 1930, Beebe judged the conditions right for a trial submergence of the bathysphere. The *Ready* put to sea. All equipment was carefully checked. The ball was swung over the side, and the steam winches lowered it empty to 2,000 feet. As the heavy sphere was hoisted, the rubber hose carrying the telephone and electrical wires began twisting on the main cable. By the time the ball broke water, the crew had a colossal one-half mile of snarled conduit hose that took them twenty-four hours to straighten out.

It was three days later before the sea was calm enough for another trial. Then on June 6, a movie camera was mounted before one of the quartz windows, the ball was lowered to a depth of 1,500 feet, and the camera was triggered electrically from the surface. When the film was developed, it was blank. But this time Barton and Beebe noted happily that there was no tangled hose; the cable and hose combination came up the same way it had gone down. Moreover, Beebe observed that only a quart of seawater had seeped into the sphere.

The diving chamber was dried out and cleaned up, and the breathing equipment installed. Then with a quick glance around and finding nothing particularly pithy to say for the occasion, Beebe squeezed painfully through the sphere's fifteen-inch opening and crouched uncomfortably on the cold steel floor, learning minutes later that there was not a single pillow aboard to assuage his discomfort. Barton crawled in behind him, and as soon as the two disentangled themselves, he put on the earphones and prepared to handle the communications while Beebe stationed himself before the windows as the observer. A winch hoisted the 400-pound door onto its studs, and the ten big brass nuts were screwed down with wrenches. Last to be closed was the four-inch-wide plug in the center of the door. When the workmen tightened the nuts with sledgehammers, the reverberations inside the sphere were so ear-shattering that Beebe thought the windows would break.

Then the big ball was hoisted up to the yardarm while Beebe and Barton watched the anxious faces of their team members below—John Tee-Van directing the man at the winch, Gloria Hollister standing by at the earphones ready to take notes, and half a score of men hauling hard to swing the sphere over the side. Dangling over the water, the ball descended, Beebe apprehensively watching the approaching side of the *Ready* as the sphere seemed to swing dangerously close to it. Next thing he knew, Barton relayed a message from Gloria Hollister who asked why the director was swearing. A fast interchange of information revealed that what had appeared to be less than a yard distance between the ship's side and the quartz-glass window was actually some twenty-five feet clearance. Beebe hastily apologized for being fooled by the optical illusion.

In a welter of foam they splashed through the sea's surface and watched the ship's hull disappear above them. Slowly the sphere dropped down through the bluish-green water passing 100 feet, then 200 feet, pausing briefly at each level while the conduit hose was clamped onto the steel suspension cable.

Suddenly at 300 feet Barton exclaimed that he was getting wet. Beebe snapped on his flashlight and examined the door. A thin trickle snaked down from the sill. There was already a pint of water pooled in the bottom of the sphere. Beebe wiped away the rivulet, but still it came. Aware that the outer pressure would push the door tighter the deeper they went, Beebe called for a faster descent.

Two minutes later they passed 400 feet, then 500 feet, periodically checking their leaks as they went deeper to 600 then 700 feet where they again paused.

Momentarily their seepage problem was forgotten as they

both stared through the quartz ports at the strangely luminous, translucent blue world surrounding them. It was unlike anything they had ever seen. "It excited our optic nerves in a most confusing manner," said Beebe. "We kept thinking and calling it brilliant. . . . I brought all my logic to bear, I put out of mind the excitement of our position in watery space and tried to think sanely of comparative color, and I failed utterly."

Beebe turned on the electric light and saw its faint yellow glow pierce the indescribable blue. Then with a flurry of sparks and sputterings the light switch abruptly short-circuited. The trouble was quickly repaired and the order sent up the wire for a continued slow descent.

Totally absorbed by concentration the divers watched the watery void gradually shift from deep blue to a dark bluish black infinity. At 800 feet they paused for their last time as Beebe sensed that they had gone far enough for this trip.

So engrossed was he with the silent, deep, dark water outside that when Barton suddenly pulled out the fan to circulate their air, the abrupt rustling startled Beebe so badly that for an instant he thought the sphere had imploded from the pressure! After that they went about their business in complete silence.

The dive lasted an hour. As the sphere was being hauled up and approached the undulating silver surface, Beebe unconsciously ducked his head when they went through the "ceiling" in a slather of bubbles.

On deck the tender, the sphere's four-inch plug, was unscrewed to the hissing escape of the chamber's compressed air. The divers' ears popped with the equalized pressure. Then began the clamorous hammering loose of the ten big nuts. When finally the heavy door was lifted off, Beebe found he was almost incapable of crawling out. He had sat so long in a cramped position that his legs hardly functioned. Moreover, he had been so totally absorbed in the experience that the sweater he had taken along as a cushion still lay untouched on the shelf inside the sphere, but his bottom bore the imprint of a monkey wrench he had sat on through the entire trip. As the divers squirmed through the small hatchway onto the deck, they thought the bright golden sunlight was hardly a match for the incredible shades of blue they had so recently enjoyed.

The bathysphere was emptied of several gallons of water, the leak sealed with a liberal coat of white lead paint, and four days later the chamber was lowered empty to 2,000 feet. It came up dry and undamaged, but the pressure had pushed three feet of the hose through the packing gland into the sphere.

When this was corrected, Barton and Beebe climbed in and were lowered to 250 feet when there was a crackling and sputtering on Barton's earphones, then silence. "My God!" he exclaimed. "The phone is broken!"

They tried signaling the surface with their searchlight but knew their efforts were useless. Suddenly both men realized how important it had been to have this link with the other world. Now the total silence engulfed them and the cold blue watery depths around them became oppressive and ominous. Then they were hauled up swiftly, pausing momentarily while workmen unclipped a hose connection during which the always observant Beebe counted twenty-four jellyfish swimming past his window. Topside investigation revealed a broken telephone wire. To repair it, 300 feet of hose were cut off and discarded.

On June 11, Beebe directed his team to a point five miles south of Nonsuch Island where earlier soundings had revealed a depth of 750 fathoms. The bathysphere was checked out for its deepest dive, 1,426 feet. For the occasion Gloria Hollister hung several freshly baited hooks around the observer's window in the hope of attracting interesting specimens for Beebe.

This time there was no test dive. The men squirmed into the chamber, put their fingers in their ears through the ordeal of the nut tightening and were then hoisted overboard.

Down they went in their slow-moving spherical elevator, Beebe clutching his copy of the classic *The Depths of the Ocean* by Sir John Murray and Johan Hjort, which accompanied him on every dive and Barton wearing his grease-stained lucky skullcap and earphones and standing by with the telephone to the waiting Gloria Hollister.

As they descended, Beebe used a spectroscope to study the gradual disappearance of colors from the surrounding water. Red was the first to go at 20 feet, followed by orange at 150 feet; by 350 feet the yellow was almost gone; at 450 feet no blue remained, just violet and a hint of green; then at 800 feet only a pale grayish white remained of the minuscule amount of light still filtering down and reaching the eye. But turning away from the spectroscope and looking out the window he saw again the enchanting blue-black of the deepening abyss.

Periodically small fish appeared before the window to investigate Hollister's baits. With his piscatory guidebook on his lap Beebe rattled off the names and descriptions of these finny visitors for his assistant who dutifully noted his every word. "Depth eight-hundred feet. Two black fish eight inches long going by, rat-tailed, probably *Idiacanthus.* Two long, silver, eel-like fish, probably *Serrivomer*. . . . Three myctophids with headlights. . . . Eels, one dark and one light. . . ." And so it went.

At 900 feet they passed through a soup of flapping snails. Beebe thought there was still enough outside illumination to read by, but when he tried it on some pica-size print, he could not make it out. At 1,000 feet the two deep-divers recoiled in horror as a huge black tentacle swung down before them showing jet-black against the blackish blue, but it was only a loose loop of their rubber hose.

At 1,050 feet they saw colored sparks of light moving through the depths. Their searchlight revealed schools of tiny hatchetfish glittering like pieces of tinsel around them.

At 1,200 feet the inner walls of the sphere dripped with condensation, but an occasional swish of their fan kept their air sweet. Beebe tied a handkerchief below his eyes to keep his breath from steaming the glass, then he concentrated on his observations "with every available rod and cone of both eyes."

The sphere continued down, sometimes passing through stratas devoid of all living things, then entering depths filled with the firefly trails of luminous fish. On several occasions when the searchlight was switched on, Beebe felt sure that he saw the shadowy movements of larger creatures just beyond the yellow cone of light. What strange new inhabitants might be observing them from the safety of the darkness, he wondered.

At 1,400 feet the sphere stopped in descent. They were over a quarter of a mile beneath the surface. Always possessed of the spirit to know "what lay over the next hill," Beebe pressed his face against the sphere's quartz window, whose outside pressure was pushing back at slightly more than 650 pounds per square inch, and looked down "into the black pit-mouth of hell itself." Recalling the words of British philosopher Herbert Spencer, he felt like "an infinitesimal atom floating in illimitable space."

Barton and Beebe had gone where no man had ever been. Yet even after having penetrated more than a quarter mile into inner space, the explorer-scientist was still poised figuratively on the brink of his shallow water reef peering longingly down into still unknown depths.

They made other dives that year, but most were studies of marine life from the shallow to midwater ranges. On one such occasion some distance from shore, Beebe was startled to see the long black sinuous shape of a sea serpent undulating across the white sand bottom to disappear in a jungle of giant sea plumes. On closer observation, however, it turned out to be a transatlantic cable lying quietly on the sea bottom.

Barton donated the bathysphere to the New York Zoölogical Society, and in 1932 the two men readied the newly painted diving chamber for another assault on the deep. Proceeding out from Bermuda the group decided to test the empty sphere. A third quartz window had been slipped into the unplugged socket made for that purpose, but there was some question of its proper installation. To check it, the steel sphere was lowered empty to 3,000 feet. It came up under laboring winches twice as heavy as it went down and almost full of water. Beebe began to unscrew the four-inch wingplug in the center of the door when it screamed and ejected a cloud of mist. The sphere had imploded; its contents were under extreme high pressure.

Beebe cleared the deck, stationed a movie photographer well out of line of fire, then he and an assistant cautiously continued unscrewing the plug. The scream dropped a few octaves and the steam thickened. Suddenly the plug leaped from their grasp and shot thirty feet across the deck, propelled by compressed air and a solid column of water. The projectile caromed off the winch and left a half-inch gouge in the harder metal. As the force of the stream slackened to a cataract, Beebe took its temperature and found it to be fifty-six degrees, indicating that the break had occurred at 2,000 feet, the depth at which this temperature had occurred.

The window was reseated, the sphere sent down and again retrieved full of water. The jet-propelled wing nut knocked another notch in the winch. The window was repacked and reseated and this time it held. The sphere came up from 3,000 feet perfectly dry.

After a few days of stormy weather the seas subsided and an attempt was made to dive. Beebe and Barton crawled inside where the director stowed his spectroscope, illuminometer, flashlight, notebook, pencils and other sundry accessories around him like a hen arranging her eggs. Then they were on their way, passing slowly down through the blue void while Beebe sharpened his powers of observation and kept up an almost steady descriptive commentary to Gloria Hollister at the other end of the telephone. As they passed into the blackness of the abyss he reported seeing luminous dots, strings and brief explosions of light. The sphere was kept dark inside and outside for maximum observation. Since its intensity tended to cook the divers, the sphere's powerful light was switched on only at brief intervals. During one period of darkness Beebe reported seeing several saber-toothed viperfish. Rethinking how he had recognized the species, he realized they had been dimly revealed by the faint blue illumination from their long curved fangs. A four-foot-long fish flashed by, revealing little more than a chain of lights; small lantern fish were so numerous that the phosphorescent glow of the adults was bright enough to illuminate the others. At 1,850 feet he saw the first deep sea squids in their natural habitat and reported, "Their great eyes, each illuminated with a circle of colored lights, stared at me—those unbelievably intelligent yet reasonless eyes backed by no brain and set in a snail."

At 1,950 feet the sphere tumbled so violently that they thought the cable had broken. Beebe cut his lip and forehead against the window ledge and Barton hit his head against the door. It was a bad scare until they learned that everything was still intact. The abrupt pitching had been caused by a sudden large wave on the surface that had tossed their tender. As the weather worsened, they were subjected to rough rolls and pitches every two or three minutes. It felt as if they were riding a wobbling yo-yo on a string.

The sphere continued down, but at 2,200 feet the bouncing became so bad that the trays of chemicals for purifying their air were falling off their racks. They called a halt to their descent. As the ball swung at its lowest level, Beebe saw an unknown species of fish. Illuminated indirectly by its own photophores, the creature was bathed in a strange blue sepulchral light. When it turned head on toward the sphere, the light vanished as if the fish had left. But Beebe knew it was still there in the darkness watching them.

The bathysphere started up. One hundred feet higher and the divers were treated to their most spectacular sight—two fish six feet long passed slowly by the sphere less than eight feet away. Shaped like barracuda but with shorter jaws which they kept open as they swam, the fishes' long fangs glowed dully with their own blue light. In the dark Beebe clearly saw their large round eyes and a single row of pale blue lights down the length of their bodies. Long tentacle-like barbels trailed from their chins and tails, each tipped with luminous lights, the front one red, the rear blue. These appendages twitched around under the fish as they swam. When Beebe switched on the searchlight he noted their ventral fins set well back on the elongated bodies. In honor of their rather loathsome appearance he named the apparitions *Bathysphaera intacta,* the "untouchable bathysphere fish."

Upon surfacing, Beebe was surprised to learn that a

Bahamian lobster which he had put in a cheesecloth bag and tied above the sphere's window as a fish bait was still alive and kicking after being subjected to a pressure of at least eight tons. The naturalist promptly retired the deep-diving *langouste* to the happier life of his aquarium.

After this dive, Barton, Beebe and the bathysphere parted company for a couple years. The sphere went into storage, Barton went off to make an underwater movie, and Beebe became involved in other scientific ventures. But by March 1934 the three were back together again. The bathysphere was collected from its resting place on exhibit at Chicago's Hall of Science Exposition, and all the elements of the new expedition were joined in Bermuda where the National Geographic Society and the New York Zoölogical Society were sponsoring a new deep dive into the abyss.

It was like old home week. Even the old *Ready* was on hand for the action scheduled to take place within a mile and a half of the same spot south of Nonsuch Island where they had made their first descent. The bathysphere was little the worse for its inactivity. A few minor changes were made to the breathing apparatus, and she was given a new coat of paint and tested extensively for several weeks. Then on the morning of August 15, with calm seas and perfect weather, it was time to take the big plunge. At 10:04 A.M., as the sphere splashed through the surface and descended, Beebe again marveled at the wondrous color change, the gradual fading of the spectrum. This time the noted bird watcher had armed himself with a pair of binoculars, and even before the sphere sank through the upper levels of light, he made a fleeting observation. Focusing the glasses on some distant dots near the surface, he identified a small ocean turbot and a flying fish for his faithful note taker, Gloria Hollister.

While the outside light lasted, they saw the usual array of small organisms. By 600 feet the spectroscope registered only gray. From then on they continued into the ever darkening depths where the scattering of sparks and lights from various marine creatures created the illusion of looking into a star-filled sky. At 1,100 feet the lights were more numerous than they had ever seen them on previous trips. Then Beebe saw something that he could not name—a delicate network of luminosity, all its large meshes aglow and moving as it drifted by with a slow ghostly waving motion.

At 1,500 feet the bathysphere paused for two and a half minutes. The searchlight was switched on. Moments later Beebe was baffled by another species unknown to science. First, four 20-inch-long arrowlike eels or elongated fish shot diagonally through the beam followed by drifting jellyfish. Then suddenly Beebe saw the strange fish as it poised half in and half out of the beam. It was two feet long, without lights, its body the buff color of dead flesh. Its eyes were small; its mouth large. As it shifted Beebe saw large filamentous fins set well back on its elongated body. Oddly enough the species had no tail, only a small knob.

His first reaction was to drag Barton to the window to verify the sight. The men were so enthralled that they said nothing for longer than the five seconds of silence Beebe had told Gloria Hollister that they would never exceed. To her urgent calls he hastily reassured her with a description of the fish which he called the "pallid sailfin," giving it a coined Greek name, *Bathyembryx istiophasma.*

At 1,680 feet Beebe was again confronted by a peculiar thing that had disturbed him on earlier dives: a spot of light would draw close to the window, then "explode" in a flash of sparks. Now he forced himself to concentrate unblinkingly on the phenomenon in an effort to comprehend what was happening. As he watched intently, a large creature approached the window and "exploded" so brightly that the red flash illuminated Beebe's face. But his rapt attention paid off. In the glare he saw a large red shrimp. When it struck the glass it emitted a phosphorescent cloud or mist, disappearing behind the miniature fireworks the same way an octopus does behind his inky smoke screen. Solving this riddle was one of the high points of the dive for Beebe.

At 1,810 feet he observed several green-glowing sea dragons (*Lamprotoxus*) and then at 2,450 feet he sensed something huge lurking in the background just beyond their beam. Fifty feet deeper he glimpsed it again—a dim oval shape twenty feet long and about a third as deep. Beebe guessed it was either a fish or a whale. For his size-conscious public he had to admit that it was the "biggest marine monster" sighted during the expedition. But he hardly gave the leviathan more than passing mention in his eagerness to get back to identifying the tinier organisms dancing in front of his window.

Finally the bathysphere stopped at 3,028 feet, over a half-mile below the surface. Here, in a blackness so intense that all other tones of black would forever pale in comparison, Beebe felt that he had reached his ultimate floor. He had descended into the perpetual night of the abyss that he had yearned for. Before his eyes he saw myriad specks of colored light from creatures that knew nothing about daylight. So accustomed were they to creating their own illumination and seeing that of others that when Beebe switched on the sphere's searchlight the abyssal organisms were completely unattracted to it, a reaction that Beebe felt was worthy of someone's further study.

Word came down the telephone wire from the surface that there were only a dozen turns left on their cable reel. Half the drum showed its wooden core. They had reached the end of their tether. The wall of the sphere was so cold to the touch that Beebe's numb fingers could no longer scribble notes. At that depth the sphere was being squeezed with a pressure of 1,360 pounds per square inch. Each window was holding back a force of nineteen tons of water. Would they care to come up? inquired Tee-Van on the telephone. Indeed they would, acknowledged Beebe with a shiver.

Otis Barton and Dr. William Beebe had penetrated the abyss and repeatedly broken their own depth records. Beebe was about as unconcerned over this fact as he was when observing the twenty-foot-long "deep-sea monster." First and last he was a scientist, a man who recorded what he saw in the hope that those who followed might use his observations as a springboard to new knowledge.

Nor did the years ever dim his ardent desire to see and learn. William Beebe never retired. In his eighty-third year he was nesting with notebook and binoculars atop a tree in Venezuela, spying on jungle birds.

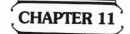

CHAPTER 11

Bittersweet Tang

 To fully appreciate the story of Dick O'Kane and the U.S.S. *Tang,* you have to know the story of Mush Morton and the U.S.S. *Wahoo.* In the early years of World War II in the Pacific, Comdr. Dudley W. Morton and his executive officer, Richard Hetherington O'Kane were one heck of a team. Sometimes the game they played with the enemy was a little unorthodox, but when the stakes were life or death the winner sometimes had to make his own rules.

Morton and the U.S.S. *Wahoo* were joined together inseparably in Brisbane, Australia, on the last day of December 1942. At first there was nothing really remarkable about this union, except perhaps that the submarine's new commander was almost fanatic to get the *Wahoo* refitted and checked out so he could get on with his part in the war. By mid-January this was done and they were on their way. It was Morton's first command, but it was certainly not going to be a routine first patrol. Mush Morton had decided to tackle a problem that had recently been bothering Operations. Somewhere along the northeast coast of New Guinea the Japanese had a major staging area in a harbor known as Wewak. Our forces knew its position only as numerical points of latitude and longitude. Morton intended to find the harbor, slip inside and raise Cain.

The only vague reference to the place was on a small map in a school atlas. Morton and his officers blew up a picture of the map, traced off the area they were interested in on the same scale as their nautical charts and they were in business.

A concensus of opinion on the coordinates settled the question of where Wewak was, so they headed for the place.

Eight days later in broad daylight the *Wahoo* slipped into the suspected enemy anchorage. The harbor was shallow, and Japanese patrol boats were around. Not the safest place even for a submerged submarine that had no place to hide. But it did not bother Mush Morton. He nosed around to see what he could find. The best prospect turned up five miles back in the harbor—an anchored enemy destroyer. The attack plan was to move up stealthily and blast the ship where it sat. The team of Morton and O'Kane went to work. The two men had worked out a unique operation, one that was later used by some of our other submarines. Instead of the commander handling the periscope and plotting his strategy from a compilation of observations, sound information and other complex data, it was Morton's belief that more accuracy could be achieved by splitting these tasks between himself and his highly capable executive officer, Dick O'Kane. The combination worked best with two men who thought almost alike. These two had gotten so good at it that in submarine matters at least they were about as single-minded as any two individuals could get. When they went to work, it was like watching the operation of a finely synchronized machine.

The *Wahoo* crept up on her target in dead silence, O'Kane taking brief glimpses of it by barely breaking water with the periscope's eye to avoid detection. Suddenly he realized the destroyer had hauled its anchor and was underway, heading toward them!

All their attack calculations changed. Now they had to have the destroyer's speed, bearing, range, all the data fed into the Torpedo Data Computer; and fast decisions made.

Then, "Standby forward. Standby one! . . . FIRE!"

"Fire one!" repeated the firing-key operator.

The *Wahoo* lurched as the torpedo left her tube and cut a white swath toward the target.

At ten-second intervals three more followed with slightly different settings fanning the torpedoes toward the target to assure a hit.

O'Kane ran up the periscope for a quick look. Cursing, he

saw the destroyer had spotted the torpedoes and was taking evasive action. "The fish are going aft. Down periscope."

"Leave it up, by God!" bellowed a thoroughly incensed Mush Morton.

The crew was stunned. Everyone knew that the destroyer's next move would be to run back full steam up the torpedo wakes to depth-charge or ram the submarine. Meanwhile the skipper waited with the scope up like a sitting duck, making a perfect target!

And that's exactly what Morton intended. The submarine lay at periscope depth bow on to the onrushing destroyer. He planned to stay right there, giving the Japanese all the target they needed, then at the last instant as they charged in for the kill and it was too late to swerve, he would fire a torpedo right down their throat!

There was nothing in the book about this tactic, and nobody had to figure their chances of survival if it failed. The *Wahoo* had already unloaded four torpedos from her bow, leaving two to go. Morton was betting everything on these last two fish.

With smoke belching from its stacks the destroyer bore down on them at full speed. O'Kane watched it come as he kept the periscope's cross hairs dead on the destroyer's sharp, widening bow.

All was silent except for the clipped, staccato statements of ranges and bearings:

"Bow angle zero. Closing fast. One three five oh yards . . . one three double oh . . . one two five oh. . . ."

At the unprecedented pointblank range of 1,200 yards, Morton's tight lips parted. "FIRE!"

Torpedo number five whooshed out and away. Ten full seconds dragged by, then the sixth and last one was fired. O'Kane stayed glued to the scope watching the twin white streaks race toward the onrushing target. The destroyer heeled, turning to starboard. Appalled, O'Kane saw the first white wake skin by its port side.

"My God, we missed!" But the words were hardly out of his mouth when the second white wake, angling more to the left, hit the target dead center. The concussion walloped the submarine like a depth charge exploding beside it. The destroyer rose into the air, bent amidships and broke in two, plummeting down in a great cloud of billowing smoke, steam and falling debris.

Diving quickly to the bottom of the shallow harbor, the *Wahoo* made knots for its entrance. Overhead, shore batteries peppered the water in the hope of scaring them into holding tight. But by the time Japanese patrol boats were on the scene, the *Wahoo* was well clear of Wewak Harbor.

Later when Mush Morton was asked how it felt to look a Japanese destroyer in the teeth while it barreled straight at him, he said, "Don't ask me, I make O'Kane look. He's the bravest man I know."

Three days after Wewak, the *Wahoo* sighted smoke on the horizon, gave chase and found two Japanese freighters steaming along on a steady course. Morton moved ahead and just off to one side of their course, intending to fire three of his bow torpedoes at each ship, timed so that when the first trio hit the lead ship the second three would be almost to the target before it could change course.

This is the way it was set up but not the way it worked. As the ship came into range, Morton realized the *Wahoo* was too close to their course of travel, so he reversed the sub to a better angle and planned to do the job with his stern tubes. Since he only carried four fish in his stern, that meant two torpedoes per ship, cutting his chances of success.

The freighters came on. The first two torpedoes were fired. Then the next two. After an interval came the thudding explosions. O'Kane ran up the periscope. The first two torpedoes hit their mark; only one of the second pair connected. Two ships with three shots. "Good shooting. Periscope down." Morton ordered the *Wahoo* swung around in case a cripple had to be polished off with a bow tube.

O'Kane looked again and was startled to see not just two ships but a third, a fully loaded troop transport that was hidden by the freighter. Three torpedoes leaped from the bow tubes toward this new target. Seconds later two of the three were hits. One ship was down by the stern, another was on its way to the bottom, but the second target ship was staggering straight back down the torpedo wakes toward the *Wahoo,* bent on ramming. Morton got off two snap shots, but only one connected. Still the hulk kept coming. There was nothing left for the *Wahoo* to do but get down fast. She blew all ballast and dived just as the careening pile of twisted steel lurched by overhead. Then she pulled up to periscope depth and O'Kane took count.

Two ships remained. The one that tried to ram them was limping away. The troop ship was sagging and dead still in the water. *Wahoo* fired a *coup de grâce.* The torpedo plowed by under the target, missing it completely. The next one went off under the ship and broke it in two, the bow sinking rapidly while the troops swarmed overboard.

The *Wahoo* chased the crippled ship and saw it joined by a tanker but was unable to catch up with either because her batteries were now low, forcing her to go slower. As the vessels moved toward the horizon, the *Wahoo* watched with her fully extended periscope and when there was no longer any chance of detection, she surfaced, still keeping the enemy in sight as she cranked up her surface diesels and executed what later became known in the silent service as the "end around." While the crippled target and its escort did a respectable seven knots, Morton pushed the *Wahoo* to a swift seventeen knots, fast closing the gap between them but on a parallel course, just out of their sight. And finally the sub pulled ahead, picked a spot in their track and got ready to pounce.

The tanker hove into range. Morton and O'Kane plotted the approach and fired a spread of three torpedoes. One connected. The tanker reduced speed but continued, wounded. Morton swung the sub to pick up the crippled freighter but he had already taken flight on a course that killed the attack plan.

By now it was dusk, too dark to see through the periscope. Morton decided to press the attack from the surface. As the *Wahoo* sliced up and out, the Japanese vessels kept up a steady zigzag course to avoid attack. For the next two hours Morton and O'Kane tried their best to get a clear shot, without success. The main problem was that they only had two torpedoes left, and both were in the sub's stern tubes. Morton even tried running the boat backward for an approach, but it was no good, the sub lacked good maneuverability. Finally Morton and O'Kane tried another idea. *Wahoo* came up close behind the tanker which was behind the freighter. As the two ships zigged to starboard, *Wahoo* held her course. When the two ships zagged to port, *Wahoo* was conveniently abeam the tanker. Morton whipped the sub around bringing her stern tubes to bear and loosed two torpedoes. The tanker buckled amidships and sank almost immediately.

Next, the freighter.

Wahoo moved in but was driven off by shell fire. She dived, but as soon as she got into position, the canny Japanese intuitively swerved away. The cat and mouse game was shredding nerves aboard the *Wahoo.* Try as they could, Morton and O'Kane could not get the wounded freighter lined up for a shot. With but two torpedoes left, they had to be positive.

Suddenly a searchlight winked on the horizon. The *Wahoo* suspected it was a Japanese escort ship, probably a destroyer that had been radioed in to help the ships under attack. Now whatever they were going to do had to be done fast. Morton furrowed his brow and tried to put himself in the Japanese freighter captain's place. What was *his* most logical move?

Of course! He would head straight for the escort. So that's exactly what the *Wahoo* did, with all screws churning full blast. She placed herself between the fleeing target and the destroyer, waited until the freighter came down the same bearing, then put an end to the game with her two last torpedoes.

The day's score for the *Wahoo:* Four ships up; four ships down. It had taken her thirteen hours to make a full sweep of things. Returning to Pearl Harbor the *Wahoo's* crew saluted their compatriots with the sub's periscope fully extended. Lashed to it was a broom.

Her next patrol was in the Yellow Sea. Again the team of Morton and O'Kane worked its magic. In nineteen days of prowling Japanese-controlled waters they sank nine ships, one trawler and two sampans, returning only because they had used all their torpedoes. Again their periscope proudly brandished the broom. After her third patrol, which accounted for three ships down and two damaged, the *Wahoo*'s luck took a turn for the worse.

The boat put in for a complete overhaul. While in dry dock the unbeatable combination of Morton and O'Kane ended. The team split up so Dick O'Kane could assume command of his own brand new submarine, the U.S.S. *Tang*. As much as Mush Morton hated losing him, he was more than proud to see his highly capable executive officer get the command for which he had repeatedly recommended him.

But from then on it was a downhill slide for the *Wahoo*. Morton requested and got a patrol into the hottest area available—the Sea of Japan. He figured this body of water between Japan and the Asiatic mainland would be a happy hunting ground if he could get the *Wahoo* through the antisubmarine minefields inside. In typical Mush Morton fashion he pulled it off by running on the surface at night over the antisub mines and busting through the straits at top speed past the challenges of the Japanese checkpoint. In fact he went through so boldly that the watch on duty did not even bother reporting it. He knew no American submarine would dare enter those heavily patrolled waters.

But Morton already had. And he found what he was looking for—fat Japanese merchant ships and tankers lulling all over the place. It was just a matter of which target to pick. The *Wahoo* went to work, firing the usual spreads that had always before brought instant hits. But now something was wrong. Time after time the deadly fish whirred away toward their targets—and kept right on going. All were misses. And then Morton realized the worst—after weeks of work getting the *Wahoo* into this "Imperial game preserve," *all his torpedoes were faulty*!

Back to Pearl he went, hot enough to spit sparks. Nobody knew whether the faulty torpedoes were sabotage or an honest accident, but Admiral Lockwood fully understood the irate skipper's feelings. When Morton finally simmered down, Lockwood asked him what he would like to do.

Morton's answer: "Load up with live fish this time and head back to the Sea of Japan."

It would have been the ultimate cruelty not to have obliged. The *Wahoo* took on a triple-checked cargo of torpedoes and burned a wide wake back the way she had come, to the Sea of Japan, Morton's long-anticipated happy hunting ground. Except for a brief stop at Midway en route, that was the last that was ever heard of the *Wahoo* or her crew.

But a Japanese report said that between September 29 and October 9, 1943, a submarine in the Sea of Japan sank four ships. This had to have been the *Wahoo.* Knowing the enemy's prior reluctance to admit kills, the number of ships sunk was probably closer to eight or more. But strangely enough, of the 468 United States submarines that the enemy claimed to have sunk, the *Wahoo* was not one of them. Like so many other submarines that never returned, she was simply listed as lost in action.

Comdr. Dick O'Kane of the U.S.S. *Tang* took it hard. His immediate response was to seek revenge for Mush Morton and the crew of the *Wahoo.* And *what* a revenge he exacted!

On the *Tang's* first four patrols, O'Kane used the same tactics he and Morton had perfected. And the old magic still worked. *Tang* sank seventeen ships, racking up the score in a remarkably short time. But absolutely nothing would ever compare to the *Tang's* fifth and last patrol, an unparalleled homage to the *Wahoo* that was never equaled.

On September 24, 1944, O'Kane left Pearl Harbor with a complement of eighty-eight men aboard the 300-foot *Tang,* and headed for the Taiwan Strait between China and Formosa. This seventy-five-mile-wide body of water looked like as fine a hunting ground to O'Kane as the Sea of Japan had to Mush Morton. It was heavily trafficked by Japanese ships carrying troops and supplies to the Philippines. O'Kane figured that if he put the *Tang* right in the middle of all that activity, it would be like shooting ducks. Except that some of these birds would be shooting back. The *Tang* carried twenty-four torpedoes, enough for Dick O'Kane to settle any traffic jam in the Taiwan Strait.

When he reached his destination, he found more activity

than he had expected. The Japanese were marshaling their forces for the greatest battle of the war in Leyte Gulf. The *Tang* promptly sank two freighters, then closed in on a cruiser and two destroyers but was driven off by shell fire. Next, O'Kane sighted a Japanese convoy of three tankers, two troop ships and escort vessels heading for the Philippines. Since the ships were traveling in two columns flanked by the escorts, O'Kane moved full speed ahead of them, put the *Tang* broadside the unsuspecting convoy and prepared to pick off the ships in the dark as they passed his bow and stern.

The blacked-out convoy moved into range. O'Kane was in the conning tower of the surfaced sub sighting the target ships with his binoculars and directing the fire from topside. At ten-second intervals the torpedoes leaped from their tubes and sped away into the night. The first tanker took two direct hits. As it mushroomed into a flaming holocaust of exploding aviation fuel, the next tanker in line caught a single torpedo that turned it into a flaming pyre. Seconds later, the third tanker caught two of the *Tang's* torpedoes and went up in a fiery explosion. The sea was suddenly as bright as daylight. The stark black burning hulks shot flames and smoke high into the air while their bright images reflected in the water. In the firelight's glare the lead transport ship saw the *Tang* and swerved to ram her.

Too late to dive, O'Kane shouted orders through his telephone. The crew leaped to collision stations; the *Tang's* diesels roared and she surged forward with a hard-right full rudder. O'Kane stayed topside where he could be the eyes for his crew. Their immediate response sent the sub on a tight inside curve across the bows of the onrushing transport. The ship turned to slice the *Tang* in two, but O'Kane called for a hard-left full rudder and scampered out of the way of the less maneuverable transport. When the tall vessel slid past the submarine's stern, Japanese machinegunners raked her decks with a hail of lead. At ten-second intervals the *Tang* fired her four aft torpedoes.

As the fish leaped away in almost converging white wakes, O'Kane saw an amazing sight. Unable to change course quickly enough to avoid a collision, the Japanese transport plowed straight into her sister ship. Amidst ripping steel and screaming men, the *Tang*'s four torpedoes struck the two entangled transports. Both ships rose into the air with a series of violent explosions that left little but huge pieces of fiery wreckage to plunge back into the sea and disappear. Incredibly, the *Tang* had sunk the entire convoy, five ships in ten minutes!

The next night another convoy showed up. The *Tang* shadowed it like a shark sizing up its prey. A pair of nervous destroyers were riding herd on two transports and a tanker. From the way the escorts were using their blinker lights and flitting back and forth, O'Kane figured that they had heard about what happened to the previous night's convoy. Once he knew their strength and bearing, O'Kane took the *Tang* ahead and lay in wait on the surface just off their track.

Out of the darkness came the column of enemy ships. O'Kane fired two torpedoes at the lead transport, shifted targets to send two toward the second transport, and emptied the bow tubes with the last two at the tanker.

All torpedoes hit their targets. It was the Fourth of July fireworks at Coney Island. And then coming through the billowing clouds of black smoke was another tanker and a freighter.

O'Kane barked orders into his telephone. The *Tang* boiled water and turned end for end to point her stern tubes at the new targets. In the time it took to maneuver the long submarine, the escort vessels saw her in the glare of the burning ships and opened fire with everything they had. O'Kane's conning tower rang like a bell from the hits, but he called for full power to outrun the angry escort bent on gunning him down.

Suddenly another destroyer loomed up out of the smoke, forcing O'Kane to make a quick decision. Should he try to outmaneuver the newcomer on the surface or dive and take his chances on a depth charging? Typically, he decided to beat the competition at its own game. Then Lady Luck intervened. O'Kane's first stern torpedo hit the transport with a shattering explosion; the second turned the tanker into a flaming pyre; and the destroyer, just as it cut across beside it, caught O'Kane's third fish, intended for the tanker, and dissolved in an ear-splitting explosion behind a column of water.

O'Kane was batting a thousand! He had left Pearl Harbor with twenty-four fish and he did not intend to return with one. His fourth target, a transport struck by a single torpedo, was still afloat. O'Kane moved in to polish it off. On command his next to last fish sped toward the crippled target. Then, to make doubly sure, he fired his twenty-forth and last torpedo at it.

As the deadly cylinder lunged out of the tube O'Kane saw something was wrong. The torpedo boiled an arcing wake to port. It was circling!

O'Kane shouted for all ahead; right full rudder. There was no time to dive. He had to dodge the runaway before it hit the sub. From the conning tower the commander and nine others watched in stunned silence as the torpedo spun a phosphorescent trail back toward the agonizingly slow-moving *Tang*.

It struck abaft the port side, instantly demolishing three compartments. The sub sank quickly by her stern. O'Kane shouted down to his men to close the hatch, but the upturned faces disappeared behind a rushing torrent of black water. The conning tower went under. O'Kane and those with him fought to get clear of the suction of the drowning submarine. As they swam, the sea shuddered with the concussion of their penultimate torpedo exploding against the crippled tanker. In the fire glare O'Kane counted nine survivors and saw the bow of the *Tang* momentarily jut up out of the water before the submarine plunged beneath the surface in a welter of exhausted air.

O'Kane and the small group of survivors started swimming toward the China coast. Almost ashore, they were picked up by a Japanese destroyer. The English-speaking interrogator soon learned who they were. O'Kane's name and reputation were well known to the Japanese as far back as his days with Mush Morton on the *Wahoo*. And now they were elated to have the infamous commander in their possession. They worked the men over with clubs and fists, and as O'Kane later remarked about his treatment, "I don't really know what *I'd* do if I got hold of people that sank all *my* ships."

The *Tang* sank to the bottom of the Taiwan Strait in 180 feet of water. Thirty men were still alive in her forward compartments. Somehow they had managed to seal themselves off from the flooded aft sections by quickly closing waterproof hatches. Now they discussed the best way to stay alive. Meanwhile, for the next two hours, unaware of the *Tang*'s self-inflicted mortal wound, the Japanese kept up an incessant barrage of depth bombing. Finally the surviving crew members decided to escape out the air locks with Munson lungs, then swim for the friendly shores of China.

Coolly they collected and burned the sub's secret papers, knowing full well that this last simple military act would further consume the oxygen and poison the small amount of life-sustaining air remaining. To make matters worse, an electrical fire broke out in the battery compartment. The men hastily crowded into the forward torpedo room and dogged tight the intervening hatch, hoping to delay the fire long enough for them to get out the air lock there.

They distributed Munson lungs and began flooding the compartment to offset the intense water pressure against the outer hatch so it could be opened. As the water rose about their waists, compressing the carbon dioxide of their exhalations to the lethal level, the fire blistered the paint on the bulkheads. One by one the men went out the escape hatch as the heat and fumes concentrated in their small compartment. When the hatch gasket started burning, the acrid stench of rubber was added to what little air was still breathable. Thirteen men went out through the lock, but seventeen that awaited their turn slowly lost consciousness in the deadly gases and slumped into the water. Of the thirteen men that escaped the submarine, five never made it to the surface and three of those that did died shortly afterward. Five survived only to be rescued by the Japanese, and when added to O'Kane's group, they made a total of fifteen. Nine of these perished as prisoners of war and six beaten, half-starved crewmen of the *Tang* lived through the ordeal to come home. Among them was Richard Hetherington O'Kane, considerably bruised and underweight but not defeated. As skipper of the *Tang*, he had set an unprecedented record. A total of 1,150 enemy ships were sunk by American submarines in the Pacific during World War II. In nine months the U.S.S. *Tang* had accounted for 30 of these. For his gallantry and bravery beyond the call of duty in this action against the enemy, Comdr. Dick O'Kane was awarded the nation's highest military decoration, the Congressional Medal of Honor. The tribute most assuredly would have pleased one Dudley W. Morton, Commander, U.S.S. *Wahoo*, somewhere in the Sea of Japan.

As long as two city blocks, her flying bridge the height of a four-story building, the U.S.S. *Triton* is the behemoth of diving machines. Powered by a grapefruit-sized chunk of uranium, the giant nuclear submarine circumnavigated the globe, covering 41,814 statute miles in eighty-four days, nineteen hours and eight minutes—entirely underwater. (Courtesy General Dynamics)

The U.S.S. *Nautilus*, first of a long line of nuclear-powered submarines whose capabilities far exceed anything ever dreamed of by the early submarine inventors. (Courtesy: Submarine Museum, New London, Connecticut)

After making its historic transpolar voyage under Arctic ice, the crew of the U.S.S. *Nautilus* stands quarters for muster as one of many tugs displays her greeting against the New York skyline. (Courtesy U.S. Navy)

Right: The U.S. Navy's forty-eighth nuclear-powered attack submarine, the *Bluefish (SSN 675)*, leaves Groton, Connecticut, for extensive sea trials following completion of dockside tests at the Electric Boat Division of General Dynamics. (Courtesy: General Dynamics)

Below: The U.S.S. *Batfish (SSN 681)* plows an impressive bow wave during sea trials. (Courtesy: General Dynamics)

Left: Launching of the nuclear-powered submarine U.S.S. *Batfish (SSN 681)* at the Electric Boat Division of General Dynamics, Groton, Connecticut. (Courtesy: General Dynamics)

Below: Artist's illustration of the U.S.S. *Nautilus* running submerged. (Courtesy: Submarine Museum, New London, Connecticut)

Artist's cutaway shows the inside layout of Jacques Piccard's mesoscaph *Ben Franklin* that took six scientists on a thirty-one-day drift mission to the depths of the Gulf Stream. (Courtesy: Submarine Museum, New London, Connecticut)

A photograph taken at great depth during the search for the U.S.S. *Thresher* reveals a cylinder similar to those carried aboard the submarine. The diagonal lines and the ball in the center of the picture is part of the lighting system for the underwater camera. (Courtesy: U.S. Navy)

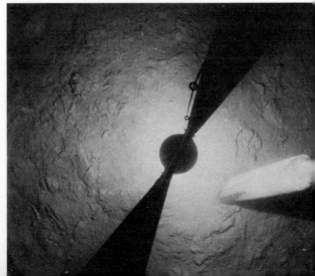

The bathyscaph *Trieste II* prepares for a dive in the Pacific while the auxiliary repair dry dock U.S.S. *White Sands* stands by in the background. (Courtesy: U.S. Navy)

Built in Switzerland at a cost of $2.5 million, Piccard's mesoscaph was designed to operate to 2,000 feet underwater but could tolerate pressures up to 4,000-foot depths. (Courtesy: Submarine Museum, New London, Connecticut)

Mute evidence of the U.S.S. *Thresher*'s fate is revealed by the underwater camera. This wreckage is an overhead view of the submarine's topside rudder. (Courtesy: U.S. Navy)

Left: Navy scientists prepare the Cousteau *Diving Saucer* for a descent off Mission Beach, California. This vehicle was used in the Navy Oceanographic Research program studying the ocean floor. (Courtesy: U.S. Navy)

Below: The research submarine *Alvin* being moved about by cranes aboard the U.S.S. *Fort Snelling.* The small submersible was responsible for finding the lost hydrogen bomb off Palomares, Spain. (Courtesy: U.S. Navy)

Below: During the search for the missing H-bomb off Palomares, Spain, CURV, the Cable-Controlled Underwater Research Vehicle that finally recovered the bomb from 2,800-foot depths, is hoisted aboard the U.S.S. *Petrel.* (Courtesy: U.S. Navy)

Left: On board the U.S.S. *Petrel* Air Force Comdr. Delmar Wilson and Naval Comdr. William Guest look over the fourth and final H-bomb recovered off Palomares, Spain, by CURV (Cable-Controlled Underwater Research Vehicle) in the background. (Courtesy: U.S. Navy)

Below: Since the *Johnson-Sea-Link* tragedy, Ed Link has built C.O.R.D. (Cabled Observation/Rescue Device) a radio-controlled underwater rescue vehicle with TV and sonar to be used in the recovery of submersibles. (Photo by W. L. Davenport. Courtesy: Harbor Branch Foundation)

Below: The *Johnson-Sea-Link* submersible rests on the bottom while a diver wearing a modified Bio-Marine rebreathing apparatus swims near the bow of the craft. Note the acrylic sphere for the sub's operators and the complexity of cables, pipes, lights, cylinders and instrument packages. (Photo by Christopher Swann. Courtesy: Harbor Branch Foundation)

Resembling a benevolent sea creature, *Deep Quest* receives a final check on the surface before descending to 8,310 feet in the Pacific Ocean. (Courtesy: U.S. Navy)

Artist's concept of the navy's Deep Submergence Rescue Vehicle (DSRV) in use. Capable of operating to 5,000-foot depths, the *DSRV-2* is designed to mate with the escape hatch of a disabled submarine and rescue up to twenty-four crewmen at a time. (Courtesy: U.S. Navy)

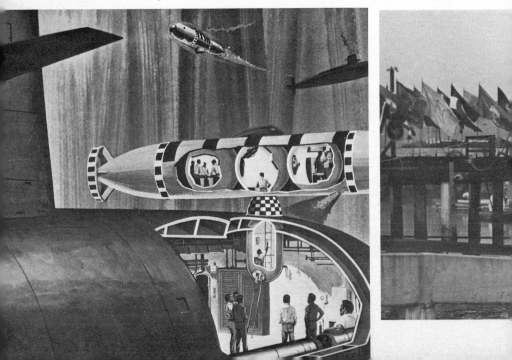

Lockheed test pilot Richard Ross, left, and Lieut. Comdr. D. Pat Raetzman, skipper of the navy's Deep Submergence Rescue Vehicle (DSRV), run through a predive check at the rescue sub's controls. The *DSRV-1*, with a depth range up to 3,500 feet, is designed to travel anywhere in the world by plane, truck or nuclear submarine to rescue crewmen of conventional-type submarines stranded on the ocean bottom. (Courtesy: Lockheed)

Front view of the Lockheed-designed research submarine *Deep Quest* in shallow water off Santa Catalina Island shows its manipulator arms. The fifty-ton submersible is designed to carry four men and a payload up to 7,000 pounds to depths of 8,000 feet. (Courtesy: Lockheed)

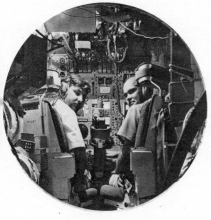

The navy's second rescue submarine, the Deep Submergence Rescue Vehicle *(DSRV-2)*, moves down a marine railway as it is launched in San Diego Bay. Capable of descending to 5,000-foot depths to rescue crewmen of stricken submarines, the fifty-foot-long submersible is part of a twin rescue system designed to move quickly to any area of the world where it may be needed. (Courtesy: U.S. Navy)

Deep Quest, with a depth range of 8,000 feet, has been used to explore the marine canyons off the Southern California coast, to obtain cores from the ocean floor and to recover flight recorders from ditched aircraft. (Courtesy: Lockheed)

CURV III, the navy's newest Cable-Controlled Underwater Research Vehicle, was instrumental in rescuing the crippled submersible *Pisces* with its two-man crew from 1,375-foot depths off Ireland in 1973. (Courtesy: U.S. Navy)

The U.S. Navy *DSRV-1* is accompanied by a diver as she submerges off San Diego, California. (Courtesy: U.S. Navy)

Autec I (*Sea Cliff*) and *Autec II* (*Turtle*) are twin twenty-six-foot-long, twenty-four-ton research vehicles patterned after *Alvin*, but larger. Possessing two mechanical arms, the pair will do oceanographic work down to 6,500-foot depths.(Courtesy: U.S. Navy)

Closeup of the instrument package attached to *Deep Star 4000* shows the array of scientific equipment used in studying the ocean floor down to 4,000 feet during a navy oceanographic research program. (Courtesy: U.S. Navy)

A crewman looks through the thick glass hemisphere window of the Naval Undersea Research and Development Center submersible *Deep View*, the first submersible with a pressure hull of glass. The fifteen-foot-long, five-ton, battery-operated vehicle is designed to operate down to 1,500 feet. The arm in the front can be manipulated to pick up objects from the ocean floor. (Courtesy: U.S. Navy)

Illustration of the relative depths attained by various diving devices from scuba to submersible. (Courtesy: Submarine Museum, New London, Connecticut)

After making several dives in Woods Hole Harbor, *Alvin* was hoisted aboard R/V *Knorr* with her trawl winch, and the vessel headed for Ponta Delgada preparatory to their involvement in Project FAMOUS. (Courtesy: Woods Hole Oceanographic Institution)

Settled in her place aboard the R/V *Knorr, Alvin* is ready for transit to the Azores and Project FAMOUS. (Courtesy: Woods Hole Oceanographic Institution)

Alvin descends on this elevator platform into the water and then moves under her own power to the dive site. Upon completion of a dive, she returns to the protected area between the pontoons of mother ship *Lulu* to be secured in her cradle and lifted again to the main-deck level of her tender. (Courtesy: Woods Hole Oceanographic Institution)

A fissure about one and a half meters wide cuts across pillow lava on the east wall of the median valley of the Mid-Atlantic Ridge. Apparatus in foreground is *Alvin's* sample-collection basket. (Courtesy: Woods Hole Oceanographic Institution)

Below: Photo from *Alvin* shows bulbous pillow lavas with cracked crust. To right is elongated or "Cousteau" pillow. (Courtesy: Woods Hole Oceanographic Institution)

Right: An artist's concept of a submersible's versatility in performing relatively complicated tasks with its operator-directed manipulator arms. (Courtesy: Submarine Museum, New London, Connecticut)

CHAPTER 12

Rickover: Nautilus Maximus

 At twilight on March 17, 1959, a long black submarine smashed through a great white plain of sheet ice and came to rest in a "skylight" at the North Pole. The scene that followed could have come from a novel by Jules Verne.

While thirty-knot polar winds howled across the ice fields, crewmen aboard the submarine raised the flags of Australia, Great Britain and the United States. In the sputtering light of red flares, a procession of men muffled in parkas and wind masks filed out onto the ice and stood at attention while their commander read them a passage from a book. Then, accompanied by torch bearers, he carried an urn solemnly past the ranks of silent men. At the edge of the ice he opened the urn and committed its contents to the wind. Riflemen fired a last volley.

The whale-shaped ship was the United States nuclear submarine *Skate*. Her skipper had just read the rites of burial at sea and consigned the ashes of Australian-born explorer Sir Hubert Wilkins to the winds of the North Pole, as he had requested before he died the previous year.

In 1931, Wilkins and Norwegian oceanographer Harald U. Sverdrup pioneered the first attempt to cross the polar ice cap underwater. Obtaining an obsolete fleet submarine they renamed the *Nautilus,* the two had Simon Lake add some special equipment for the unique voyage. Since Wilkins hoped to ski the submarine along the underside of the ice pack in a sort of upside-down-sled manner, Lake mounted a pair of wooden ski-like runners to the boat's superstructure. The plan was to duck under the ice, give the sub enough positive buoyancy to bring the runners in contact with the frozen undersurface, then "ski" over the ridges and slopes, surfacing whenever necessary for air and battery recharging in any open-water splits in the ice. Wilkins knew these "polynyas" or "skylights" existed, because he had seen them in a plane from the air.

Unfortunately, however, before the two men could pull off the feat, things went wrong. Testing the antiquated submarine under the ice floes 500 miles from the pole almost proved more than the crew could bear. Wilkins reported that as the *Nautilus* bumped along under the ice, the faintest scratch against the frozen undersurface resounded inside the submarine like the ripping of giant strips of calico. Heavier thuds thundered like the continuous shocks of earthquakes. The experience was described as "quite terrifying." After a few such tests the crewmen were less than enthusiastic about their endeavor. While the cantankerous submarine had more than its share of breakdowns, its troubles were compounded when two of the crew sabotaged the boat's diving planes to avoid having to make another nightmarish trip under the ice.

Despite these setbacks, Wilkins and Professor Sverdrup pressed on, forcing the damaged sub under the ice with great difficulty. After floundering around for several days until frost formed on the *Nautilus'* bulkheads, the crew's morale hit bottom. With the ice-battered old *Nautilus* almost a candidate for Davy Jones' locker, Wilkins was forced to admit defeat and limp home.

Twenty-eight years later, however, thanks to the *Skate,* the intrepid Australian explorer finally reached his destination, all of which probably would not have happened for at least several more decades had it not been for Capt. Hyman George Rickover, the controversial father of the atomic submarine.

Ever since Cornelius Van Drebbel covered a boat with skins, and sank it in the Thames so that he could row underwater, people have been a little chary of submarine inventors. With or without cause these innovators have been called everything from crackpots to geniuses, with few epithets missed in between. And this was the case with Rickover, a man whose close friends spoke of him as being "one of the most gentle, warmhearted and unselfish men" they had ever met, "one with a keen sense of humor." Yet he was the same Rickover whom biographers, journalists, co-workers, industrialists, politicians and comrades-in-arms often saw in another light. Combining all their descriptions produces an interesting composite of the man they described as "a wiry dynamo with a thin, serious face, close-cropped white hair and a tongue like a whip. A dynamic, inquisitive man who pushed and prodded leaders of industry to get what he wanted, who trodded on the toes of everyone from seamen to admirals; a down-to-earth, no-nonsense, hard-working officer who snapped at congressmen, told off senators and took verbal potshots at both civilian and military officials, a man whose personal initiative and drive got jobs done while at the same time his dynamic personality either engendered complete respect and blind devotion from his co-workers or stimulated them to compare him favorably with the real Captain Bligh or the fictional Captain Queeg. And somewhere in that description was the real Captain Hyman Rickover, who apparently took pleasure in his work, no matter what it was.

Even in high school young Rickover was more industrious than most students. He thought nothing of putting in seven hours in school, and then seven more hours of hard work. This combination of work and study precluded Rickover's developing any outside interests or friends. He simply had no time for them. The same single-minded devotion to his studies and work followed him into the Naval Academy where he was known as a serious, asocial ensign who spent more time with his books than he did with friends.

Three years after his graduation in 1922 he was made electrical officer aboard the battleship *Nevada* where his reputation for diligence and hard work grew along with his hunger for education. A few years later he earned a master's degree in electrical engineering at the Naval Academy, followed by advanced courses at Columbia University's School of Engineering. After that, Rickover decided he wanted to get into submarines. He applied for the service, but since he was twenty-nine years old, the board rejected him as over age. Rickover promptly hurtled this minor obstacle by putting his problem before the admiral, who as luck would have it had been his commanding officer aboard the old *Nevada*. This time his application was accepted. Rickover trained at the rugged submarine school at New London, Connecticut, and became the engineer officer for a Simon Lake–designed submarine, the S-48.

Within a year he completely overhauled the submarine and put it in better working condition than it ever was before. Next he was transferred to a rust-bucket of a minesweeper, the U.S. *Finch* stationed in the Yellow Sea. The dilapidated, dirty, rust-caked *Finch* was the kind of ship the navy knew it had, but no one really cared to admit it. If anyone asked her whereabouts, she was usually off in some distant sea prowling the backwaters by herself. Then came the efficient, the diligent Captain Rickover on an irrevocable collision course. In a twinkling the *Finch*'s crew was organized to knock off the ship's coats of rust and add several coats of paint. Meanwhile, the Japanese invaded China, and the *Finch* was caught in the crossfire, but this small detail did not slow Rickover's face-lifting program. The crew of the *Finch* never forgave him for it.

During World War II Rickover was made chief of the electrical section at the Bureau of Ships. With his usual penchant for looking around to see how he might improve a situation, he found ample room for his talents in the catalogs listing the thousands of spare electrical parts that went into the navy's ships. Discovering many duplicate listings of parts, he undertook the challenging job of reclassifying the whole catalog system. With that completed, Rickover took a closer look at some of the parts and found many that could be improved. He therefore redesigned the parts, pressured the various companies into making the changes or chance losing their government contracts, and achieved his goal despite stepping on a few toes along the way.

In 1944, Rickover, now a captain, was assigned to another problem area, the navy's giant supply depot in Mechanicsburg, Pennsylvania. It was so bogged down by inefficiency and red tape that vital parts were only trickling to the fleet. This was just the kind of challenge Rickover enjoyed. He hit the beach at full bore, wiped out a small army of inefficient people, and after an explosive organizational battle, he shaped up the survivors until supplies were being dispatched 25 percent faster than before. With equal dispatch, Rickover cleaned up two subsequent major assignments; he revamped and speeded up the fleet repair facilities at Okinawa in 1945 and speedily supervised the mothballing of the fleet at the end of World War II.

By 1946, with a reputation for getting jobs done no matter how difficult they were, Rickover was sent to Oak Ridge, Tennessee, to represent the navy in a joint military-civilian effort to figure out practical applications for atomic energy. Rickover's group consisted of several top-flight civilian engineers and several junior-grade navy officers with outstanding engineering backgrounds from the Bureau of Ships.

After learning something about the capabilities and limitations of atomic energy, Rickover's group decided that nuclear energy could be used to power an atomic submarine. Inside of six months after his arrival at Oak Ridge, Rickover and his fellow engineer Lieut. Comdr. Louis H. Roddis submitted a report to the Bureau of Ships in which they stated their findings indicating that the navy could have a nuclear-powered ship within the next five to eight years. The navy liked the idea but considered the officers' opinions overoptimistic. This time Rickover was up against his biggest challenge.

For the next few years he fought to get his project accepted. In the process he managed to alienate almost everyone he came in contact with. Pushing himself into a round-the-clock effort, he expected nothing less from his co-workers. When the navy dissolved his team, leaving him a man without a command, he simply redoubled his efforts. One morning he might be in Washington trying to drum up enthusiasm for his nuclear reaction among the navy's upper echelons, that afternoon he might be doing the same thing with scientists at Oak Ridge and that night he would be wading through a mountain of paperwork related to the same subject. Finally, he sparked enough interest in the scientists at Oak Ridge that they spent all their spare time working on the project. Rickover was elated. All he had to do now was sell the idea to the navy's top brass.

Firmly believing that the shortest distance between two points is a straight line, even if it bisects six admirals, Rickover went directly to the top, detailing his project in a letter to the then chief of naval operations, Adm. Chester Nimitz. In a masterful piece of persuasion that took him two months to write, Rickover emphasized two points, the practical importance of an atomic submarine and the feasibility of the Bureau of Ships working in conjunction with the Atomic Energy Commission to produce it.

With the help of high-ranking naval officers sympathetic to Rickover's plan, the letter moved swiftly through channels and was approved by Admiral Nimitz and the secretary of the navy. Everything looked rosy until the Atomic Energy Commission vetoed the idea. That efficiently blocked Rickover's plan for the next two years, but it did not put the determined man out of combat. He tightened his belt and dug in all the harder. Working through channels, Rickover was instrumental in bringing about the abolition of the old, inactive, nuclear-power group at the Bureau of Ships which was replaced by a new nuclear branch with himself as its head. Rickover now had a substantial platform from which to operate; he had a command again.

By 1949, with a reshuffling of personnel in the Atomic Energy Commission, the winds of change blew more favorably for Rickover. When the new head of the Atomic Energy Commission saw a need and added a new division called the Naval Reactors Branch, who was selected to lead it but Captain Rickover.

There was little to hold him back now except the usual bureaucratic red tape. With a reasonable appropriation to work with, Rickover had his beachhead and was ready to escalate the battle. Working with the navy, Westinghouse engineers decided to attack the problem by building a large model of the nuclear power plant and gradually reduce it to the size that would fit into a submarine, an approach that Rickover saw might take years. After some rather heated discussions, Westinghouse decided to try Rickover's way— build a model reactor of the size that would go into the submarine. Moreover, Rickover insisted that as modifications were made on the prototype they be used immediately on a second model that would be constructed with only a short time lapse after the first. This approach gave results at least five years sooner than if the project had been done the other way.

Rickover refused to tolerate red tape, excuses, mediocrity or inefficiency. Like a man obsessed he put himself heart, body and soul into the project, frequently working around the clock to speed the operation to its completion. And as usual he expected a comparable effort from his co-workers, an attitude that made him about as popular with some of them as he was with the paint-chipping crew of the *Finch.*

When the Electric Boat Company in Connecticut was given the contract for building the first United States nuclear submarine to be named the *Nautilus,* they had no illusion about what they were getting into with Rickover. He was a perfectionist and he demanded perfection of those who had anything to do with the project.

As it progressed from the planning stage to the construction stage, Rickover gave no quarter. When engineers ran into trouble meeting specifications, Rickover held the line and would not give an inch. The submarine had to be perfect throughout. He refused to alter the smallest specification. Parts manufacturers had to come up with the exact items requested, or as far as Rickover was concerned, the parts were so much junk.

Fifty-foot models of the *Nautilus* were built and repeatedly blown to bits with miniature depth charges to test the boat's weaknesses. Once when Rickover learned that the navy planned to test depth charges on one of its old World War II submarines, he saw to it that key parts of the *Nautilus* were put aboard the target sub. Later when the parts were returned to him and some had not withstood the impact of the underwater explosions, he bounced them back to the manufacturers with ear-scorching disapproval, making them feel almost unpatriotic for offering him such "junk" in the first place. As a result, red-faced manufacturers tried harder. The parts were redesigned and proved to be 100 percent improved. Rickover was fighting just as hard to personally see his pet project to a perfectly successful conclusion as if he were fighting for his life in an honest to goodness full-scale war. He fought his greatest battles with his three lifelong foes—inefficiency, mediocrity and bureaucracy, taking on all opposition, military and civilian alike, until he bested them with his sheer boundless energy and determination.

In 1951, the Navy Selection Board convened to decide which captains were to be made admirals. With his unblemished record of outstanding achievements Captain Rickover was considered a prime candidate. But the Board passed him over. If the fact bothered Rickover, he never mentioned it. He was too busy consolidating loose ends in his project.

The following year, 1952, the public became aware of the *Nautilus'* construction and Rickover's contribution to the project. In recognition of this and "for exceptionally meritorious conduct in the performance of outstanding services to the government . . ." the secretary of the navy awarded him the Legion of Merit. It was his second such honor. He earned his first in World War II. The following day the Navy Selection Board convened to select its admirals. For the second time, despite his remarkably outstanding military career and the award of two Legions of Merit, Rickover was passed over. His friends could not believe it. To be passed over twice by this promotion board meant that there would not be another time; the officer under consideration was usually retired within the next six months.

But this was not Rickover's intention. He tried to convince his friends that the Board had made an unbiased decision, but they knew better. One close friend in particular sacrificed his own career to try and right the wrong. During the next six months, Lieut. Ray H. Dick wrote or spoke to every senator or representative that would listen to him, pleading with them to speak up about the Rickover affair. So fervently did he argue his case that Sen. Henry Jackson and Rep. Sidney Yates joined the cause to help Rickover. Highlights of their speeches were picked up by the press, and in due course, public opinion turned the tide. In July 1953, during the regular meeting of the Navy Selection Board, Capt. Hyman George Rickover, despite his tongue-lashing, brow-beating, ego-shattering ways, was promoted to the rank of rear admiral. But it was a hollow victory for Rickover, saddened by the loss of the friend who had helped him make it possible. On January 5, 1953, completely exhausted from his physical and moral battle, thirty-one-year-old Lieut. Ray Dick was admitted to Bethesda Naval Hospital where he died that night of a heart attack.

In January 1954, the determined man who had conceived, directed, badgered, bullied and fought for the atomic submarine finally saw his efforts bear fruit. Within the eight years Rickover originally predicted, the United States launched the *Nautilus*, its first atomic submarine. More fabulous than Jules Verne ever dreamed, she was a huge, black, $90 million supersub longer than a football field and capable of traveling underwater for more than 100,000 miles on the power of a nuclear mass no larger than a baseball. From the moment she entered the water, her performance and reliability constantly amazed submariners throughout the world. By February 1957, while a second atomic submarine, the U.S.S. *Seawolf,* was completing her initial cruise and a third atomic sub, the U.S.S. *Skate,* was about to ride down the ways, the *Nautilus* had logged some 60,000 miles, more than twice the distance around the world, using only a golf-ball-sized chunk of uranium from her original nuclear core. While other submarines had difficulty holding high speeds submerged for more than an hour, the *Nautilus* averaged an incredible 19.1 knots on one 265-hour submerged voyage. Then in July 1958, the *Nautilus* was ordered on a top-secret history-making voyage called Operation Sunshine. Under the capable guidance of thirty-seven-year-old, Tennessee-born Comdr. William R.

Anderson, the atomic submarine was to proceed from Honolulu to Portland, England, passing from the Pacific to the Atlantic by traveling under the Arctic ice cap.

As the *Nautilus* left her Pacific port, another United States nuclear submarine, the U.S.S. *Skate* under thirty-eight-year-old Ohio-born Comdr. James F. Calvert, slipped out of Connecticut's Thames River, bound for the Arctic. Her top-secret orders read that she was to: "Develop techniques for surfacing in ice packs. . . . All other items are subordinate to this one. . . . If nuclear submarines are to be useful in the Arctic, they must have access to the surface." Calvert's job was to learn how.

At 2315 on August 3, 1958, the *Nautilus* passed under the North Pole and surfaced five days later to radio the historic news to the chief of naval operations with the laconic message: "NAUTILUS NINETY NORTH."

On August 9, as the *Skate* approached the great ice cap and came up to periscope depth for a position fix, she heard the first news of the *Nautilus'* success from a British broadcast. Although the missions of the two submarines were quite different, the *Skate's* crew was disappointed in being beaten to the North Pole. Commander Calvert took the submarine under the ice and traveled 600 miles to pass beneath the North Pole nine days after the *Nautilus.* Forty miles from the Pole on the Pacific side, the *Skate* surfaced in a sheet-ice skylight or polynya. Before returning to base, the nuclear submarine repeated the maneuver in eight different localities, putting her back against the ice and breaking through to surface.

The next year on a return trip to the polar ice cap, the *Skate* crashed through a thick skylight to become the first submarine in history to surface at the North Pole. And there, on March 17, 1959, the *Skate's* crew brought the valiant Australian Arctic explorer, Sir Hubert Wilkins, to his final resting place.

What Rickover began with his *Nautilus* has resulted today in a United States nuclear-powered submarine fleet numbering at this writing 128 ships—not boats, as submarines are generally called—because they have indeed achieved the size and power of surface ships. This includes the largest and most powerful submarine in the world, the U.S.S. *Triton,* 447.5 feet long, the length of two average city blocks, her flying bridge towering forty-one feet above water, the height of a modern four-story building. Powered by a grapefruit-sized chunk of uranium, the *Triton* is the first vessel to carry two nuclear reactors, enabling her to generate the horsepower of a light cruiser. The whole world was given an example of her capabilities when on February 16, 1960, the nuclear submarine with a complement of 184 officers, crewmen, scientists and technicians, sailed from Groton, Connecticut, on a voyage duplicating Ferdinand Magellan's voyage around the world from 1519 to 1522. Unlike the Portuguese navigator's tedious three-year journey, the *Triton* circumnavigated the globe in eighty-four days, nineteen hours, and eight minutes. Moreover, she made the whole trip underwater, logging a total of 41,814 statute miles, partly surfacing only twice, once to transfer a sick seaman off Argentina and again off Spain to honor the country from which Magellan sailed.

After two and a half years of operation in which she covered more than 110,000 miles, the $109 million underwater giant was no longer considered a "first line" submarine. Chalking up a final first for her record, the *Triton* was decommissioned on May 3, 1969, and became the first United States nuclear submarine to be relegated to the "mothball fleet."

But bigger and better prospects are on the horizon. To be launched in 1978: the first of ten proposed supercolossal, nuclear-powered, strategic-missile submarines—the *Trident.* This behemoth will be nearly as long as *two* football fields, possess a sharklike fin or dorsal "sail" two stories tall and displace more than 16,000 tons, a weight five times greater than the first of her kind, Rickover's *Nautilus.* More than just a submarine, the *Trident* will be a fully mobile intercontinental-ballistic-missile launching field carrying twenty-four missiles, each with multiple nuclear warheads, capable of being launched from any sea or ocean in the world toward any target 6,000 miles away. As the mightiest submarine in the world, the *Trident* will run faster, deeper and more silent than any of her predecessors. Her nuclear reactor will propel the submarine some 400,000 miles—about eight years of cruising—without need to refuel. The proposed fleet of ten such submarines will cost an estimated $13 billion, but military officials feel this is a small price to pay for what has been described as the "mightiest deterrent to attack that mankind has yet devised—a weapon that can wreak devastation upon an enemy no matter how destructive his initial attack may be."

And after *Trident*, what?

CHAPTER 13

Piccard: To the Realm of Eternal Calm

On a quiet Thursday morning in August 1932, a sleepy-eyed, nine-year-old boy stood on a sun-dappled field in Switzerland and watched a huge balloon climb up into the clear blue sky until it disappeared. In the enclosed gondola beneath the balloon was the boy's father, Auguste Piccard, a physics professor who at that moment was setting a world record by soaring to the incredible height of 55,557 feet, higher than man had ever gone before in a lighter-than-air craft. But what had most impressed young Jacques Piccard about this historical event was his being awakened at one o'clock in the morning in preparation for it. As he watched his father set a world record for going up, little did the youngster realize that one day he would set a world record for going in the opposite direction.

The elder Piccard, a tall, large-framed man with a high-domed head framed by long, light, wavy hair, was not always interested in balloon ascensions. Long before he had worked out the problems of exploring the stratosphere, he had envisioned an underwater vessel that would take him to the most profound depths of the ocean. With growing interest he read of Dr. William Beebe and Otis Barton's efforts to break the depth barrier in their bathysphere. A month after Piccard set his high-altitude record, Beebe and Barton made their deepest dive of 1932, taking their steel sphere down to a record 2,200 feet off the southern coast of Bermuda. Piccard fully appreciated the significance of their efforts but he thought their methods both primitive and dangerous. On every dive their lives depended on the strength of a single, slender, steel umbilical cord. When their support vessel rode over a wave, the bathysphere received an amplified jolt. Surely, thought Piccard, this was an inadequate platform from which to make serious scientific observations. There had to be a safer, more practical method than that. How much better it would be if the underwater vessel had its own ballast and buoyancy systems. That way it could maintain stability at any depth simply by dropping ballast to achieve the desired degree of buoyancy.

Piccard lacked the means to put his ideas into practice until the late 1930s when the Belgian government's scientific research fund, *Fonds National de la Recherche Scientifique,* provided the financial assistance he needed. Piccard immediately set to work on his "bathyscaph," a word coined from Greek meaning "deep boat." Construction of the vessel he called the *FNRS-2* (*FNRS-1* was his stratosphere balloon) was interrupted by World War II, but by then the divers' compartment, a pressureproof, hollow steel sphere, had already been cast. Piccard completed the rest of the submersible after the war, suspending the seven-foot-diameter sphere beneath a sixty-five-foot-long, thin-walled, steel, dirigible-shaped float. The operating principle of the bathyscaph was quite unique. The float was the submersible's buoyancy chamber. But instead of being left empty and therefore capable of being crushed by underwater pressures, it would be filled with high-octane gasoline, an almost incompressible lighter-than-water liquid that would give the boat its lift. To make the boat sink, two silos contained iron pellets held in place by electromagnets. Descent could be stopped at any depth by touching a button that cut the current to the magnets and released a shower of pellets. After that the boat could go no deeper until it took on more ballast. Jettisoning all the pellets would allow the *FNRS-2* to float to the surface. The submersible's diving chamber was designed to withstand a pressure of 13,000 feet, the average depth of the oceans. But unfortunately, its sixty-five-foot-long buoyancy float was not as sturdily constructed. When the bathyscaph was completed in 1948, Piccard took it off the west coast of Africa for a series of unmanned test dives. The submersible went down to 4,600 feet, automatically dropped its ballast and floated to the surface. But during recovery by a surface vessel in choppy seas, the thin-walled steel float was so badly damaged that any further tests were out of the question.

Piccard realized that his design would have to be modified with a sturdier buoyancy float. That meant costly changes during a postwar period when money for funding ambitious scientific projects was not easy to obtain. But funds or not, there was no shortage of enthusiasm in the Piccard camp. For Auguste's son, now a six-foot six-inch, quiet-spoken, intense young man, had joined his father and more than matched his eagerness to get on with the challenging project. Jacques had been educated at schools in Belgium and Switzerland. While majoring in economics at the University of Geneva he interrupted his studies in 1944 to join an Alpine Infantry Division of the Free French Army. A year later he was discharged as a sergeant decorated with the Croix de Guerre. Completing his studies, Jacques graduated in 1946 and put in a year of graduate work. He then went to Trieste where he intended writing an economic history of the free state, but it was never completed. In November 1948, he was at his father's side watching the first experimental unmanned dive of the *FNRS-2* with its unfortunate ending. Also on hand to witness the demonstration of the revolutionary new diving vessel were representatives of the French Navy Underseas Research Group headed by Commandants Philippe Tailliez and Jacques-Yves Cousteau.

After the test the Piccard's went home to a barrage of newspaper publicity criticizing their "waste" of funds for the project. As a result, the moneylenders tightened their purse strings, and the Piccards were left with nothing more than a frustrated desire to somehow negotiate the critical impasse.

The means were found, but they came with an unexpected development. Despite France's involvement with a war in Indo-China, Cousteau engineered an agreement between the Belgian and French governments to build a new bathyscaph. Belgium turned over the *FNRS-2* to the French research group, and Piccard was invited to assist as a "scientific adviser" in the building of a new bathyscaph at the group's facility in Toulon. But primarily what the Frenchmen intended to do was simply add another stronger buoyancy float to the steel sphere already built for the *FNRS-2,* this one designed the way the French wanted it. As a result of differences of opinion, Piccard and the Frenchmen had a falling out. Within a year he quit the project and went to Switzerland and Italy to try and raise funds for a new bathyscaph in which he alone controlled how it would be built. In the surprisingly short time of only fourteen months, the professor and his thirty-one-year-old son, Jacques, raised the money and completed their third bathyscaph. Since most of the funds for its construction came from Switzerland, with most of the industrial and technical aid coming from Italy, the new submersible flew the Swiss flag and was named the *Trieste* for the city where much of it was built. This diving machine was a marked improvement over its predecessors. Although it resembled the French *FNRS-3* which was launched just two months before the *Trieste,* its steel sphere was forged rather than cast, therefore enabling it to withstand greater pressures and achieve deeper depths. The stronger buoyancy tank was now more streamlined like a boat's hull to facilitate towing and, like its French counterpart, it contained an entry shaft through the tank into the sphere so the divers could enter and leave while the boat was afloat. On the *FNRS-2* the divers entered the sphere by a hatch and had to remain inside for up to twelve hours while the bathyscaph was in the water having its float filled or emptied of high octane gasoline.

In August 1953, after making a short test dive to 300 feet off the Isle of Capri, Professor Piccard and Jacques descended to 3,500 feet off Ponza Island. It was a smooth dive into the black void illuminated only by the *Trieste*'s searchlights directed downward. Looking out through the viewport, Jacques told his father that he saw the bottom approaching. Suddenly the scene was obscured by a thick gray soup that reminded Jacques of wheat flour. They had hit bottom and gone through it, half burying the sphere in soft silt. The divers were not alarmed since they figured if they went in so easily they could just as easily lift out of it. But fifteen minutes later when Jacques touched the button that released some of their iron pellets, they did not float out. He dropped another load from the silos, and this time the silt disappeared as they rose swiftly to the surface.

A month later, after carefully studying the details of their earlier dives, they descended to the remarkable depth of 10,395 feet off Naples. The dive was a complete success. Since they were not in the business to break records, Professor Piccard went back to teaching and turned the bathyscaph over to Jacques.

Meanwhile the French were testing their bathyscaph, the *FNRS-3*, and had in fact reached a record 6,888 feet before the Piccards' deep dive. The following year, on February 15, 1954, Frenchmen George Houot and Pierre Willm climbed aboard the *FNRS-3* off the coast of Dakar, Africa, and descended io what was then man's deepest penetration of the ocean, 13,282 feet. On the bottom, over two and a half miles down, their sphere was squeezed by a total outside pressure of 68,000 pounds. In the yellow beam of their searchlight the men were surprised to see a six-and-a-half-foot-long, big-eyed shark that may have never known anything but this watery world of perpetual darkness. The men had planned to remain at this depth for three hours, but after only thirty-six minutes their stay was abruptly cut short when one of the electromagnets failed and released one of the 1,300-pound batteries carried both for a power supply and as a quick-release form of ballast. Seconds later the bathyscaph re-sounded with a dull rumble as another magnet cut loose and let a second big battery slide off into the sand. By then the boat was soaring toward the surface at a rapid rate, and Houot grabbed their ultrasound key and tapped out a dash-dash, the single letter *M*, meaning *Je monte*—"I ascend." To the surface tender and escorts this code letter was the signal to scatter so that the bathyscaph would not come up and crash into one of their keels. Seventy-five minutes after leaving the bottom, the *FNRS-3* surfaced 1,100 yards from her tender, and the men were picked up. "The *FNRS-3* will go no deeper than we have taken her," said her pilot, George Houot. "That is her habitat."

But the success of this dive started the French navy thinking about building a bigger and better bathyscaph, one strong enough to reach the bottom of the deepest hole in the oceans—the Challenger Deep in the Mariana Trench, 200 miles southwest of Guam. There vessels recorded depths ranging from 35,000 to 38,000 feet. Since the French navy was eager for a French bathyscaph to set that world record, it immediately began work on a super dive-boat to be called the *Archiméde.*

Periodically Jacques Piccard made shallow-water dives in the *Trieste* with scientists interested in studying marine life along the Mediterranean coast. But since a single dive meant purchasing 18,920 gallons of gasoline and nine tons of iron pellets for jettisoning (the latter at a cost of $866.25), Père Piccard and his son were not overly active with their boat. Then good fortune came along in the form of an American oceanographer named Dr. Robert Dietz.

Jacques had been invited to lecture in London when he met Dietz who worked for the U.S. Office of Naval Research. The two talked together, and it did not take Dietz long to realize that Piccard's *Trieste* was the answer to a whole new world of oceanographic research. Jacques told him, however, that he and his father had already offered to let the U.S. navy use the boat but that they were turned down. Dietz returned to Washington and waged a one-man campaign to persuade the navy that the *Trieste* was a boat they seriously needed. Meanwhile he raised enough money to bring the Piccards to America where they persuaded influential scientists that the submersible was an essential research tool and encouraged them to pressure the navy into purchasing it. The indirect approach worked. In the summer of 1957, American oceanographers evaluated the *Trieste* during a series of Mediterranean dives, and the following year, the U.S. navy bought it.

It was no secret that the French were building a super bathyscaph at Toulon to reach the bottom of the Challenger Deep. With their anticipated dive date two years off, the Americans decided to beat them to it with the *Trieste.* A new, more strongly forged sphere was quietly ordered from the Krupp Steel Works in Germany. There was little difference in size; however, the new cabin had five-inch-thick steel walls forged in three sections bonded together by epoxy resin. During a test dive of the new bathyscaph in deep water off San Diego, the pressure cracked one of the seals so loudly that the divers thought the sphere had imploded. But no further damage was done.

A date was set for the Challenger dive. Late in the summer of 1959 the submersible was made ready. In January 1960, while surface support vessels searched for days to echo-locate the deepest part of the Mariana Trench, the *Trieste* was making its long laborious tow from Guam, 200 miles away. Bad weather and high seas were hard on the cumbersome boat. By the time she reached the Trench, she looked more like a battle casualty than a vessel about to embark on the deepest dive into inner space. The rough crossing had demolished several of her instruments. Since replacement parts were unavailable, the divers would either have to do without or improvise. The assault on the abyss was to be attempted by Jacques Piccard and a young U.S. navy submarine officer, Lieut. Don Walsh, who was in charge of the *Trieste.* The two men checked out the boat as best they could. An hour before the scheduled dive, the searching surface craft finally found the deepest part of the Trench and dropped marker flares.

The *Trieste* was towed into position. Walsh and Piccard climbed aboard and dogged tight the hatch. Right on schedule at 8 A.M., they began their dive. Since the submersible's tachometer that told the vessel's rate of descent and ascent had been destroyed in the crossing, Piccard had to use his watch and depth gauge to get this information. The dive was to last for nine hours, with a planned descent rate of three feet per second to 26,000 feet, two feet per second to 30,000 feet, then one foot per second the rest of the way to the bottom to assure them of a soft landing.

As the surface light faded from a bright blue-green to the deep royal blue marking the outer limits of the abyss, the bathyscaph began its long journey into what Jacque's father,

Auguste Piccard, called, "the realm of eternal calm." The two men were cramped and uncomfortable in the tight confines of the sphere. Outside their Plexiglas portholes the water was black. They reached Beebe's region of perpetual night and went beyond, without fanfare past 13,282 feet, Willm and Houot's deepest penetration of the ocean with the *FNRS-3*; and then they were at more than twice that depth. . . . "Four five zero zero fathoms," intoned Piccard, intently watching the depth gauge. Their rate of descent was slowed to two feet per second now. Then, at 30,000 feet, their rate was slowed to one foot per second.

Suddenly, at 32,500 feet a resounding crack startled the men. They checked carefully but found nothing wrong. Since everything seemed intact, they continued on. Finally, five hours and six minutes after they left the surface, they reached a soft mud bottom at the incredible depth of 35,800 feet—over seven miles down! In the yellow glow of their floodlights they saw a member of the flatfish family swimming around nonchalantly where the water pressure was exerting a stupendous squeeze of over seven tons per square inch! This was the first verification that active fish could exist at such depths. Walsh radioed the news that they had reached the bottom of the Challenger Deep. After a short while they began their ascent up through the seven miles of water between them and the surface, and at 4:56 P.M., four minutes ahead of schedule, the hydronauts broke through the undulating silver mirror into the bright sunshine world of air.

Observers cheered when the *Trieste* appeared on the surface. But as time passed and neither man emerged, there was growing concern for their safety. Meanwhile, on the *Trieste*, Piccard and Walsh found their entry shaft through the gasoline envelope completely flooded. For twenty minutes they were trapped in the sphere until the column of water could be ejected by compressed air. The cause was later found to be a cracked Plexiglas port in their outer hatch cover—the sound they had heard near the bottom.

Word flashed around the world that the *Trieste* had reached the bottom of the Challenger Deep. Then, several days later, it was learned that there had been a slight miscalculation. The *Trieste's* depth gauge was set for fresh-water and had not been recalibrated for saltwater. While they had actually reached 35,800 feet, their gauge read 37,800 feet. Sonar probes had reported depths ranging from 35,000 to 38,600 feet. Somewhere in the Mariana Trench there was still a hole at least a half mile deeper than the *Trieste* had gone. The error took nothing away from the outstanding achievement. The two men were flown to Washington where President Eisenhower awarded Piccard the navy's Distinguished Public Service Award and Walsh the Legion of Merit.

On April 10, 1963, the nuclear-powered U.S. submarine *Thresher* with her compliment of 129 men was lost on a routine test dive 220 miles off the Massachusett's coast. All resources of the United States navy were used to search for the missing sub. Modern research vessels with special sonar equipment and underwater cameras joined the massive operation. In San Diego, the *Trieste* was loaded aboard a freighter that headed for the site. Four months after the sinking, following repeated dives, the *Trieste* found the *Thresher's* grave in 8,400 feet of water. Twisted steel debris was scattered so far and wide that one of the bathyscaph's pilots said it resembled a junkyard. The 300-foot-long submarine had imploded from water pressure of up to two tons per square inch forcing one of the vessel's many valves.

By the end of 1963, the U.S. navy had built and launched an improved version of Piccard's bathyscaph, the *Trieste II.* The new vessel was bigger, better powered and had more advanced instrumentation.

Jacques Piccard served as a consultant to the U.S. Office of Naval Research until 1966. Shortly after he was honored for his Challenger dive, however, he returned to Switzerland to begin work on the idea of a new diving boat that his father had discussed with him in October 1953. "With modern kinds of steel and even with Plexiglas," said Auguste Piccard, "one hull could be made lighter than water that would still descend to respectable depths—intermediate depths. If it's lighter than water, we don't need a float. . . ." Thus was born the idea for a middle-range diving boat, a "mesoscaph." Initial designs were drawn, but finding a backer was another problem. When Jacques learned that Switzerland was planning a national exposition to be held in Lausanne in 1964, he suggested that the mesoscaph be built for the affair so that visitors could tour the bottom of Lake Geneva in it. The exposition's steering committee liked the idea, funds were made available for the boat's construction, and in 1963, Jacques launched the mesoscaph *Auguste Piccard,* named for his father, who had died the previous year. Capable of diving to a depth of 3,500 feet, the 165-ton underwater boat was cylindrically shaped with a conning tower in the stern. Outside she looked like a submarine; inside like a commercial airliner. Electrically powered propellers were mounted aft, large hydraulically controlled dive fins forward. The boat could carry forty passengers who sat along both sides of the wide cabin compartment in comfortable swivel seats, each with its own porthole. Sixty-one floodlights along the keel illuminated the scenes viewers would see while an externally mounted television camera showed them how the submarine looked from outside. The fish in Lake Geneva must have been startled to see this Cyclopean metal monster with its forty glass eyes descend among them nine times a day. But in the course of the Convention the mesoscaph made 13,000 dives and took 33,000 people to the bottom of Lake Geneva in over 300 feet of water without mishap.

When the Convention was over, Piccard's backers put the mesoscaph up for sale, asking $2 million, far more than it cost to build. No one was particularly interested in paying that much for a used mesoscaph, even if it was Switzerland's first and only submarine. Eventually, however, the price fell to a more reasonable $100,000, and the *Auguste Piccard* was sold to a large American company. Presently it is being used by offshore oil interests in the Arabian Sea.

One morning in 1965, Piccard was contacted by a representative of the Grumman Aircraft Engineering Company (now Grumman Aerospace Corporation) who asked if he would be interested in working with them. A meeting was arranged, and negotiations began in New York where Piccard learned that the Grumman Company, which was then working on the lunar module for the Apollo missions, wanted to get into submarine research. This was generally true for most of the big American aircraft manufacturers, who were anticipating reductions in the role of warplanes, with expanding interests in the sea. While keeping most of its personnel involved with aircraft matters, the company was opening up a submarine division to be called Grumman Ocean Systems. Would he, they asked, care to suggest some worthwhile projects for their new division?

Piccard had three in mind, ideas he had been considering for several years. They chose his most ambitious project—a mesoscaph code-named the PX-15, built to explore the depths of the Gulf Stream. A five-year collaboration was agreed upon, and once the project's goals were clarified, construction of the mesoscaph, PX-15, was begun in Monthey, Switzerland, in March 1967.

Piccard had estimated the cost of the boat at $1 million, but by the time it was built and fully equipped, the cost went to $2.5 million. To help defray expenses, Grumman sought to interest other members of the scientific world in contributing to the project. Piccard proposed to spend one month drifting at different depths in the Gulf Stream as the current moved northward along the East Coast of the United States at a rate of up to five knots. It would be an unprecedented opportunity to study current conditions, marine life and the capacity of a crew to live in virtual isolation for a prolonged period of time. The latter was of particular interest to the National Aeronautics and Space Administration, (NASA) who saw it as a significant correlation to the space program. The Naval Oceanographic Office saw the project as a possible means of learning something about the mysterious Deep Scattering Layer. Ever since modern man has learned how to bounce sonic and ultrasonic waves between the ocean's surface and its bottom, he has been puzzled by a strange phenomenon. Sometimes, at different depths, mysterious layers appear in the water mass that reflect these signals and give the impression of a bottom where none exists. Through the years countless scientific efforts have tried to learn what the layers consist of, but so far the only answers we have are theoretical. Since the layers rise closer to the surface at night and descend to between 1,500 and 4,000 feet during the day, scientists have speculated that they may be dense thermal layers or great concentrations of marine life, possibly plankton, squid or small fish. So far, however, the theories have never been proved. The navy felt that the *PX-15*'s Drift Mission would be a good way to learn the answer.

In early 1968 the *PX-15* was completed. The 130-ton, fifty-foot-long, ten-foot-beam steel mesoscaph was designed to operate to depths of 2,000 feet, with a safety factor of two, meaning that it could withstand pressures up to 4,000 feet. She was driven by four 25-horsepower, direct-current motors externally mounted with propellers on the vessel's four corners. These would propel the *PX-15* up or down, forward or backward. The electricity supplied by twenty-five tons of lead-acid batteries in the keel provided enough energy for the submersible to remain submerged for extended periods. Buoyancy was controlled by external ballast tanks that could be filled or emptied by compressed air. An additional five tons of iron-shot ballast could be dropped for an immediate ascent in an emergency. A conning tower on the bow contained the entry hatch.

Living accommodations inside the spacious hull would support an eight-man crew for up to six weeks. Special chemical air-scrubbing equipment provided a constantly reusable air supply. There was ample room inside the mesoscaph's cabin for a considerable volume of scientific instruments, and since the hull was lined with twenty-five viewports, the submersible would make an excellent platform from which to carry out subsea observations and tests. In honor of the multitalented man of science who first made a true study of the Gulf Stream and had a chart of this "river in the Sea" published in 1770, Piccard appropriately renamed his new mesoscaph the *Ben Franklin.*

After exhaustive tests in Switzerland, the mesoscaph was shipped to West Palm Beach, Florida, where more trial runs were made and the submersible was finally readied for her Drift Mission. Some two thousand applicants wrote Piccard asking to be taken along on the month-long journey through the depths of the Gulf Stream. But only a select six-man crew was picked to go, each man a specialist in his own field. Grumman representative and captain in charge of the mesoscaph was ex-submariner, Don Kazimer, whose many years of sea service and experience in handling the submersible qualified him for this responsible job. His adjutant, navigator-engineer Erwin Aebersold, was the builder-designer of the control centers for both the *Auguste Piccard* and the *Ben Franklin* and a close Swiss friend of Jacques Piccard. U.S. Navy Oceanographic Office representative, Frank Busby, an oceanographer and civilian research submarine expert, would be evaluating the *Ben Franklin* for features applicable to future navy and civilian submersibles. Acoustics specialist and oceanographer Ken Haigh, on detached duty from the British Royal Navy for two years with the U.S. Navy, would record the characteristics of sound-wave transmissions at depth. Seeking information that might help similar teams manning space stations, NASA engineer Chet May would keep count on the viral and bacterial growth aboard while testing and observing the others during the month-long isolation. Last of the six-man crew was Jacques Piccard with what he considered the somewhat pompous title of "Expedition Leader."

On July 14, 1969, the navy support vessel *Privateer,* which would follow on the surface and maintain radio contact with the mesoscaph throughout the mission, towed the *Ben Franklin* thirty miles off West Palm Beach into the main flow of the Gulf Stream. At 8:54 P.M. the submersible cleared the surface and descended for an hour to 1,500 feet, hovering thirty feet above the white sand bottom where the reduced current carried them northward at about one-tenth knot. Outside their viewports the mesoscaph's searchlights pierced the exceptionally clear water where only a few plankton and shrimp welcomed their arrival.

As the underwater voyagers soon learned, the Gulf Stream's depths were not as proliferous with fish as they had suspected. In fact the entire trip proved rather uneventful with the exception of some unusual highlights.

At 6:09 A.M. on the morning of their fourth day, while drifting at a depth of 832 feet, a strange incident occurred.

Piccard had just turned in and the others were occupied elsewhere when Frank Busby, who was working in the aft laboratory, glimpsed something through the porthole. As he rushed to the window, he saw a six-foot-long broadbill swordfish swimming agitatedly back and forth beside the submersible. A companion fish lurked in the background. Abruptly the nervous broadbill squared off and zoomed in to attack the 130-ton mesoscaph, striking the steel hull just below one of the Plexiglas portholes with enough of a wallop to be heard clearly by Busby and Ken Haigh. Busby hurried forward for his camera, but by the time he returned the attackers had departed.

Periodically the submersible was taken up to shallower depths or dived down to the bottom, always with the scientists observing and recording what they felt and saw while highly sophisticated instruments measured and recorded data. At times the bottom appeared rough and uneven. Once what appeared to be a general deposit of manganese nodules was in reality ripple marks in the sand. At a depth of 1,320 feet the bottom was quite broken up with long strange traverse marks as if made by moving objects. The keels of submarines? wondered Piccard. Unlikely, he decided, since it was too deep for anything but research submersibles.

On Wednesday, July 23, Piccard awakened to find that during the night, while they were drifting deep in the Stream parallel to the Georgia coast, the mesoscaph was caught up in a series of internal waves. Although the crew felt nothing, the *Ben Franklin*'s depth graphs recorded that she rode waves that took them up 100 feet in twelve minutes followed by a rapid descent of 165 feet in two minutes—all occurring within a water mass moving northeastward at a little over two knots.

Off Charleston, South Carolina, the fickle Gulf Stream suddenly ejected them. Caught in one of the many eddies that swirl off the main current the same way tornadoes might spin off from a hurricane, the mesoscaph was forced to surface. As it slowly ascended, Piccard happened to look out the porthole and, in a rare moment of absolute water clarity, he saw the sunlight reflecting on surface waves through 300 feet of water. It was also during this period that the men saw several large sharks and a barracuda, more fish than they had seen in all the previous twelve days of their drift.

Preserving their isolation on the surface by keeping their hatch closed, the crew maintained radio contact with their support vessel while it towed them thirty miles back into the middle of the Stream. On course once more the *Ben Franklin* descended leisurely into the depths, leveling off at 1,900 feet. There again, as usual during the deep dives, the temperature of the noninsulated cabin reflected that of the colder water surrounding the mesoscaph, this time dropping to a chilly fifty degrees. To keep warm the scientists did calisthenics, a rather tiring solution to an uncomfortable condition that bothered them periodically during the entire trip.

On August 5, at a depth of 650 feet, they saw their first large shoal of fish. Identified as *Thunnus alalunga,* longfin tuna, they accompanied the mesoscaph for almost a day and a half. When the submersible blew one of its ballast tanks, the school of tuna rushed into the column of air rising to the surface and frolicked like youngsters in a bubble bath.

At eight o'clock on the morning of August 14, approximately 300 miles southeast of Halifax, Nova Scotia, the *Ben Franklin* surfaced, and the Drift Mission was officially over. Although the scientists had failed to find the mysterious Deep Scattering Layer, the expedition was considered a complete success. In thirty-one days the mesoscaph had covered over 1,500 nautical miles, recording a tremendous amount of oceanographic data that would take months, possibly years, to evaluate. Hundreds of hours of magnetic tapes including those with sonic "maps" of the ocean floor, 848 pairs of bottom photographs and 65,000 others made by automatic cameras filming activities inside the mesoscaph for NASA had to be analyzed.

While her crew was flown home in a Grumman Company airplane, the *Ben Franklin* was towed at a somewhat more leisurely pace back to New York where she underwent modifications for future ocean research projects. Mechanical arms were added so that marine and geological specimens could be collected, a special core drill would take bottom samples, and an air lock would enable divers to leave and enter the mesoscaph at any desired depth.

While continuing as a consultant to Grumman Oceans Systems, Piccard plans and designs new submersible research vessels of the future, concerned now more than ever with the growing problems of preserving our pollution-endangered oceans. He feels that if the conquest of the sea is a sign of mankind's progress, that same progress threatens our ecological systems, suffocating life in the sea as well as on land. "Earth, with its population of nearly four billion, is a small, self-sufficient capsule traveling in space," says Piccard. "If we want it to continue its journey without mishap, we must keep it clean and livable . . . this means we must give even more consideration to what we put into [the oceans] than to the wealth their exploitation affords."

Whatever new food or energy resources are yet to be found within the unknown depths of the oceans, you can be sure that one of the men leading the way to these new frontiers will be Jacques Piccard, in one of his marvelous diving machines.

CHAPTER 14

Cousteau: Master of the Deep

"UFO SIGHTED AT SEA," read the newspaper caption. The following story told about a skin diver who saw what he described as a saucer-shaped aircraft hovering over the surface of the sea off Catalina Island. According to the eyewitness the craft seemed to be sucking up seawater through a transparent pipe. The story ended as do most such sightings with the UFO marshaling its forces and soaring off into the blue. Then, in 1959, in a more remote part of the world, another saucer was sighted at sea.

This time a scuba diver was making his way along the bottom in sixty-five feet of crystal clear water off the West Indies island of Guadeloupe when he saw a sight that started his adrenal glands pumping. Coming toward him just over the tops of the sea fans was a large, yellow, saucer-shaped object. It did not stop until it almost reached the diver, who suddenly threw up his hand as if to ward it off. Surprisingly, the saucer came to an immediate halt, hovering in the water in front of the man. Two shiny discs seemed to be observing him with alien curiosity. The diver gestured to his left as if hoping to make the apparition go away. Instead, the saucer quickly sideslipped to the left. The diver waved his right hand. Obediently the saucer darted quickly to the right, pausing near a tall, vaselike sponge. Momentarily the man seemed undecided, then he did a very strange thing. He held up his hands, palms inward, and motioned with his fingers. The saucer advanced. The diver continued to beckon like a crewman bringing a plane into a carrier deck. The saucer obeyed, slowly advancing until it was hovering inches over the sponge without disturbing it. Then, with an abrupt sign of dismissal from the diver, the craft tilted back, pointed its glassy eyes upward and with an audible hum it darted off into the blue beyond the reef. The diver in turn swam back to his ship.

The man who appeared to have been directing UFO traffic was inventor, author, and underwater pioneer, Jacques-Yves Cousteau, who had just returned from observing a trial run of his newest invention, a two-man jet-propelled Diving Saucer. The miniature submarine was designed to explore the depths that range out to the Continental Ridge, the sloping offshore shelf that extends down to about 600 feet of water before it drops off abruptly into the abyss. Cousteau wanted an underwater vehicle that was small, highly maneuverable and capable of complete mobility. It meant taking the best of what had been done before and shrinking it into a small, light, hydrodynamically shaped hull that could be propelled in any direction with the least effort and the most efficiency. Between the dream and the accomplishment lay a multitude of problems. But putting his inventive mind to work on such matters was something Cousteau had been doing since he was a boy.

Born in St. Andre-de-Cubzac, France, in 1910, he was eleven years old when one day he found himself in possession of a set of blueprints for building a 200-ton marine crane. Young Cousteau looked them over, then built a four-foot model. Cousteau's father, a lawyer, was so proud of his son's handiwork that he showed the model to an engineer friend. The man examined it closely and asked who had helped the youngster. "No one," replied Jacques' father. "He did it all by himself."

The engineer then told Père Cousteau that he could be justly proud of his son because the boy had added an element that was not in the blueprints and it had improved the crane to such a degree that he thought the part was patentable.

It made little difference whether it was a marine crane or a toy boat; young Jacques Cousteau was interested in all matters nautical. After schooling in New York he entered the Brest French Naval Academy and, in 1933, graduated second in his class. Following a round-the-world cruise on a French navy training ship and a tour of duty commanding a naval base in Shanghai, Cousteau transferred to a naval aviation school in France. Before completing his training as an aviator, however, he was involved in a serious auto accident that crushed his ribs and broke both his arms. One of his shattered arms became so badly infected that the surgeon wanted to amputate it to save his life. But Cousteau objected so adamantly to losing his arm that the doctor resorted to saving it with drugs instead. Eight months after the accident he was still unable to move more than one finger. Hoping to exercise it into shape, Cousteau transferred back to the fleet and was stationed in Toulon where he spent many hours each day swimming in the Mediterranean with his friends Philippe Tailliez and Frédéric Dumas.

About sixty miles up the coast a well-known American writer named Guy Gilpatric was practicing a new sport he called "goggling." Around 1929, Gilpatric grew so curious to see what things looked like underwater that he plugged the ventilating holes in an old pair of flying goggles with putty, painted over it and went down for a look. After finding that he had made himself a wonderful pair of windows into the sea and delighted in the fantastic new world he saw there, Gilpatric wrote books and magazine articles expounding on this marvelous sport of goggling. In 1936, Cousteau heard about the sport from Dumas, and before long the three friends acquired some South Sea island–type pearl-diving goggles and found themselves as enraptured with the sport as Gilpatric. Soon Cousteau was experimenting with ways for a diver to stay longer underwater. Although his efforts were interrupted by World War II, the ideas were never far from his thoughts. When France fell, Cousteau joined the French underground where his distinguished service earned him the *Légion d'Honneur* and the *Croix de Guerre.* Despite the Occupation he continued diving in the Mediterranean, often under the very noses of the Germans. While they considered him a harmless eccentric, Cousteau noted their naval movements and passed the information on to Allied intelligence.

As his diving progressed, Cousteau began using a self-contained apparatus patented by a French naval captain, Yves le Prieur. It consisted of a steel cylinder of compressed air carried on the diver's back with a hose connecting it to a full face mask. The constant air flow was regulated by turning a valve. Since there was no way for the unit to maintain the same air pressure as the surrounding water pressure, it was safe only for shallow-water dives. Moreover, the constant flow of air meant that much was wasted, limiting the diver's time underwater. Cousteau felt that the Prieur equipment could be greatly improved with a valve that adjusted automatically to the water pressure and gave a diver air only when he inhaled. But how could he obtain such a device?

When someone told him that an engineer named Emile Gagnan might be able to help, Cousteau obtained forged papers and went to Paris to see him. Cousteau explained his needs, and Gagnan showed him a special valve he had designed for controlling the flow of fuel to vehicles powered by cooking gas. Combining the valve with a few minor components, Gagnan built the first demand regulator. On a freezing day in January 1943, the two men drove to an isolated stretch of the Marne River near Paris to try it out. Cousteau donned his air cylinder coupled to the Gagnan regulator and submerged in the icy water. For the first time he got air only when he inhaled, and no matter how deep he went, the air pressure remained the same, the regulator adjusting itself automatically to the surrounding water pressure. This occasion marked man's first completely free and untethered step into inner space. With a few small modifications to the hose and mouthpiece, Cousteau gave the world the Aqualung.

Toward the end of World War II, he tried without success to interest the Allied navies in his new invention. Returning to France, Cousteau teamed up with his old friends Tailliez, Dumas and others to form the first French Undersea Research Unit. There was a whole new underwater world to explore, and these young men were anxious to begin. When his naval duties interfered with his new undertaking, Cousteau requested and got a leave of absence from the navy to pursue his underwater work. A nonprofit corporation supported by the contributions of friends led to his acquiring the *Calypso,* a 360-ton British minesweeper which he turned into a highly sophisticated, floating, marine research laboratory. On this ship he and his friends of the French Navy Group for Undersea Study and Research set forth filming and exploring their way through the Mediterranean and the Red Sea, unearthing and excavating Greek and Roman treasure argosies. In 1953, he wrote of these adventures in a book, *The Silent World,* and filmed them for a documentary of the same title. Both book and film were immediate successes throughout the world.

In the following years Cousteau broadened his investigations, yearning always to penetrate deeper into that mysterious blue realm of inner space. In 1951, while the *Calypso* was in the Red Sea, and her divers were skimming down the vertical face of a deep reef, they paused at the limit of their range as did Beebe, looking down through the many fathoms of clear blue water, stopped from going further by the barrier of the depths. Cousteau pondered what a diver needed to let him pass into this forbidden zone. First he considered encasing him in a suit of pressure proof armor but almost immediately rejected this idea because the armor would prevent complete mobility. This led to his considering a small two-man vehicle employing a principle of locomotion that would give it as much maneuverability as an unencumbered diver. After threshing out the problems with his technicians Cousteau had them build the Diving Saucer, a tangerine-shaped hull consisting of two 3/4" steel half-shells six and a half feet in diameter capable of withstanding the crushing force of 3,300 feet of water. Three hulls were made. On a test in which the first hull was to be lowered empty into the ocean, the crane's cable broke and the Saucer hull, ballasted by a heavy piece of iron on a thirty-foot chain, plummeted to the bottom in 3,300 feet of water. There was no doubt that the hull was strong enough for that depth, because years later the *Calypso* was able to echo-locate the Saucer still intact and floating thirty feet above the bottom on its chain tether.

Hull number two was outfitted, this one named the *Denise* in honor of the wife of the group's dedicated electrical engineer, Jean Mollard. The Diving Saucer or *La Soucoupe*, as the French called it, was highly innovational. The flattened-sphere steel hull was concealed inside a bright yellow, streamlined, outer fiber-glass jacket. Instead of propellers the *Diving Saucer-2* was driven by an electrical water pump that operated two hydro jets, one on each side of the forward section of the Saucer. Seawater was jetted swiftly out through the two hydraulically operated nozzles. Power came from five batteries hanging between the flooded inner and outer hulls. The Saucer had no rudder or diving planes; it was controlled entirely by the position of the jet nozzles which could be swiveled in a full circle. To turn either to starboard or to port, the flow was decreased on the side toward which the submarine was to turn.

Inside the pressurized cabin, the pilot and his passenger lay prone on comfortable foam-rubber mattresses. A continuous instrument panel surrounded them with barometer, compass, depth gauges, ammeters, hydraulic pump, sonar equipment and a rebreathing system that removed the carbon dioxide from their cabin air and replenished the oxygen. Before each passenger was a small Plexiglas observation port. Outside lights illuminated the area in front of the Saucer. The vessel's logbook was a tape recorder. As a safety precaution the cabin equipment included two Aqua-Lungs so that if the *DS-2* was ever trapped on the bottom, the men could release compressed air from one of the cylinders until the cabin pressure equaled the outside water pressure, enabling them to open the hatch and ascend with the Lungs to the surface. Ballast consisted of a fifty-pound chunk of pig iron that was dropped after each dive. A reservoir of mercury controlled the submersible's diving angle. By pumping the heavy metallic element to a forward or an aft chamber, the pilot could change the Saucer's diving angle much as did the sliding weight in Wilhelm Bauer's *Sea Diver*. This method, however, was a bit more reliable.

After Cousteau saw the Diving Saucer in action with his Aqua-Lung, he and pilot Albert Falco decided to see how well the *DS-2* functioned at the extremes of her depth range. The hydronauts entered the top hatch, closed and battened it down. Cousteau started the rebreathing apparatus; oxygen hissed into the cabin. The men made themselves comfortable on their foam "diving couches" and looked out through their individual Plexiglas ports as the crane lifted the *DS-2* over the side and deposited her gently on the rolling surface of the sea. The tackle was released; Falco turned on the hydraulic plant. Water rushed out the port and starboard jets, and the Saucer moved forward. A soft blue glow lit the inside as the submersible tilted for a power glide down through the depths at 1.5 knots, the roiled sea limiting visibility to about fifty feet. Falco turned on the sonar, whose three transducers were pointed up, down and straight ahead, to echo-probe what they could not see.

Bottom dropped away from the *DS-2*, but at about 250 feet the Saucer suddenly stopped descending. It seemed to be caught and suspended in space by some invisible force. Falco prepared to take on water ballast, but Cousteau told him to wait. He realized that they were simply floating on a thermal layer of colder, much denser water. Before long the Saucer cooled and lost its buoyancy; once again it descended down through the colder water. Inside, feeling the chill, the men donned sweaters.

At 360 feet the Saucer neared bottom, but something was wrong. It reacted sluggishly. Falco shut off the jets. In the silence they heard the rattle of escaping bubbles. One of the batteries outside the hull had short-circuited. Gas pressure had cracked its waterproof housing and was escaping. Although not immediately dangerous to the men, Cousteau ordered the Saucer back to the surface. Falco dropped the fifty pounds of external ballast. The Saucer began rising but then it began to sink again. Cousteau stripped the safety tape off a lever and pulled it to disengage a 330-pound emergency weight. This time the *DS-2* floated swiftly to the surface.

The *Calypso* sailed for the Mediterranean. New batteries and battery boxes were built for them at Marseilles. Falco and Cousteau tried the deep dive again, this time off the island of Corsica. At a leisurely pace the *DS-2* glided down through the blue, paralleling the steep gray slope of the featureless bottom, then at 400 feet they approached a black horizon. It was the end of the shelf; the beginning of the Continental Slope. Falco brought the Saucer to a soft landing two feet from the drop-off. For a moment the two men looked with awe at the sharp demarcation line between the shelf and the abyss. Then, after checking all their equipment, Falco turned on the jets, and they went over the edge. Mercury was levered into the forward cylinder, the Saucer tilted forward thirty-five degrees, and they glided down the steep slope like a slow-motion skier. Except for an occasional octopus or school of small fish, there was little to be seen at these depths. They continued downward for so long that Cousteau felt like an amateur yogi standing on his head. Two hours from the time they left the surface, the *DS-2* touched down at 1,000 feet. And there, in the silence of a watery world over three times deeper than man could go with the Aqua-Lung, Falco and Cousteau toasted their successful dive with a bottle of wine.

After a while they levered mercury aft, dropped their weight and began a gradual ascent, steering the Saucer in ever widening S curves upward. At 500 feet they saw rock spires rising from the bottom like church steeples. In a playful mood Falco sent the Saucer weaving through them, spinning and twisting, sometimes even caroming off a spire like a billiard ball bouncing off on a reverse course. Cousteau turned on powerful lights and filmed the kaleidoscopic colors of marine life festooning the spires, then they parked the Saucer at 200 feet while they ate their lunch. When Falco complained of a headache, Cousteau tested their cabin air and found that they were breathing 2 percent carbon dioxide. Back to the surface they went after their four-hour tour of the slope. The dive was a complete success; the tests were over.

From 1960 to 1964 the *DS-2* made some 130 dives for Cousteau and scientists doing underwater research work in the Mediterranean. In September 1962, off Marseilles, Cousteau and his underwater research group put down history's first manned habitat on the floor of the ocean. It was called Continental Shelf Station No. 1 or Conshelf 1.

In the habitat's cylindrical cabin, Albert Falco and Claude

Wesley remained under 35 feet of water continuously for a week, emerging during the day to perform underwater tasks for up to five hours in depths down to 85 feet. This successful achievement prepared the way for Cousteau's Continental Shelf Station No. 2 (Conshelf 2), the first human colony on the ocean floor. While surface ships supported the project, five Aqua-Lung divers that Cousteau called "Oceanauts" established an underwater community on Sha'ab Rummi (Roman Reef) twenty-five miles from Port Sudan. The sunken colony consisted of four main buildings and eight auxiliary structures. Five of the marine research team lived in the main habitat for a month under 35 feet of water, working up to five hours a day in depths to 100 feet without decompression. Two experienced divers operated out of an advanced station with a compressed helium and oxygen atmosphere for a week in 85 feet of water, emerging to dive on compressed air down to 363 feet without decompression. The community's underwater taxi was the *DS-2* with her own dome-shaped hanger on the bottom of the sea. Like the vessel it housed, the hanger was unique. To facilitate launching the sub, it was open on its underside, the sea kept out by compressed air. The *DS-2* hung from the center of the slightly pointed dome on an electrical winch that would lower her through the floor opening into the water. While she was hooked to the ceiling, however, a folding floor covered the hanger's lower opening so that mechanics could service and recharge her batteries in comfort.

Before arriving at Roman Reef, Cousteau had tried the *DS-2* in the Gulf of Aden, diving on a rock reef called Arab Shoal. As the Saucer patrolled the reef she picked up an escort of some thirty large, bold sharks who kept her company throughout the dive.

When four of the *Calypso* divers swam down with an antishark cage to photograph the sharks at night, they found themselves the immediate center of attraction for an audience of some seventy circling sharks. Since all four men could not fit into the shark cage, the leader pushed the least experienced of the divers inside while he and his three companions sat back-to-back atop the cage and rode it to the surface, fending off the attacking sharks with cameras and floodlights. After they boarded the ship safely, someone suggested that it would make interesting movie footage if the DS-2 could be filmed amidst the maddened shark pack. So Falco and Cousteau glided down into the melee of sharks in the Diving Saucer while two of the divers descended with the movie camera and powerful floodlights in the antishark cage.

The performance started as planned, with the glittering-eyed sharks swimming alongside the DS-2 while the cinematographers took their pictures. Suddenly, however, Cousteau and Falco were surprised to see both photographers drop their camera equipment and start dancing wildly around the inside of their cage, slapping at their ankles and generally behaving in a most bizarre way. Swirling around the men were what appeared to be swarms of white gnats. The divers signaled to be hauled up promptly and, by the time Falco and Cousteau were taken back aboard the Calypso, they saw the decks red with blood. The men were being treated for small vicious wounds all over their ankles, the only areas left exposed by their diving suits. The miniature attackers were "sea mosquitoes," tiny plankton crustations thought to be isopods with bites as vicious as tiny piranhas.

During the five-minute decompression stop just before reaching the surface, one of the divers said that he was so tortured by the voracious sea mosquitoes that he was tempted to open the cage gate and take his chances with the sharks.

Considering these experiences in the Gulf of Aden, Cousteau built antishark grilles around the entries to all the colony's habitats. The sharks, however, proved less numerous than expected and confined their activities to the outskirts of the colony.

Early one morning, at 2 A.M., Cousteau and Falco decided to take a submarine cruise in the DS-2 to see what was happening on the ocean floor at that hour. As the Saucer jetted out into the surrounding blackness, Cousteau switched on the headlights. Two patrolling sharks moved out of their way. The gray rocky escarpment dropped from beneath them. The down-looking sonar traced an uneven slope until they reached 160 feet below the surface, the bottom of the reef.

Falco landed momentarily to adjust their buoyancy. Then

he turned on the jets, pumped mercury into the forward cylinder, and they tilted over the sharp edge of the drop-off to glide in a slow graceful zigzag down the rocky face of the cliff. At 200 feet the water seemed as thick as soup with concentrations of microorganisms that attracted great numbers of squid and small fish. Could this be the mysterious Deep Scattering Layer? Cousteau believed it was.

At 325 feet the men found a horizontal ledge from six to thirty feet wide that ran along the wall like some prehistoric highway. Surface sonar had not picked up this feature before, but it had been sighted on every dive in the Red Sea. As the Saucer moved along the shelf, Cousteau theorized that it might be an ancient seashore marking the water level eons of years in the past during one of the glacial periods when seas were much lower.

Four hundred feet down the *DS-2* again came to a halt on a paper-thin invisible barrier between hot and cold bodies of water. Gradually as the submarine cooled, it sank of its own accord into water sixteen degrees colder than that just above it.

At 900 feet the *DS-2* leveled off over a sloping sand bottom dotted with huge boulders. Visibility was 100 feet, and in the glare of the headlights the men saw great numbers of squid, spiny lobsters and, at the base of a cliff, a bed of crabs carpeting the bottom by the millions. Cousteau was struck by the irony that just above them in the lands bordering the Indian Ocean there were millions of half-starved people living in a world where man was reaching for the moon but had not yet learned how to fish these crabs.

At dawn Falco dropped their fifty-five pound ballast weight, and the *DS-2* soared back up the cliff face to the green waters of the living reef.

Thirty-two days after populating Conshelf 2 and carrying out complex underwater research work on Roman Reef, the Oceanauts returned to the surface. Not only had they set a record for man living and working underwater, but it was the first time that a submarine had ever been housed, serviced and operated from a hanger on the bottom of the sea. Cousteau felt that when future test installations moved into deeper water, supplying Oceanauts with an atmosphere of hydrogen and oxygen would make it possible to establish a settlement at minus 800 feet. "From this station," he said, "the Oceanauts may swim to a depth of 1,200 feet. That will be the ultimate Conshelf station. We will then have crossed the Dropoff Line to the Continental Slope. On to Conslope One!" But before these plans materialized, problems of a more serious nature loomed on the horizon.

In 1967, Cousteau, joined by his son, Philippe, who had first been strapped into an Aqua-Lung and shown the underwater world of the Mediterranean when he was four years old, set off with a team of scientists aboard the *Calypso* on a six-year diving and filming odyssey through the seas of the world. Television audiences everywhere thrilled to their adventures. But in their travels the underwater explorers saw more than they had anticipated. To Cousteau, who but thirty years before had pioneered scuba diving in a sea where all forms of marine life were richly abundant, it was discouraging to find that this was all changing. Industrial pollution and man's wholesale destruction of marine life were taking their toll on the once bountiful seas.

"Man is just beginning to explore the seas to know them, and already he has discovered that they are dying," he said sadly.

And in 1973, Philippe wrote, ". . . anyone who has visited the undersea world recently can attest to the spoilation and disheartening signs of a sick environment. . . . Unless we change the course of things right now, species of fish and other sea life will disappear before we can even understand what they once were. . . ." In a plea to divers everywhere to give up spearfishing and enjoy the thrills of the hunt with an underwater camera, Philippe Cousteau summed up the feelings of both himself and his father when he said, "The burden of saving the seas falls most squarely on those of us who have seen the pristine beauty. . . . It is our responsibility to begin the revolution that will free the seas. . . . Whatever we do to our seas, we do to ourselves."

Captain Nemo could not have said it more eloquently.

CHAPTER 15

Mutt and Jeff: Search for the Missing H-bomb

At dusk on Sunday, January 16, 1966, an eight-engine B-52 jet Stratofortress of the Strategic Air Command (SAC) lifted heavily off the air-force runway at Goldsboro, North Carolina. For the crew of Bomber 256, it was the beginning of another routine air-alert mission. Since 1961, SAC had kept bombers in the air every second of the day or night, flying one of four "watchdog" routes that stretched across the globe. Each mission lasted twenty-four hours and each bomber carried four hydrogen bombs capable of more destruction than man has ever known. If an enemy launched nuclear missiles at the country, SAC's airborne Stratofortresses would be in position to strike back.

As the huge plane climbed for altitude, the crew of Bomber 256, code-named Tea-16, settled into their normal flight routine. The plane would not land again until its mission was over. Periodically in the next twenty-four hours it would be met by huge flying tankers and refuel in flight. Meanwhile it would fly a predetermined course called Chrome Dome—a triangular route eastward over the Atlantic, across Spain into the Mediterranean, north along enemy territory, then westward and back to base.

As it had so often in the past, the mission went like clockwork. All that broke the routine were the refueling procedures. The first, over the Atlantic, went smoothly as usual. At dawn over Spain, they were met by a tanker from

Madrid's Torrejón U.S. Air Force base and refreshed a second time with some 40,000 gallons of jet fuel. Then on out over the Mediterranean they flew, following the long triangular course of the Chrome Dome route that finally brought them back to southern Spain and their last fuel rendezvous. This time a tanker from Morón, the American base near Sevilla, met them just in from the Mediterranean coast at an altitude of six miles over an area SAC called the Saddle Rock refueling zone. The operation would take ten to fifteen minutes. Both crews had done it hundreds of times. The lumbering KC-135 fuel tanker stayed ahead and above the bomber; the planes were cruising about 450 miles an hour. From the tail of the tanker the boom operator sent out the long telescoping hollow metal tube that would carry the fuel. He alone directed the coupling, guiding the bomber pilot by radio and flashing lights into the proper position for a hookup. As the open mouth of the bomber's fuel tank approached the long stingerlike appendage, the tanker's boom operator said calmly over his radio, "Watch your enclosure, Tea-16." He meant that the bomber was drawing up too quickly to the boom nozzle. Throttles were eased. Another approach began. Then suddenly it happened. The tanker's nozzle missed its target and struck the B-52's longeron, the metal spine running the full length of the plane. Aerodynamic stresses started crumpling the whole structure. Simultaneously fire raced up the tanker's boom and touched off 40,000 gallons of jet fuel. In the ensuing fireball the tanker's four-man crew was incinerated. Flames shot through the disintegrating bomber, but before it too was consumed, most of the crew managed to eject and parachute to safety. Of those seven, three were killed. The fiery fallout of the collision rained down from 30,000 feet onto an area of land and sea roughly ten miles square. Somewhere in all that scattered debris were four unexploded hydrogen bombs with the power of 1 million tons of TNT, enough to atomize southern Spain.

Witnesses to the disaster came from the small village of Palomares, a cluster of white adobe houses baking on the dusty saffron-colored slopes leading to the sea. They saw the fireball, then the parachutes. Boats headed for the men that landed at sea. One fisherman saw a parachute with what he supposed was a dead man below it fall into the sea and disappear. He noted the place then went on to pick up the other survivors.

Within hours convoys of searchers arrived from the American bases at Morón and Torrejón. A tent city was erected. Teams searched through the main concentrations of debris and questioned eyewitnesses. Long ranks of men roamed the countryside hunting the scattered pieces. And one by one what they were looking for was found. The first hydrogen bomb was discovered in a dry riverbed, its tangled parachute beside it. Number two turned up stuck in the ground on a hill behind a cemetery. Within twenty-four hours after the accident, number three was found in a tomato patch beside a garden wall. But no matter how hard the searchers looked, the whereabouts of the fourth and last hydrogen bomb remained a mystery. More and more U.S. airmen arrived. A massive air and land search began. Helicopters patrolled patterns from above. The arid hills and plains on all sides of Palomares were gone over foot by foot. Nothing but burned fragments of the collision were found. A hydrogen bomb the length of an automobile and as big around as a garbage can had somehow completely vanished. To add another headache, two of the three bombs that had been found had been damaged enough to release quantities of radioactive plutonium. Since the wind was spreading the contamination faster than the clean-up crews could collect it, villagers were asked to vacate their houses while these operations went on.

Various U.S. naval vessels appeared off the coast opposite Palomares. Their sounding devices indicated possible debris from the collision on the bottom, but the navy divers were unable to find anything resembling the bomb. Since it was thought highly probable now that the bomb had gone down at sea, the fishermen who had seen the parachutes were again questioned closely. An effort was made to reconstruct exactly what had happened—how and where the bombs would have fallen. This eventually resulted in a big chunk of ocean being considered a likely zone. The sector was divided into search areas, and the navy divers went to work. When they had worked to their depth limits, calls went out for more deep-water equipment. The Perry *Cubmarine,* a two-man submersible, was flown in from Florida. It could operate down to 300 feet. Reynolds Aluminum Company sent their submersible, the *Aluminaut,* a seventy-eight ton giant designed to dive to 15,000 feet, and from the Woods Hole Oceanographic Institution came the more diminutive *Alvin,* a twenty-two-foot-long, seventeen-ton minisub that could carry three men in a tiny sphere to 6,000 feet. Other sophisticated equipment included Westinghouse's five "acoustic fish," Ocean Bottom Scanning Sonar, a Decca radio navigation system for charting the search from shore, and underwater television cameras to be towed on diving sleds.

After a spate of bad weather and a lengthy delay tuning up all the sophisticated electronic machines, an intense sea search got under way. Where divers left off, the minisubs took over, painstakingly checking out each deep-water sonar contact. As time passed and the search area widened, Rear Adm. William S. Guest, commander of the Sixth Fleet Task Force, ordered to help the air force find its wayward bomb, summed up the situation with an accurate if unnautical allegory: "It isn't like looking for a needle in a haystack," he said. "It's like looking for the eye of a needle in a field of haystacks in the dark."

Everything now hinged on what the deep-diving vehicles could turn up. The most likely area where the bomb might be was divided into checkerboard squares; each section being searched thoroughly before moving to the next. Particular attention was given to the report by a fisherman, Francisco Simo, who pointed out the place where he had seen a large gray parachute come down with a "dead man" and disappear from sight, but none of the fatalities had landed at sea; moreover, the only gray chutes aboard the B-52 were attached to hydrogen bombs. So if Simo was right about what he saw and where he saw it, they might be close to the bomb.

Since it was smaller and more maneuverable than the other

submersibles, the *Alvin* was picked to make her first search dive on the spot pointed out by Simo. The bottom would be a combination of mud flats, cliffs and ravines. It was hoped that the *Alvin* could negotiate all these irregularities without overlooking anything. But since it was in deep water, the only illumination available would have to come from the sub itself. It would be slow, tedious work, but no one was more anxious to get the job done than the *Alvin*'s crew, William Rainnie, Marvin McCamis and Valentine Wilson. All three were ex-navy submariners who had worked together long enough now on the *Alvin* that they functioned as a smooth-running team. To them their deep-diving vehicle was more than just a beautiful piece of finely tuned machinery. They had helped create the *Alvin*; it was a part of them.

On February 14, Rainnie and McCamis took the *Alvin* down to 1,800 feet to look around the bottom. Their lights revealed a drab mud plateau. Fish, shrimp and plankton abounded. They searched for six hours before coming up with a record of current measurements. This information fed to the computer would give them another valuable piece to the puzzle: the angle and direction the bomb had taken as it drifted down toward the bottom.

In the weeks that followed, both the *Alvin* and the *Aluminaut*, the Mutt and Jeff of the submersibles, engaged in almost round-the-clock dives, searching one sector after another. The only new clue that turned up was the *Aluminaut*'s discovery of a big chunk of the B-52's fuselage. If heavy debris was that far out, it meant that the bomb might be too. The search area widened.

For some time now the submersibles' crews had noticed tracks along the muddy bottom. Sometimes they were caused by trawlers, sometimes by avalanches or fish. On the first of March, however, one of the *Alvin* observers spotted a track that looked different. It was about two feet across and curved as if it might have been made by the passage of a round, barrel-shaped object. They followed it down the muddy bank, their visibility limited to the twenty-foot-wide yellow glare of the *Alvin*'s floodlights. Then, at 2,800 feet with their batteries growing weak, bottom currents swept them off course, and they lost sight of it. They surfaced to try again the next day.

The next day, however, the *Alvin* was ordered into another sector. The navy was not impressed by bottom scratches. If sonar reported nothing down there, there was no use wasting any more time in that sector. Not even when the *Aluminaut* stumbled onto cannonballs and what was believed to be the wreckage of a Spanish galleon. Meanwhile, the *Alvin*'s crew chafed to get back onto the mystery track, at least long enough to follow it out and dispel their lingering suspicions.

The opportunity came a few days later when the sub was not scheduled for search duty. On their own, *Alvin*'s crew went down searching for the odd track. After a long hunt they found it. This time a navy commander was along as an observer. When he saw the track, he agreed that it was the right size to fit the bomb. But again it was too late to follow the trail; they had to return to the surface to charge the sub's batteries.

The next day they tried again, skirting the base of a cliff where they had last seen it. As they picked up the marks again, they saw signs of an avalanche. Then, hot on the trail, they abruptly realized that they had wandered under a huge mud overhang. If it fell, it could easily bury both them and the bomb. Rainnie carefully put the *Alvin* in reverse and eased out from under the treacherous shelf. After more than seven hours of searching down to 2,700 feet without finding anything, they were again forced to come up.

Meanwhile the *Aluminaut* was having her share of trouble. Arthur Markel, the sub's no-nonsense skipper was as devoted to his costly piece of diving machinery as the *Alvin* crew was to theirs. So when Markel and his men set out, ballasted for a 1,200-foot dive, and their boat nose-dived into a muddy bottom at 600 feet, Markel was understandably a little put out with the navy's sonar error. The heavily weighted sub plowed down the embankment to deeper water. When it came to rest, Markel released the vessel's load of lead-shot ballast, but the *Aluminaut* was stuck tight. There were three alternatives. If the sub stayed where it was, the men would suffocate and die. If they blasted off the keel, the sealed cabin would rise uncontrolled to the surface, chancing a collision with the bottom of a navy vessel. The third possibility was that they could somehow get the sub loose from the sucking mud without sacrificing the keel, which Markel knew would probably terminate their role in the search. With the last alternative the best choice, Markel tried rocking the boat free. All efforts failed until he got the crew in a group and ran them toward the sub's stern. After a few "laps" down the length of the boat the seesawing action did the trick. The *Aluminaut* pulled free and floated slowly to the surface with enough mud jammed into her understructure to take the men two days of cleaning before getting the boat back to its normal diving weight.

On March 15, two weeks after her crew had sighted the track for the first time, the *Alvin* made her 128th dive. This time McCamis and Wilson took her down with observer Arthur Bartlett from Woods Hole. Rainnie stayed on the surface as their radio contact. As the *Alvin* reached the bottom near the base of a cliff, she almost landed on the odd track they had been seeing. The crew was excited. This time they kept the sub well clear of the bottom, knowing only too well how the clouds of stirred-up silt could obscure their visibility. As they hovered over it, Wilson shot pictures of the groove with a camera mounted outside the sub. Topside Rainnie heard their comments:

"Better pitch 'em real fast," said McCamis.

"I'm clicking," said Wilson. "I don't know what it is, Mac, but there's two tracks that come down here and converge!"

"Okay, okay, snap pictures."

Once they had the track, they turned the sub around and began following it backward. Twice before they had lost it going forward simply by overshooting. Now they were trying it in reverse.

Overhead, sonar was keeping a check on them. They were working down a steep slope at 2,450 feet when they some- how lost the track. After wandering around for twenty minutes they picked it up again, followed it to the south and almost lost it. As it gouged its way down into a steep muddy gully, the *Alvin* drew closer. Then Rainnie heard the startled exclamation, "That looks like a parachute! . . . A chute that's partly billowing."

"Could be!"

"Open up with the pictures."

They photographed the big parachute. Cautiously they hovered above it. Something was tangled under the chute. They saw what looked like a fin. The navy's code name for discovery of the bomb was to be "Benthosaurus," in case any unfriendly vessels were monitoring the proceedings with sensitive listening gear. For simplicity's sake, the *Alvin*'s crew settled on the code words "bent nail." But in his excitement, McCamis reported a "rusty nail," as he called for a position fix.

"Echo, this is *Alvin*. Bill, get as good a position on us as you possibly can. I think we got a big rusty nail down here. . . . We found a sixty-foot parachute and we believe we have a fin of the bomb in sight. It's underneath the parachute."

"Rog-er!" was the enthusiastic reply from surface sonar.

The *Alvin* had trouble holding her position against the currents. Again they lost their find as loose silt swirled up and engulfed the sub. They searched gullies down the steep incline for twenty minutes before reaching 2,650 feet and sighting it again. This time they drew alongside the chute for a close look. They were certain of what they had found now.

"Echo. This is *Alvin*. How do you read me?"

"I read you loud but not clear," came the reply.

"I think we have enough identification. We'd like to skip clear of this area. There's several straps hanging down loose. There isn't any doubt in our minds about what we see. It's wrapped in the chute, but part of it shows. The thing is still lodged on a very steep slope. We got a good look at it. It's exactly the shape we've seen in the pictures."

"*Alvin*. This is an A1 job. Outstanding."

"Thank you."

The minisub was asked to hold its position until the *Aluminaut* arrived on the scene to take over while they surfaced. That was the longest wait the *Alvin*'s crew had to endure. They "parked" the boat in the jaws of a crevice to maintain position against the currents, then waited in the darkness for eight hours before the *Aluminaut* arrived. For McCamis the underwater rendezvous of the two submersibles was almost as dramatic a moment as the discovery of the bomb. In the total darkness of the deep he saw a greenish glow approaching them from the south.

"It was beautiful, the most beautiful thing I ever saw," he said later. "A great silvery-pink monster, it looked like, with great green phosphorescent eyes coming up silent through the water. I dreamed of seeing something like that, but I just thought it was a dream. I never thought I'd see it."

The *Aluminaut* had been delayed for the installation of a pinger, an electronic device which was to be placed near the bomb so that vessels could relocate the site simply by zeroing in on the electronic beeps.

When word spread that the *Alvin* had found something, Francisco Simo, the Spanish fisherman who was now known among his friends as Paco de la Bomba, went out to look at the area.

"*Si, Si,*" he nodded excitedly. "This could be it. I was not far from here when I saw it come down." Later measurements revealed that he was exactly a thousand yards away. The navy had marked the spot with a buoy.

The problem now was how to recover the bomb. With her bow buried in the mud slope to hold her place in the currents, the *Aluminaut* "bomb-sat" for twenty-one long hours while the *Alvin* recharged her batteries and had a mechanical arm installed. Then the little sub rejoined her watchful cohort on the bottom, pulling down with her a 3,500-foot light line in her two-fingered claw. The idea was to anchor the light line, then use it as a guide to bring down a heavy hauling cable to attach to the bomb. The *Alvin* buried the anchor in the mud wall, but that night a storm swept away the line, anchor and marker buoy. Plan number one was aborted.

The next idea was to drop one of the camera sleds near the bomb with trailing 300-foot hooked lines which the *Alvin* was to collect in her mechanical claw and attach to the parachute shrouds. This sounded as if it might work. The little sub followed the loaded sled to the bottom and tried to transfer the lines to the shrouds. Between the whimsical currents, the flaying lines and the less than dexterous mechanical arm, the attempt was a failure. "Copilot Val Wilson likened their efforts to "a drunken Swede trying to eat spaghetti with chopsticks." Plan number two was scrubbed.

The next five days of stormy weather delayed the operation. But in the lull navy technicians busily made a device called the "poodl." It consisted of a main line attached to several coiled lines. The invention was fastened to a ship's anchor and dropped to the bottom just eighty feet from the bomb. The *Alvin* was to uncoil the lines and attach them to the parachute shrouds. Unfortunately the coils were impossibly tangled. With her mechanical claw the *Alvin* then secured the main single line to six of the parachute's risers, and the navy decided to see if it could be raised this way. A surface winch went into action. The bomb shook free of the muddy slope. Up it came, slowly, 50 . . . 75 . . . 100 feet off the bottom. Then the line snapped and the bomb dropped back to the bottom again. So much for plan number three.

While the *Alvin* rejuvenated her batteries, the *Aluminaut* hurried down to secure their wayward charge. The sub reached the spot to find the parachute gone. So was the bomb. The pingers had dropped off and the whole thing was lost again! Admiral Guest's ulcer went on a rampage. The crews of the submersibles were sick. Surface personnel who were aware of the succession of problems were equally depressed. It was a gloomy situation that went from bad to worse. No one could believe that the bomb had strayed more than 100 yards away from its original site. The *Alvin* and the *Aluminaut* searched the area night and day to the point of exhaustion. They saw the track the bomb had made as it was dragged up the slope before lifting off the bottom, they saw anchor tracks, towed equipment tracks, their own tracks and the long, wide, downhill bomb track that had first led them to the target, but there was still no chute and no bomb. It had vanished as surely as if it had sprouted wings and flown away, or simply dropped into a cavernous black hole on the bottom. The latter possibility was considered gallows humor because, not far downhill from where the bomb had rested, the bottom dropped off a cliff to 3,000 feet, leveled briefly for a shelf, then plunged down to 3,600 feet. The mere thought that it might now be at that depth was enough to raise a crown of sweat on the toughest sonarman's brow.

The search concentrated on the uphill quadrant, the direction the bomb was being pulled when the cable broke. Although the bottom track was there and had been scrutinized many times, it took an observation by Commander Boykin, who accompanied the *Alvin* on a dive, to point out an irregularity in the track. The first part had a "cookie-cutter" mark as if the bomb had jammed its fins in the mud shortly after being moved, and the rest of the track was made by the anchor flukes after the bomb broke free. That could mean that the bomb may have fallen free faster than they had thought. The *Alvin* searched downhill, finding nothing but the same old track. Wilson thought he saw some variations along its edge, but the possibilities of the bomb sliding back down its old groove was too farfetched. Or was it?

The next day the *Alvin* went down 3,000 feet to explore the southern sector below the track. The sub examined the mud bottom, found nothing and began working her way up the slope, pausing every fifty feet to run parallel search patterns. First the crew began seeing chunks of mud that had fallen from above. Then, minutes later, McCamis announced calmly, "There it is."

It was the lower end of the sixty-foot fully extended chute. They still could not see the bomb, but it had to be nearby. Rainnie sent up the code word that they had found the chute; then they waited while surface vessels got a fix on their position. The bomb was at a depth of 2,800 feet; about 120 yards west southwest of where it was first found, then lost.

Not long after the bomb had disappeared, the navy had ordered another unique piece of underwater equipment from California to assist in the operation. It was called the CURV, an abbreviation for Cable-controlled Underwater Research Vessel. This rather strange-looking apparatus consisted of ballast tanks, lights, underwater television cameras and a mechanical claw—all mounted together as a compact unit completely controlled by cables from the surface. Originally designed to recover test-fired torpedoes, its maximum depth of operation was 3,000 feet, well within reach of the bomb, providing it did not roll any further down the slope.

Odd as it may seem, in all this time, no one as yet had had a good clear look at the bomb. It was still hidden by the chute. Although the *Alvin* attached pingers to the canopy, she was still unable to unwrap it from the shape beneath it. Finally CURV was maneuvered down to attach a rope to the parachute's apex and draw it aside. Then the robot was to put a big shackle on the bomb itself so it could be raised. The *Alvin* dove down to oversee the action. Upon reaching the spot the crew was shocked to find the bomb and the chute gone! It was lost for the third time!

Fortunately, however, Admiral Guest's ulcer hardly had time to react to this new turn of events when the *Alvin* tracked the missing bomb to its new resting place 300 feet away. First Val Wilson saw an edge of the billowing chute. The *Alvin* moved closer. Suddenly without warning the nylon canopy blossomed out in the current, and with all its ensnaring risers the chute plastered itself against the sub's viewport. If it had reached a little farther, the *Alvin* would have been entrapped in the nylon shroud as surely as was the bomb. With utmost care Wilson backed the sub away from the deadly mantle, heaving a sigh of relief that was echoed from every ship on the surface.

On April 6, the CURV was again sent down to secure a second and a third line to the parachute shrouds. The work went on through the night. Every time the surface manipulators moved the CURV's claw, the television camera view was blotted out by clouds of silt that took fifteen minutes to settle. But the efforts continued until the fate that almost claimed the *Alvin* finally stilled the CURV. The billowing chute draped over the vehicle's engines entangling everything so securely that the robot could not move.

Despite the bad luck, everyone was relieved that it was not the *Alvin* trapped in the chute on the bottom. But this was the last straw, the ultimate disappointment. The only thing worse that could happen would be for the bomb to roll off the cliff and drop into the inaccessible abyss.

Something had to be done. Two lines were secured to the parachute which in turn was secured to the CURV. Admiral Guest did the only thing that there seemed left to do. He ordered the lines drawn tight to see if the CURV could be worked free.

Groaning, the winches turned slowly. The cables drew taut, then slack. The rolling seas made it impossible to tell when the slack was taken up. But the coils came in, and a man called out the depth from a mark on the line.

"Twenty-four hundred feet still out!"

"What? What did you say?" someone asked. "That can't be right."

The man at the winch showed him that it was. A shout went up. "Hey, did ya hear that? *She's 400 feet clear of the bottom!*"

A crowd rushed aft. Could it be possible? A quick check proved that it was. Admiral Guest was notified. CURV's television cameras were turned on to reveal the parachute and its deadly cargo moving up smoothly through the water mass. If during this entire bomb-hunting operation there was ever a need for prayer, this was it. CURV, the chute and the H-bomb were now swinging and spinning on the end of two incredibly thin lines over the chasm itself. If the lines parted now, the whole thing would plummet down to 3,000 feet and probably beyond.

But the lines kept coming a foot at a time, the long tedious, nerve-wracking pull lasting an hour and forty-five minutes. And then it surfaced, the CURV first, its tanks, tubes and mechanical claw looking oddly out of place atop the billowing white canopy on which it perched. "Look at that ol' CURV," someone yelled gleefully, "riding her like a sleigh on a hill of snow!"

On Thursday, April 7, two months and twenty-one days after it was lost, the fourth and final H-bomb recovered from the Palomares air accident was gently secured aboard a U.S. Navy ship and sailed home. With it went a universal sigh of relief.

CHAPTER 16

D/RVs:
The New Generation

 We have seen the evolution of the more conventional diving machines from Alexander the Great's legendary glass barrel to the mammoth indefatigable nuclear-powered submarine. Now it seems that history is repeating itself and we are going back once again to the basic, uncomplicated shape of Alexander's pressureproof capsule. This new generation of sophisticated diving machines is called Deep Research Vessels (D/RVs). Most laymen can recognize them on sight because "no two are ever alike, most of them look like something from outer space, and they cost a fortune to build." Their sole function is to take man and the tools of his trade to the ocean bottom to explore, gather samples or make observations. Some of these vehicles belong to the navy and are intended for military purposes; but most belong to private industry and are used for special deep ocean investigations.

D/RVs are true submersibles and are differentiated from submarines in that they require the assistance of a surface support vessel. Many, particularly those developed during the golden age of submersibles from 1965 to 1969, were the product of an affluent society. In the rush to get into the sea simply because it was the thing to do, some companies spent large sums of money hastily building diving vehicles designed for no more specific purpose than to go underwater. Other industries, however, took advantage of our advanced aerospace technology and more carefully built vehicles designed for special jobs. Indeed, many of these D/RVs with their clusters of tanks, tubes, aluminum cylinders, acrylic domes, externally mounted mechanical arms, searchlights, cameras, core drills and complicated instrument packages look like they might be more at home on some galactic star than at the bottom of the ocean. But appearances are no deterrent. At present there are probably some one hundred such submersible vehicles in the world; about fifty of them are in the United States. Since all require crews and surface support vessels, their cost of operation is not exactly inexpensive. If, for example, you or your company wished to lease a small underwater vehicle capable of diving to the relatively shallow depth of 1,000 feet, you could probably get the submersible with its 100-foot-long surface support ship, its special handling gear, its twelve-man crew and insurance to cover everything for about $5,000 a day. A larger submersible, good down to 10,000 feet, with crew, ship and insurance would run about $18,000 to $20,000 a day, depending upon the length of the lease. This is why many D/RVs spend a lot of time in storage.

Since most of the members of this generation of deep-diving submersibles seldom resemble each other, here are some examples of the variety of vehicles and their characteristics: In 1964 the Electric Boat Company of Reynolds International launched the *Aluminaut*. Originally designed for a depth of 20,000 feet this figure was later revised to 15,000 feet. The fifty-foot-long vehicle weighing seventy-eight tons and carrying a five-man crew is constructed of concentric rings of aluminum bolted, rather than welded together, to form a cylinder. It has four viewports, two mechanical arms and can take core samples four feet long.

Also built in 1964, the *Alvin*, a twenty-two-foot-long, seventeen-ton research submersible, is owned by the Woods Hole Oceanographic Institution and bears a striking resemblance to Walt Disney's tugboat cartoon "Little Toot." The three-man, 6,000-foot-depth vehicle that played such an important role with the *Aluminaut* in the recovery of the wayward H-bomb off Palomares in 1966 was itself lost in October, 1968, during a launching accident in which it plunged to a depth of 5,500 feet. The following year it was recovered in a remarkable salvage feat by none other than the big member of the Mutt and Jeff team, the *Aluminaut*.

Perry Submersibles started out with their first *Cubmarine* (PC-3X) built in 1960 that was operational to 150 feet and went on to construct six other *Cubmarines* capable of diving to the mid-depth ranges of the continental shelf. They are designed for making observations and simple salvage. The 1968 *Shelf Diver* with its twenty-five viewports, mechanical arm, core drill, rock drill, TV cameras and diver's lockout hatch has been used for inspection of underwater pipe lines owned by Shell Oil Company.

Deep Star 4000 is another submersible that has enjoyed a popular press. Vaguely reminiscent of Jacques Cousteau's *Diving Saucer, Deep Star 4000* was based on a Cousteau design and built under his guidance by Westinghouse in 1965. The nine-ton, eighteen-foot-long, yellow steel capsule with two 5-inch-thick Plexiglas viewports, mechanical arm and bow cameras has been used in hundreds of research dives down to its operational depth of 4,000 feet. In the last few years the battery-powered, highly maneuverable vehicle has carried out extensive research dives for the United States Navy. It was the prototype for Westinghouse's *Deep Star 20,000*, a thirty-six-foot-long, thirty-two-ton vehicle launched in 1972 and designed to be used down to 20,000 feet as a deep-sea search vehicle.

In 1970, Jacques Cousteau updated his design of the *Diving Saucer* by using a hull originally made for the *Deep Star 4000* to create the *Diving Saucer SP-3000*, a twenty-foot-long, twelve-ton vehicle with a cruising speed of two to three knots and capable of operating down to 9,000 feet. The same year, the navy designed and built the radically different *Nemo*, a sixty-six-inch-diameter acrylic sphere mounted atop disks containing the vehicle's life-support system. Inside the sphere one or two crewmen in shirtsleeve comfort can winch their underwater elevator up or down a cable attached to an anchor on the ocean floor. With a range down to 600 feet the *Nemo* will take men to the bottom to observe construction.

As an alternative to the usual use of acrylic plastic, the navy built *Deep View*, a sixteen-and-a-half-foot-long, five-and-three-quarters-ton vehicle whose entire bow section is capped, for the first time in any submersible, with a glass (borosilicate) hemisphere. Propelled by four 5-horsepower electric motors the craft can dive to 1,500 feet.

One of the highlights of 1970 was the launching of the navy's first Deep Sea Rescue Vehicle, the *DSRV-1*, built by Lockheed Missiles and Space Company for depths down to 3,500 feet. This fifty-foot-long, fiber-glass-hulled, forty-seven-ton, torpedo-shaped vehicle was the first of its kind designed to search out a nuclear submarine in distress, mate itself to the submarine's escape hatch and take on up to twenty-four men from the downed combat submarine. This vehicle was followed in May, 1971, by Lockheed's *DSRV-2*, capable of carrying the same number of survivors but operational to a depth of 5,000 feet. The big advantage of these Deep Sea Rescue Vehicles is their air weight of about thirty-five tons, enabling them to be transported quickly by land, sea or air to any place in the world. Moreover, the DSRVs can be carried, launched and recovered from a mother submarine while submerged or even if necessary while under ice.

Unfortunately, however, since they lack a means of mating with any of the many different research minisubs in use today, the DSRVs can only be used with submarines. Otherwise there might have been a different ending to the undersea tragedy that occurred in the summer of 1973.

On Sunday, June 17, the *Johnson-Sea-Link*, a twenty-three-foot-long, nine-ton research submersible designed by inventor-oceanographer Edwin Link, set out on a routine dive twenty miles off Key West, Florida, in several hundred feet of water. The $2 million minisub resembling a cross between a rotorless helicopter and a space module was donated to the Smithsonian Institution for oceanographic research by industrialist J. Seward Johnson and the designer, Link. Loaded with safety devices, she was operational to 1,500 feet. Her crew were all experienced men: the vessel's pilot, Archibald ("Jock") Menzies, thirty, an ex-commercial diver; Robert Meek, twenty-seven, an ichthyologist and scientist; Albert

Stover, fifty-one, a twenty-year navy veteran and expert submariner; and E. Clayton Link, thirty-one, supervisor of Life Support Systems and son of Edwin and Marion Link.

On this dive Menzies and Meek were in the submersible's forward compartment, a six-foot-diameter, four-inch-thick acrylic sphere; Stover and Link were in the rear compartment, an aluminum in/out air lock enabling divers to enter or leave the minisub underwater. There was no passageway between the two compartments.

The object of the dive was to collect some fish traps and check on the fish population surrounding an artificial reef made by the wreckage of an old navy destroyer, the *Fred T. Berry*, scuttled the year before.

Shortly after reaching the wreck in 360 feet of water, the *Sea-Link* was swept off course by an unusually strong current and became entangled in the dangling cables and debris of the sunken warship. Unable to work the minisub free, Menzies radioed for help. The message was quickly relayed by Ed Link from the submersible's surface support ship, *Sea Diver*, to the U.S. Submarine Naval Base at Key West. The U.S. Coast Guard flashed the news to the chief of naval operations in Washington, and with agonizing slowness, help started on its way.

From nearby Key West came the U.S.S. *Tringa*, a submarine rescue vessel, which spent the next five hours getting herself properly positioned and anchored over the site. Meanwhile, aboard the submersible, the men were running out of air. Lethal carbon dioxide from their exhalations was increasing. In the forward compartment where the four-inch-thick acrylic sphere insulated them from the forty-degree Fahrenheit water outside, Menzies and Meek took the Baralyme chemical out of their broken "scrubber" that absorbed their carbon dioxide and put it in an air-conditioning fan so it could continue to be effective. The move probably saved their lives. In the rear of the sub Stover and Link were not doing so well. The aluminum compartment quickly took on the water's temperature, reducing the effectiveness of the chemical scrubber. In an effort to restore it, the two men increased their compartment's air pressure, then rubbed the pieces of Baralyme over their arms and faces, hoping their body heat would help it absorb carbon dioxide.

It was after 10:30 Sunday night before the first rescue attempt was made. Two helmet divers from the *Tringa* were lowered on a platform and got within fifty feet of the submersible before the currents and swaying debris drove them back. A second attempt failed. A third try put the divers within ten feet of the entrapped sub, but the swift currents and debris kept them from going further despite Menzies' and Meek's radioed urging, "Keep coming! Keep coming!" as they watched them from the acrylic sphere.

The next morning the navy submarine *Amberjack* arrived with two small submersibles with mechanical arms from Perry Submarines. Both were launched off her deck, but one had a sonar malfunction and the other was only able to get within sixty feet of the *Sea-Link* before she was forced to surface to avoid being swept into the dangling wreckage herself.

All hope now hinged on a navy diving bell flown in from San Diego, California. Two scuba divers were lowered in the bell but got no closer than forty feet over the entrapped submersible before they too were stopped by the wreckage. By now, Stover and Link were unconscious in the rear compartment; Menzies and Meek said their air supply would not last much longer.

Then, after taking twenty-three hours to reach the scene, the oceanographic research ship *A. B. Wood* arrived. No one really felt the *Wood* could contribute anything to the hopeless situation; however, her skipper and crew rigged a closed-circuit television camera and sent it down on a cable. Over the radio, Menzies weakly reported that he could see it but that it was on the wrong side of the *Berry*. The camera was retrieved, a grapple hook attached to the cable beside it and the rig lowered again. This time Menzies directed its positioning by radio until it hooked the minisub. Minutes later the cheering crew hauled the *Sea-Link* to the surface. Menzies and Meek were taken aboard the *Tringa*, none the worse for their harrowing experience. The minisub was rushed to Key West where the rear compartment underwent lengthy decompression, but it was too late for Link and Stover who were dead from carbon-dioxide poisoning.

Although Edwin Link did not appear at any of the subsequent investigations, he wrote the following letter to the officer in charge of the Coast Guard investigation:

> The tragedy of the situation is that with an adequate undersea rescue system and equipment, this loss need never have occurred. Had it been a modern nuclear submarine with 100 men entrapped, the result could not have been the same. The Navy and Coast Guard have recognized the problem for years, but with inadequate funds have not been able to develop such a system. It is inevitable that as man continues to invade the ocean depths, similar accidents are bound to occur in spite of every precaution. The sole remedy—rapid, effective submarine rescue systems, must be developed and kept in strategic locations. The technical knowledge of such a system has been available since the loss of the nuclear submarine *Thresher* ten years ago, but it has not been implemented.

A similar tragedy was narrowly avoided a few months later when, on October 30, 1973, the two-man British crew of the twenty-nine-foot-long submersible *Pisces*, Robert Mallinson, thirty-five, and Roger Chapman, twenty-eight, were making a telephone cable survey off the coast of Ireland when the accident occurred. While the minisub was on the surface, it was fouled by a cable being hauled in by its support vessel. The after hatch was torn off; the compartment flooded, and the sub with the two men inside sank to a depth of 1,375 feet.

As soon as the call for help went out, the Naval Undersea Center at San Diego responded by sending its unmanned CURV III to the scene. Just six and a half hours later, the updated model of the same device that had successfully picked up the lost H-bomb was surface manipulated in a search for the missing sub, guided by its built-in, closed-circuit television camera. It dove down 1,375 feet to find the crippled *Pisces* and attached a heavy cable so that the submersible and the men could be hauled to the surface. Despite being trapped for seventy-five hours and fifty minutes, Mallinson and Chapman emerged from their ordeal in excellent condition but with their oxygen supply almost exhausted.

Quick action and the improved hardware of modern technology saved the men of the *Pisces*. The following year, fully aware of the need for more vehicles designed to aid unconventional submarines, inventor Ed Link completed work on C.O.R.D. (Cable Observation/Rescue Device) a radio-controlled underwater vehicle with TV and sonar to be used in the recovery of stricken submersibles.

Compared to the early efforts to develop diving machines, modern man is making rapid progress. He knows how to design the vehicles but unfortunately he has not yet learned how to use them to maximum advantage. As advanced as we seem to be technologically, we have not yet even begun to employ this knowledge in the greater development of the existing potential. The oceans of the world hold vast untapped stores of food, fuels and minerals. But until we solve the problems of their recovery, these resources might as well be on another planet. Still, as we probe outer space, so too have we made the first tentative efforts to explore the deeper recesses of inner space, the ocean world. In the summer of 1974, scientists from two nations took a major step into this alien environment with Project FAMOUS—the French-American Mid-Ocean Undersea Study.

Preliminary work on the project began several years earlier. The site selected for study was a dark, rugged wasteland comprising the largest feature on earth—a 40,000-mile-long ridge that girdles the globe like the seam of a giant baseball. But since the ridge bisects the bottom of the mid-Atlantic Ocean under more than 9,000 feet of water, it is understandable why less is known about it than the mountains of the moon.

For years scientists have suspected the rift valley stretching along the ridge of being the birthplace of new ocean bottom. But nobody knew for sure if this was true or how exactly it worked. Theoretically, it is here that volcanic action slowly pushes fresh material up through the earth's mantle, forcing apart huge sections or plates of the earth's surface in the process and contributing to the long-known but little-understood phenomenon of continental drift.* To prove their theory the scientists planned to take a closer look at that ocean bottom to determine what was happening there. The site chosen was a section of mid-Atlantic Ocean floor 250 miles southwest of the Azores. Three years of intense study by surface ships photographing, surveying, mapping and sampling the bottom had set the stage. Now it was time for three deep-diving submersibles to take the scientists down to examine the area. The French would use their bathyscaph *L'Archimède* shaped similar to Piccard's *Trieste I* with its pressure sphere and gasoline envelope buoyancy float. Although designed for maximum depths and heavy payloads, she was less maneuverable than their second sub, the *Cyana*, formerly the Cousteau-designed *Diving Saucer SP 3000* with a depth range of 10,000 feet. The Americans would rely on the highly maneuverable *Alvin*, hero of the Mediterranean H-bomb search. Now, however, "Little Toot" was outfitted with a new titanium hull enabling her to dive to depths down to 12,000 feet. Each vehicle was equipped with special tools, baskets and manipulator claws for collecting bottom samples during an anticipated forty-odd dives into the submarine mountain range.

The American scientists selected to make these dives included Dr. James Heirtzler, the U.S. chief scientist for FAMOUS, Dr. Robert Ballard and Dr. Wilfred Bryan, all of the Woods Hole Oceanographic Institution; Dr. Robert Keller of the National Oceanic and Atmospheric Administration's Atlantic Oceanographic and Meteorological Laboratories, Dr. Ian MacGregor of the University of California, Dr. James Moore of the U.S. Geological Survey and Dr. Tjeerd H. Van Andel of Oregon State University.

After several test dives in Woods Hole Harbor in early June, 1974, *Alvin* was winched aboard the R/V *Knorr* and lashed down for her trip to the Azores. Two and a half weeks

---

*It is generally believed that all the continents once fitted together like pieces of a jigsaw puzzle. About 225 million years ago the land masses gradually split apart from each other and began separating. Scientific opinions are also divided, but the rate of drift is thought to range from one to two centimeters up to one or two inches a year.

later the ship arrived at Ponta Delgada with *Alvin's* catamaran-type tender, *Lulu*, in tow. After a few test dives and with the full complement of scientists aboard the *Knorr*, the team moved to its assigned position over the mid-Atlantic Ridge, and on June 29 the dives began.

Lulu dropped transponders to the ocean-floor perimeter of *Alvin's* intended dive range. In conjunction with sonar and computerized navigation techniques, these bottom-moored acoustical reference points would enable both *Alvin* and her mother ship to keep track of each other. *Lulu* positioned herself about equidistant between the transponders, and *Alvin* was lowered into the water on a platform between the tender's twin pontoons. While the sub was steadied with Manila lines, two scientists and the submersible's pilot crossed on a small metal plank from one pontoon to the sub. With everyone aboard, *Alvin* moved out from between *Lulu's* hulls at the stern, lines were cast off, and *Alvin*, under her own power, moved a short distance away from her tender and stood by on the surface.

With the closing of *Alvin's* hatch, the pilot went through a routine checklist by underwater telephone with *Lulu*. Over the phone the voices sounded distant and hollow.

"Is the underwater identification light on?" asked the voice on *Lulu*, referring to a brightly flashing strobe on the sub.

"Affirmative," replied *Alvin's* pilot.

"Roger. Dive when ready," instructed the tender.

Two wet-suited divers made a final check to be sure the hatch was tightly secured.

Levers moved, switches closed, *Alvin's* ballast tank filled with water, and she started down. Aboard *Lulu*, the support crew followed her anxiously on the instruments tracing her descent.

Inside *Alvin* a recorder constantly monitored the depth of the submersible from the surface, height off the bottom, time and heading. As the sub sank into the darkness, her outside floodlight was switched on. Looking out through one of the viewports, Dr. George Keller, one of the two scientists aboard, recalled getting the impression that he was seeing a "reverse snowfall effect" as the submarine sank rapidly through water filled with tiny sea creatures. There followed a long, gentle descent into the black abyss.

When *Alvin's* sonar indicated their approach to the bottom, pilot John F. Donnelly jettisoned the sub's descent weights. *Alvin* jerked upward as the two packets of thick plates dropped free. Donnelly switched on the vertical propeller and the craft continued descending.

Over two miles down, where water pressure exerted a two-ton per square inch squeeze on the *Alvin's* hull, the crew of the submersible saw bottom when they recognized the huge black blob below them as the sub's shadow thrown on the sea floor by her own floodlights. A cloud of silt kicked up by the jettisoned weights rolled down current like a puff of smoke. *Alvin's* propellers whirred, and the tiny craft moved forward, hovering just above the sea floor. Thus began an eerie odyssey that would be repeated on each dive that *Alvin* made in the weeks to come. Some of the project scientists recalled vivid impressions of those experiences.

"It took a couple of dives to get over the 'oh wow!' feeling and begin to think about the meaning of what you see in a total context of sea-floor spreading," said Dr. Ballard. "Looking at the Mid-Ocean Ridge from *Alvin* is like looking at the Rockies in a heavy fog—you can see the details, but you never get a panorama of the countryside," observed Dr. Keller. "My impression of the bottom," recalled Dr. Heirtzler, "is that a giant had been walking around crushing things. It's obviously a horrendous place to be, very busy with earthquakes and volcanic eruptions. . . ." For an accurate record of his impressions Dr. Bryan continuously taped his observations: "We're coming up to a very sharp crest here, many broken blocks right up to the crest, very large fractured pillows. And now we see a very large bulbous pillow off to the left . . . very much older lava and broken . . ."

The rough topography of the terrain was due to a variety of odd-shaped lava formations typical of volcanic eruptions. The divers named them according to their shapes. Dome-shaped formations appeared to be bulbous pillows. Dr. Tjeerd Van Andel thought they looked "exactly like baked potatoes with a crack on top and sour cream coming out." Elongated forms were called "Cousteaus," for the well-known French ocean-ographer. Pillows with their tops lifted off from a second eruption were "trapdoors," ribbonlike extrusions were "toothpaste," and when fingers of lava draped over a crest it was a "haystack."

After many exploratory dives it became obvious to the FAMOUS scientists that the area of recent volcanic activity was confined largely to a 500-foot-wide section of sea floor on either side of the valley midline. Of particular interest were the fissures, the rips and stress marks that were clues to the movement of the sea floor.

As *Alvin* moved slowly over the bottom, the men stared at the black, jagged crevasses that appeared out of the inky darkness of the near freezing water to be illuminated for the first time ever in the yellow circle of light generated by the submersible. On one excursion into the area, *Alvin* stopped on the brink of one of the largest cracks the men had ever seen.

"We could see as much as eighty feet down into that fissure," recalled Dr. Ballard. "Do you remember the old movies where the earth opens up and swallows everyone in huge cracks? Well, that is geological fiction on land, but down there it happens. My reaction was to just sit still and look. We didn't say anything or do anything. Seeing that crack was like getting a lollypop too big to fit in your mouth. We realized that we were the first human beings to see that fissure, and because of its remoteness, we'll probably be the last. It is a heady feeling to realize you are witnessing the spot of the creation of the crust of the world."

Geologists had long debated whether the earth's sections or "plates" were pushed apart by the upwelling lava or were pulled apart by unknown forces. Had they been pushed, there would be compression features—buckled crust, heaped material—but none were found. Instead, the scientists saw large and small fissures every one hundred feet or so, all running parallel to the midline of the ridge, indicating that powerful forces had wrenched apart the bottom here.

On every dive the *Alvin* took samples. Manipulated adroit-ly from inside the sub, her hammer, crowbar or core drill separated the test materials from the bottom. Then, while cameras whirred, dutifully recording the events, *Alvin's* manipulator claw delicately picked up the rocks and deposited them in various baskets for the scientists.

In the course of their wanderings over the bizarre volcanic landscape, the observers noted with surprise the abundance of sea life in this perpetually cold, black world over two miles down.

"It was really quite a zoo down there," reported Dr. Bryan after exploring a traverse canyon cutting across the rift valley. "We saw lots of dog-faced fish—big ones." Some were three feet long. Others, called *benthosaurs*, rested on the bottom, using their pectoral fins and tail as a tripod. Once, the *Alvin* surprised an umbrella-sized octopus and saw a three-foot-long squid, numerous eels and rat-tail fish. At other times they saw no more than a puff of silt where some deep-sea creature had swiftly departed. In one place the bottom was covered with tiny horseshoe crabs. The *Alvin's* prop wash scattered them like leaves in an autumn breeze.

Meanwhile, in the northern part of the rift valley, the French *Archimède* and *Cyana* were seeing similar sights. Scientists aboard the *Cyana* found rich iron and manganese deposits caused, they suspected, by geothermal "hot springs." In an effort to help their French colleagues locate the springs, U.S. scientists aboard the R/V *Knorr* spent several evenings going back and forth over the French dive area photographing and probing the depths with sensitive thermal detecting equipment. A thermal sensor was even mounted on the *Cyana* for a bottom search, but the attempt was unsuccessful.

By summer's end and the conclusion of the study, Project FAMOUS had compiled an impressive record of achievements. The three submersibles had made a total of forty-four dives. *Alvin* accounted for seventeen of these, during which the research submersible covered twenty-nine kilometers of sea floor in eighty-one hours of submerged time. She stopped at eighty-one sampling stations, brought back 867 pounds of rocks and took 17,000 photographs. On the surface, the R/V *Knorr* made forty-five dredge stations and towed cameras over eighty kilometers of sea bottom, photographing it, giving the Americans a grand total of some 50,000 photos of the sea floor, plus video tapes and moving pictures—enough research material to keep scientists busy for years to come.

While it is still too early to appraise the total value of Project FAMOUS, it is not too early to praise the effort that took scientists to the ocean's depths to see firsthand the Mid-Atlantic Ridge, known now to be a huge linear volcano believed to have been erupting for millions of years, pulling the continents slowly apart and giving birth to new ocean bottom.

Using sophisticated diving machines powered by small nuclear reactors and batterylike fuel cells already developed by our space technology, tomorrow's ocean-research projects will take us to the outer limits of inner space. Fleets of hydrodynamically shaped vehicles of special alloys, glass or plastic, will carry men to the continental shelf and beyond for exploration, research, mining, prospecting, aquaculture and salvage. Since much of what man accomplishes in these depths will depend upon how long he can stay there, underwater communities will appear. Pods of habitats, some inflatable, some of plastic, will grow along our continental shelf like mushrooms, their inhabitants venturing forth in pressurized vehicles to perform their useful work.

With three quarters of our planet underwater and our land resources rapidly being depleted, there is no question where future man must turn to survive.

Appendix

Evolution of Diving Machines

**333 B.C.
to 1972**

333 B.C. (circa) •Legendary descent of Alexander the Great in glass barrel.

1531 •Guglielmo de Lorenca's diving bell used to find sunken Roman galleys in Lake Nemi, Italy.

1538 •Two Greeks demonstrated diving bell for Charles V, Toledo, Spain.

1552 •Diving bell demonstrated by Adriatic fishermen in Venice, Italy.

1578 •Englishman William Bourne's theoretical diving boat with ballast-tank bulkheads operated by jackscrews.

1597 •Italian Buonaiuto Lorini described iron-bound wooden diving bell with diver platform.

1620 •Dutchman Cornelius Van Drebbel built first operational submarine boat with air purification system used on Thames River, London, England.

1640 •Frenchman Jean Barrie patented diving bell used for shipwreck salvage near Dieppe, France.

1665 •Diving bell used to salvage cannon from shipwreck in Tobermory Bay, Mull, Inner Hebrides.

1677 •Frenchman Dr. Panthot of Lyons employed improved Spanish salvage methods with a diving bell, Cadaques, Spain.

1680 •Giovanni Borelli designed a diving boat with folding oar blades, Italy.

1689 •Improved method of supplying diving bells with surface pumped air invented by Dr. Denis Papin, France.

1690 •Englishman Edmund Halley built a superior diving bell supplied with fresh air by weighted casks and set longest deep-dive record: sixty feet for ninety minutes.

1715 •Englishman John Lethbridge invented truncated, cone, wood diving machine with leather arm sleeves; dived to seventy-two feet.

1772 •Frenchman Le Sieur Dionis rumored to have built underwater boat capable of four-and-a-half-hour underwater journey.

1774 •Englishman John Day converted fifty-ton schooner *Maria* to heavily ballasted "submarine," dived it to 130-foot depth off Plymouth, England, to become first recorded submarine fatality.

1776 •American David Bushnell invented hand-powered submarine *Turtle* used to attack H.M.S. *Eagle* by Sgt. Ezra Lee in New York Harbor during American Revolution.

1800 •First practical hand-powered submarine boat built by American inventor, Robert Fulton, in France. Six-hour dive, Brest.

1820 •English smuggler Captain Johnson built 100-foot-long submarine to liberate Napoleon from St. Helena for £40,000, but Napoleon died too soon.

1825 •Captain Johnson offered to sell France five submarine boats with compressed-air supply; French refused.

1831 •Spanish inventor Cervo failed to survive first trial deep dive of wooden sphere to 200 feet when it imploded.

1834 •French submarine inventor Jean Baptiste Petit lost with his submarine during a dive.

1850 •Wilhelm Bauer built sheet-iron submarine *Brandtaucher* with which he single-handedly confronted Danish blockaders at Kiel and panicked the fleet into flight.

1851 •Bauer, Witt and Thomsen made first submarine escape from *Brandtaucher* at Kiel, Germany.
•American shoemaker Lodner D. Phillips built two 50-foot-long, hand-cranked submarines in which he and his family dived up to ten hours in Lake Michigan.

1855 •Bauer's submarine *Le Diable-Marin* made 134 record dives at Kronstadt, Russia.

1863 •Frenchmen Simeon Borgeois and Charles-Marie Brun built first compressed-air-driven submarine, the 140-foot-long *Plongeur*, tested successfully to twenty-foot depths.

1864 •Confederate submarine *Hunley* attacked and sank Federal blockade ironclad U.S.S. *Housatonic* off Charleston, South Carolina; was herself destroyed with entire crew in the encounter.

1868 •Submarines driven by compressed air built in Russia.

1869 •Jules Verne's *Twenty Thousand Leagues under the Sea* published.

1872 •U.S. Navy bought Oliver Halstead's twenty-two-foot-long submarine, *Intelligent Whale*, that drowned thirty-nine men during tests.

1878 •American inventor John P. Holland built the *Holland I* submarine in Paterson, New Jersey; powered it by steam.

- Englishman Rev. G. Garrett built steam-powered submarine *Resurgam*; after successful tests, built and sold three more to Russia, Greece and Turkey.
- Successful steam-driven submarine built by Theodore Nordenfelt in Sweden.

1881
- First practical electrically driven submarine, the eleven-ton *Goubet*, built by French inventor Goubet.
- John P. Holland's *Fenian Ram* powered by four-horsepower gasoline engine built in New Jersey.

1884
- Josiah Tuck's thirty-foot, electric-driven submarine *Peace Maker* with diver's lock tested successfully to sixty-five feet, New York.

1885
- Garrett and Nordenfelt built sixty-ton *Nordenfelt I* driven submerged on steam reservoir; sold to Greece.

1886
- Englishman J. F. Waddington built thirty-seven-foot-long submarine *Porpoise* operated by seven-horsepower electric motor.
- First practical forerunner of today's submarine designed by Frenchman Dupuy de Lôme: the cigar-shaped, sixty-foot-long, six-foot-wide, steel-hull *Gymnote*, powered by electricity; completed by Gustave Zédé. Still in French Naval Service in 1907.

1887
- Lieut. Isaac L. Peral built and demonstrated his seventy-three-foot electric submarine *Peral* on thirty-foot dives, Cádiz, Spain.
- Bronze electric submarine, sixteen-foot *Goubet II* built by Frenchman Goubet; operated four years successfully.
- *Nordenfelt V*, a 125-foot, 160-ton, 1,000-horsepower submarine built by Nordenfelt, sold to Russia, wrecked en route.

1890
- *Gustave Zédé*, a 160-foot electric submarine designed by Ramazotti, built at Toulon, France, in service to 1901.

1892
- Italian submarine, eighty-foot electric-powered *Pullino*, had three propellers.

1894
- American inventor Simon Lake built small wooden submarine with wheels, the *Argonaut Jr.*, included diver's air lock.

1897
- Italian Piatti del Ponzo and Frenchman A. Delisle built steel sphere *La France* with external claws, electric lights, telephone; lowered to 165 feet.
- Simon Lake built the *Argonaut*, a three-wheeled, iron, thirty-foot-long, electric-powered boat with air lock.

1900
- First U.S. Navy submarine commissioned—the *Plunger*, by American submarine designer, John P. Holland.

1902	•Italian inventor Giuseppe Pino built wheeled chamber for underwater salvage, Italy.
1908	•Frenchman Abbé Raoul built wheeled "fishing submarine" with telephone, searchlight, mechanical claws; tested to 325 feet, Toulon, France.
1916	•German cargo submarine *Deutschland* crossed Atlantic.
1917	•Germany declared unrestricted submarine warfare.
1918	•Miniature submarine called "underwater chariot" used by Italians Raffaele Paolucci and Raffaele Rossetti to sink battleship *Viribus Unitis* at Pola, Yugoslavia.
	•British built two giant aircraft submarines.
1927	•A. R. McCann, U.S. Navy, designed rescue bell for submarines.
1930	•Roberto Galeazzi built *Butoscopic Turret* and dived to 700 feet, Italy.
	•Americans William Beebe and Otis Barton descended to 1,400 feet in Barton's *Bathysphere* off Bermuda.
1932	•Beebe and Barton reached 2,170 feet in *Bathysphere* off Bermuda.
1934	•Beebe and Barton reached 3,036 feet in *Bathysphere* off Bermuda.
1936	•Italian Lieuts. Teseo Tesei and Elias Toschi designed and built first practical electric underwater chariots for warfare.
1938	•Auguste Piccard designed and built the bathyscaph *FNRS-2* in Belgium; intended as deep-diving submersible.
1940	•Midget submarines (one- and two-man enclosed types), Japan.
1943	•Twenty-four torpedo-plane-carrying submarines launched, Japan.
1945	•Two of the largest submarines ever built—3,500 tons each, carrying three torpedo planes, designed and launched, Japan.
	•*Official Submarine Warfare Losses in World War II:*
	•Britain, with 218 submarines, lost 76 submarines.
	•United States, with 288 submarines, lost 52 submarines.
	•Germany, with 1,072 submarines, lost 705 submarines.
	•Japan, with 181 submarines, lost 130 submarines.
1948	•Auguste Piccard launched and tested bathyscaph *FNRS-2,* empty, to 4,600 feet off Dakar, Africa; damaged on recovery.
1949	•American Otis Barton lowered to 4,500 feet in his bethoscope off California.
1952	•Construction begun on Capt. Hyman Rickover's project-

ed first U.S. atomic submarine, *Nautilus*, by Electric Boat Company.

1953 •Bathyscaph *Trieste* launched and tested to 10,400-foot depth off Ponza Island, Italy, by Auguste and Jacques Piccard.

1954 •French bathyscaph *FNRS-3* with George S. Houot and Pierre Willm descended to 13,287 feet off Dakar, Africa.

1955 •United States launched first atomic submarine *Nautilus*, the 323.7-foot-long prototype for an ever-growing fleet of such ships cruising under nuclear power.

1958 •Comdr. William R. Anderson took U.S. atomic submarine *Nautilus* from Pacific to Atlantic under the polar ice cap via the North Pole.

•U.S. nuclear submarine *Skate* crossed under North Pole from the east; surfaced in open-water polynyas of ice cap.

1959 •United States launched longest submarine ever constructed: the 447.5-foot-long nuclear submarine *Triton* with two nuclear reactors.

•U.S. nuclear submarine *Skate*, under Comdr. James F. Calvert, surfaced through ice at North Pole.

1960 •Commanded by Capt. Edward L. Beach, the U.S. nuclear submarine *Triton* circumnavigated the world underwater. After traveling 110,000 miles, the $109 million *Triton* was first nuclear sub relegated to the "mothball fleet," in 1969.

•Frenchmen Jacques-Yves Cousteau and Albert Falco descended to 1,000 feet in *Diving Saucer* off Corsica.

•Jacques Piccard and Don Welsh descended to record 35,800 feet in navy bathyscaph *Trieste*, Challenger Deep, Pacific.

1962 •French navy bathyscaph *L'Archimède*, manned by Frenchmen Georges Houot and Pierre Willm, explored six-mile depths of the Japan Trench.

1963 •U.S. nuclear submarine *Thresher* sank on sea trials in 8,400 feet of water, 260 miles off New England coast. Bathyscaph *Trieste* with Lieut. Comdr. D. L. Keach, Comdr. J. W. Davies and Lieut. Comdr. A. Gilmore found and photographed debris.

•Jacques Cousteau's Continental Shelf No. 2 underwater community thirty-five feet down on Sha'ab Rummi Reef, Red Sea, established first submerged submarine base in air-filled dome for *Diving Saucer*, 1,000-foot-depth vehicle powered by water jet.

•Benthos V, Lear Sigler, submersible of two tons, 600-foot depths.

•Jacques Piccard launched mesoscaph *Auguste Piccard,* a mid-range vehicle designed for 3,500-foot depths, Switzerland.

•*Star 1,* ten-foot-long submersible designed for 200-foot depths; experimental use of fuel cell, owned by Philadelphia Maritime Museum.

1964 •Jacques Piccard's mesoscaph *Auguste Piccard* made 13,000 dives, taking 33,000 sightseers to bottom of Lake Geneva (over 300-foot depths) during Swiss National Exposition, Lausanne.

•Submersible *Aluminaut* launched by Reynolds Submarine Service, United States. All-aluminum vehicle with two mechanical arms, four viewports, core sampler. The fifty-one foot sub was designed for 15,000-foot depths but operates at 6,250 feet.

•D/RV *Alvin* launched by Woods Hole Oceanographic Institution, United States; twenty-two feet long, seventeen tons; designed for 6,000-foot depths.

•*Asherah* launched, seventeen-foot, 4.2-ton submersible used by University of Pennsylvania Museum for underwater archaeology.

•*Yomiuri,* forty-eight-foot, 41-ton D/RV; seven ports, arm, cameras; 1,000 foot depth; Japan.

•*Cubmarine (PC-3B)* launched; eighteen-foot, 2.3-ton minisub built by Perry Submersibles, United States. Operational depth 600 feet. Earlier models: *PC-3X,* 1960, 150 feet; *PC-3A,* 1962, 300 feet.

•*Deep Jeep 2000,* ten-foot-long, 4.5-ton submersible built by Naval Ordnance Test Station as experimental vehicle using viewing optics; operational depth 2,000 feet.

•Auguste Piccard's *Trieste I* Bathyscaph sold to the U.S. Navy (1958); was extensively rebuilt to become *Trieste II.*

1965 •Westinghouse Electric Corporation launched *Deep Star 4000,* eighteen-feet, 9 tons, with cameras, two viewports, mechanical arm; operational depth 4,000 feet; used for scientific research by U.S. Navy.

•*Submanaut* launched, a ten-foot, two-ton, plywood and laminated epoxy fiber glass vehicle designed for 1,000-foot depths; used at 200 feet.

1966 •*Alvin, Aluminaut* and Perry *Cubmarine* used in search for H-bomb lost near Palomares, Spain, after aircraft collision.

•*Pisces I* launched, sixteen-foot, 7.5-ton D/RV with three

viewports, mechanical arm, cameras, TV; operation depth 1,800 feet; owned by International Hydrodynamics, Canada.
- *Star II* launched; seventeen-foot, 4.3-ton D/RV with six viewports; operational depth 1,200 feet; Electric Boat Division, owner.
- *Star III* launched; twenty-four-foot, ten-ton D/RV with five viewports, mechanical arm; operation depth 2,000 feet; donated to Scripps Institution of Oceanography.

1967
- *Deep Diver,* twenty-three-foot, 8.2-ton submersible built by Perry Submarines; operational depth 1,335 feet.

1968
- U.S. nuclear submarine *Scorpion* lost at sea; cause unknown. Remains found in over 10,000 feet of water 400 miles southeast of Azores and photographed by deep-sea remote cameras.
- Jacques Piccard's mesoscaph *Ben Franklin (PX-15),* built by Grumman Aircraft for midwater use; fifty feet long, 130 tons, powered by four 25-horsepower electric motors; operating depth 2,000 feet.
- *Beaver IV*, a twenty-five-foot, 16-ton D/RV built by North American Rockwell Corporation; ten ports, diver air-lock hatch, cameras, manipulator arms, designed for oil work, operational to 2,000 feet.
- *Deep Quest*, forty feet, fifty-two-tons, designed and built by Lockheed Aircraft Company. The submersible has camera, core sampler, TV, video tape, navigational computer, is operational to 8,000 feet.
- *Dowb*, a seventeen-foot, 9.6-ton D/RV with TV, cameras and unique 360 degree optical viewing system, designed for depths to 6,500 feet by General Motors Corporation, United States.
- *Nai'a (PC-5)*, a twenty-two-foot, five-ton submersible with ten viewports, manipulator arm, designed for pipeline survey and inspection by Pacific Submarines.
- *Nekton,* a fifteen-foot, 2.2-ton vehicle used in Alaska for geological exploration; has core drill, viewports, mechanical arm, cameras; built by General Oceanographics for 1,000-foot depths.
- *Paoli I*, a fifteen-foot, two-ton submersible designed for 1,000-foot depths by Anautics Corporation.
- *Shelf Diver*, a twenty-three-foot, 8.5-ton submersible designed for Shell pipeline inspection with twenty-five ports, diver's air-lock hatch, mechanical arm, core sampler, rock drill, TV cameras; operational to 800 feet by Perry Submarines.
- *Shinkai*, a fifty-nine-foot, 100-ton submersible with two

viewports, cameras, TV, sonar, navigation and scientific equipment, for fisheries and geological research up to 1,960 feet, Japan.

- *Serv*, a ten-foot-long, two-ton D/RV with ten viewports, TV, cameras, core sampler, mechanical arm, built by Lintott Engineering Ltd., England.
- *Sea Cliff* and *Turtle*, two submersibles alike, twenty-five feet long, twenty-one tons, resembling *Alvin* design; twin arm manipulators on each vehicle, viewports, for deep-submergence research and work; operational to 6,500 feet, by Electric Boat Division.
- Research submersible *Alvin* accidently sank in 5,051 feet of water 120 miles south of Cape Cod; no casualties.

1969
- *Alvin* recovered by combined effort of *Aluminaut* and research ship *Mizar*.
- Mesoscaph *Ben Franklin (PX-15)* drifted depths of Gulf Stream from Florida to south of Nova Scotia, 1,500 miles in thirty-one days, collecting oceanographic data; with Jacques Piccard, Don Kazimer, Erwin Aebersold, Frank Busby and Ken Haigh.
- *Deep Star 2000*, twenty-foot long, nine-ton submersible with two viewports, cameras, mechanical arm, TV, designed for 2,000-foot depths by Westinghouse Electric Corporation.
- *Pisces II/III*, twenty-foot long, twelve-ton D/RV with manipulator, three viewports, cameras and TV, designed for depths down to 3,000 by Vickers/HYCO.
- *Sea Cliff,* a twenty-six foot, twenty-four-ton D/RV that is a copy of the *Alvin*, but larger, with two mechanical arms, designed for 6,500-foot depths; owned by Woods Hole Oceanographic Institution.
- *Sea Fleas* (2), a 9.5-foot-long, 2.6-ton vehicle designed by Jacques Cousteau to carry a man and camera; used for filming underwater series; operational to 2,000 feet.
- *Turtle*, a twenty-six-foot long, twenty-four-ton D/RV, sister vehicle to *Sea Cliff*, designed for 6,500 feet; used by the U.S. Navy for military oceanography.
- *Vast Mk III*, ten-foot-long, 1.2-ton vehicle with single large viewport, air ballast, maneuverable, designed for 250 feet. Eight Mk III's built as private submersibles by Underwater Vehicles, Inc.
- *NR-I*, a 136.4-foot-long, 400-ton, nuclear-powered ocean engineering and research vehicle built for the navy by General Dynamics Electric Boat, external lights and TV cameras, remote-controlled manipulator, vari-

ous recovery devices, viewports; remote grapple, fixed TV mast, and fitted with wheels for "bottom crawling"; operational to 2,000 feet; intended for Continental Shelf exploration and research.

1970
- *DSRV-1*, the U.S. Navy's Deep Submergence Rescue Vehicle, fifty feet long, thirty-seven tons; designed for rescuing crewmen twenty-four at a time from sunken submarines by mating with vessel's escape hatch. Transportable by land, sea or air; operational to 5,000 feet; built by Lockheed.
- *Nemo*, a deep-submergence vehicle, six feet long, one ton; an acrylic sphere attached to life-support disks. Vehicle drops its anchor, one- or two-man crew winches vehicle down its own cable; operational to 600 feet.
- *Guppy*, an eleven-foot, 2.5-ton tethered vehicle that powers down 3,000-foot line; three viewports, manipulator, owned by Sun Shipbuilding, used in Alaska.
- *Perry PC-9*, a twenty-two-foot long, 10.5-ton cubmarine-type submersible designed for 2,000-foot depths by Perry Submarines, used for pipeline inspection; owned by Brown and Root Construction.

1971
- *DSRV-2*, U.S. Navy's second Deep Submergence Rescue Vehicle with same characteristics and capabilities as the *DSRV-1*.
- *Deep View*, fifteen-foot-long, five-ton D/RV, the first submersible to use glass (borosilicate) as a forward viewing hemisphere; battery operated; designed for 1,500 feet by Naval Underwater Center.
- *Diving Saucer (SP 3000)*, a twenty-foot-long, twelve-ton, third-generation DS developed by Jacques Cousteau and OFRS, using Vasco Jet 90 hull originally for *Deep Star 4000*. Operational depth to 10,000 feet.
- *Makakai*, a deep-submergence vehicle with acrylic sphere mounted on aluminum frame and two pontoons, built by U.S. Naval Undersea Research and Development Laboratory, Hawaii. Operational to 600 feet with one- or two-man crew.
- *Trieste II, (X-2)* Navy bathyscaph, modified float, pressure sphere, propulsion system and mission equipment; protective supports now hide sphere; fitted with external TV cameras, manipulator, computerized digital navigation; designed operational depth 20,000 feet. Fitted with fuel-cell power plant, 1973.

1972
- *Argyronete*, an eighty-two-foot-long, 300-ton, Deep Submergence Vehicle with Diesel electric power, 450-

mile range, lockout chamber, designed for depths to 1,970 feet by COMEX/IFP, France.

•*Deep Star 20,000*, a thirty-six-foot-long, forty-two ton, Deep Submergence Vehicle able to carry out deep-search missions; designed for depths to 20,000 feet by Westinghouse Electric Corporation.

Bibliography

Abbot, Henry L.: *Beginning of Submarine Warfare*, The Shoe String Press, Inc., Hamden, Conn., 1966.

Anderson, Hillary Houser: "Edwin Link, The Triumphs and Tragedies in One Man's Quest to Launch Man-in-Sea," *Skin Diver*, vol. 21, no. 11, November 1973.

Anderson, Comdr. William R., with Blair, Clay, Jr.: *Nautilus 90 North*, The World Publishing Company, Cleveland, 1959.

Barnes, Robert H.: *United States Submarines*, H. F. Morse Associates, Inc., New Haven, Conn., 1944.

Beach, Capt. Edward L.: *Submarine*, Henry Holt and Company, Inc., New York, 1952.

Beebe, William: *Half Mile Down*, Duell, Sloan & Pearce, Inc., New York, 1934.

Calvert, Comdr. James: "Up though the Ice of the North Pole," *National Geographic*, vol. CXVI, no. 1, July 1959.

Cohen, Paul: *The Realm of the Submarine*, The Macmillan Company, New York, 1969.

Cousteau, Jacques-Yves: "Diving Saucer Takes to the Deep," *National Geographic*, vol. 117, no. 4, April 1960.

Cousteau, Jacques-Yves: "At Home in the Sea," *National Geographic*, vol. 125, no. 4, April 1964.

Cousteau, Jacques-Yves, with Dugan, James: *The Living Sea*, Harper & Row, Publishers, Incorporated, New York, 1964.

Cousteau, Jacques-Yves: *World without Sun*, Harper & Row, Publishers, Incorporated, New York, 1965.

Cousteau, Philippe: "Reconsidering the Speargun," *Skin Diver*, vol. 22, no. 12, December 1973.

Cross, Wilbur: *Challengers of the Deep*, William Sloane Associates, New York, 1959.

Davis, Sir Robert H.: *Deep Diving and Submarine Operations*, Saint Catherine Press Ltd., London, 1951.

Dugan, James: *Man under the Sea*, Harper & Row, Publishers, Incorporated, New York, 1966.

Houot, G. S., and Willm, P. H.: *2000 Fathoms Down*, E. P. Dutton & Co., Inc., New York, 1955.

Hubbell, John G.: "Trident: Super-Deterrent of the Deep," *Reader's Digest*, vol. 102, no. 613, May 1973.

Idyll, C. P.: *Exploring the Ocean World,* Thomas Y. Crowell Company, New York, 1969.

Keach, Lieut. Comdr. Donald L.: "Down to Thresher by Bathyscaph," *National Geographic,* vol. 125, no. 6, June 1964.

Lake, Simon, and Corey, Herbert: *Submarine,* D. Appleton-Century Company, Inc., New York, 1938.

Lewis, Flora: *One of Our H-Bombs Is Missing,* McGraw-Hill Book Company, New York, 1967.

Link, Edwin A.: "Tomorrow on the Deep Frontier," *National Geographic,* vol. 125, no. 6, June 1964.

Marx, Robert F.: *Sea Fever,* Doubleday & Company, Inc., Garden City, N.Y., 1972.

Marx, Robert F.: "Florida's Mini-Sub Disaster," *Argosy,* vol. 377, no. 1, November 1973.

Moore, John E., ed.: *Jane's Fighting Ships,* McGraw-Hill Book Company, New York, 1973–74.

Morris, Richard K.: *John P. Holland, 1841–1914,* United States Naval Institute, Annapolis, Md., 1966.

Parons, William Barclay: *Robert Fulton and the Submarine,* Columbia University Press, New York, 1922.

Piccard, Auguste: *Earth, Sky, Sea,* Oxford University Press, New York, 1956.

Piccard, Jacques: *The Sun beneath the Sea,* Charles Scribner's Sons, New York, 1971.

Rush, C. W., Chabliss, W. C., and Gimpel, H. J.: *The Complete Book of Submarines,* The World Publishing Company, New York, 1958.

Shenton, Edward H.: *Exploring the Ocean Depths,* W. W. Norton & Company, Inc., New York, 1968.

Shenton, Edward H.: "Where Have All the Submersibles Gone?" *Oceans,* vol. 3, no. 6, November–December 1970.

Soule, Gardner: *Undersea Frontiers,* Rand McNally & Company, New York, 1968.

Stewart-Gordon, James: "The Wet World of Jacques-Yves Cousteau," *The Saturday Evening Post,* November–December 1973.

Sweeney, James B.: *A Pictorial History of Oceanographic Submersibles,* Crown Publishers, Inc., New York, 1970.

Verne, Jules: *Twenty Thousand Leagues under the Sea,* The Heritage Press, New York, 1956.

Wagner, Frederick: *Submarine Fighter of the American Revolution,* Dodd, Mead & Company, Inc., New York, 1967.

Williams, Harry T., and the Editors of *Life* magazine: *The Union Restored*, The *Life* History of the United States, vol. 6: 1861–1876, Time-Life Books, New York, 1963.

Wyckoff, James: *Who Really Invented the Submarine?*, G. P. Putnam's Sons, New York, 1965.

Index

About the Author

Robert F. Burgess is a journalist who has written for numerous national publications, and author of many books, including *Sinkings, Salvages and Shipwrecks.* Mr. Burgess lives in Florida.